For Ron Halstead
from Charles Villiers.

for "auld lang syne!"

Start Again, Britain

The author

Start Again, Britain

Charles Villiers

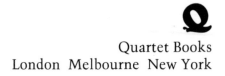

Quartet Books
London Melbourne New York

First published by Quartet Books Limited 1984
A member of the Namara Group
27/29 Goodge Street, London W1P 1FD

Villiers, Charles
    Start again, Britain.
    1. Laissez-faire   2. Great Britain —
    Economic conditions — 1945–
    I. Title
    338.6'1'0941   HC256.6

    ISBN 0-7043-2480-6

Phototypeset by AKM Associates (UK) Ltd.
Ajmal House, Hayes Road, Southall, London
Printed and bound in Great Britain

Contents

Acknowledgements

The author and publisher are grateful to the following for their kind permission to include the various charts and graphs, photographs and cartoons which appear in this book:

Associated Newspapers Group plc and John Kent; Associated Press; Basic Books Inc; *British Industrial Performance* (NEDO 1983), graphs reproduced by permission of Her Majesty's Stationery Office; the Cabinet Office; Michael Daley; the Department of Trade and Industry; *Economist*; *Financial Times*; Methuen Educational; the Press Association; Brian Reading, whose cartoon is reproduced by courtesy of the *Guardian*.

Preface

Had Britain's industrial performance been better, Sir Charles Villiers would not have had to write this book . . .

He lays the blame for Britain's decline fairly and squarely on the shoulders of management in business, administration, the public services and education. I agree with that. In a few years' time, North Sea oil will be nearing depletion and Britain will no longer be able to live off it, as now. In the interim, British management has the mammoth task of innovating and investing in new products and processes, and training a new generation of British industrial people.

To succeed against international competition and achieve a turnaround, management will need not so much the intervention or regulation of government, but rather its full-blooded collaboration – government acting as the shrewd coach and cheerleader, while businessmen and managers everywhere perform as captains of their teams. Charles himself had the experience of captaining a vast team at British Steel. It can be made to work as well in Britain as in competitor countries; as well in the private as in the public sector. His prescription follows that route. Not everyone will agree with each of his proposals, but they form a coherent set of new ideas to cure the British disease.

Charles has had an exceptionally wide experience as banker, soldier and administrator, Managing Director of the old Industrial Reorganization Corporation, Chairman of the Northern Ireland Finance Corporation and recently as Chairman of British Steel. It was he who had the unenviable task of closing ten steel works, making many thousands of people redundant and refusing to lose (no one wins) one of the most critical strikes in British industrial history. His contribution was crucial and made the task of his successors that much easier. He is now deeply involved in job creation and the work of small business.

It follows that his views are based on real life at the sharp end. He has dedicated *Start Again, Britain* to present and future managers in Britain. They would be well advised to 'read, mark, learn and inwardly digest' (whether or not they come to agree with it) because, as he says, 'the management *of* anything *is* everything'.

Michael Edwardes
London, 1984

Overture:
Sit Down, You're Rockin'
the Boat!*

'Why rock the boat?'

'Well, our industry *has* run down, our oil *will* run down and we *shall* run down into one hell of a mess, unless we turn around and start again.'

'Yes, yes, of course, but life is very pleasant if you have a job or a decent pension, and it should see us out.'

Thus the unacknowledged conspiracy to go gently down together. Many people are asking, 'What on earth *is* going on?', and others, 'What's next, when inflation *has* been beaten down?' This book tries to answer those questions, omitting the problems of Britain's relations with Europe and other countries. I believe we have to get ourselves right before we start telling others what to do.

In addition to being a Jack of many financial trades in the private sector, I have worked in one way or another for the last seven British governments and watched them struggling with Britain's core problems. I became deeply disenchanted with 'as is' in Britain – it was quite unnecessary for us to be so unsuccessful; this endangers the good things done in the past and the prospects of a good life in the future. At one time we seemed to take leave of our traditional common sense.

I went back to what are to me the great start-again moments in

* Nicely-Nicely in *Guys and Dolls* by Damon Runyon

our history – the invasions by the Anglo-Saxons and then by the Normans, the defeat of the Spanish Armada, the first Industrial Revolution, the two great Reform Bills and the establishment of the welfare state. In each case there was a new regime, a new way of doing things, a new hope and an old fear lurking in the background. I became convinced that once again Britain is ready for a new start; what is more, I saw signs of a new beginning in the places where Britain most needs change and movement.

To describe the whole of British life would take many volumes. To describe the new start, now in train, can be done by picking out some starting points and seeing how the change is coming, or not coming. It is coming hesitantly, too slowly, and Britain is still losing ground. Change has to be accelerated, if it is to be effective. This can be done, but not in traditional ways, nor by the traditional people, nor by sticking to the old ideas and attitudes. Nearly forty years of the welfare state have given us a valuable social service, but they have stunted our capacity to create the wealth to pay for it. If we don't soon get around to improving all our assets, human and material, we shall lose what we have gained.

The pressures upon Britain to start again are very strong. First, there is the fact that much of British industry is approaching the point of no return in its long decline and simply *has* now to turn around. Second is the new industrial revolution, the computer and the microprocessor, which is changing everything in factories, offices and homes. Third is the force of competition from Japan and other newly industrialized countries in East Asia. Fourth is the need to pay for social security, with its ever-increasing costs. Fifth is the pressure of unemployment, now near its all-time high. Sixth is the growing insistence of British people to have 'a say', as individuals, on the shop floor and in the offices. Seventh is the fact that Britain is living off North Sea oil, a wasting asset if ever there was one; it will not be long before we are net importers of oil again.

I believe, therefore, that we have now to move on to a new position, to a natural successor to the welfare state, taking with us social security for the old and the young, for the sick and the disadvantaged, for the retired and the unemployed – those whom I call 'the needy', for short. This new position we might call the development state. Chalmers Johnson, Professor of

Political Science at the University of California, recently wrote: 'Throughout the fifties the Japanese government operated and perfected what is recognized today as a model of the state-guided capitalist developmental system.' This he distinguished from 'the American regulatory state'. I distinguish it from the British welfare state and call it the development state.

Britain should not, indeed cannot copy the Japanese, but Japanese experiences are of the greatest possible interest because, under the pressure of events, Britain has started to move in the same direction. My phrase 'development state', is shorthand for a new British purpose and strategy and set of ideas.

The main purpose of the development state in Britain would be the long-term improvement of Britain's real economy, and all that bears upon it. It would develop all Britain's assets: men, women, skills, experience, machines, bricks and mortar, minerals and, of course, our financial assets. This would be done by voluntary collaboration between government, management, schools, colleges, customers and workforce, leaving companies to compete freely in the market places. This purpose would take priority over everything except national defence, dignity and liberty – and you don't get much of them if you can't afford to pay!

This proposition is the main theme of this book and I make no apology for hammering away at it through to the final chapters, which outline some of the new machinery of the development state.

The development state would be different from the welfare state. In place of what is soggy, tolerant of error, slack and defensive it would be ambitious, positive and creative. It would not be content to batten down the hatches, wait for the storm to blow over and then carry on as before. It would continually be looking for new opportunities. 'Better' and 'more' would be its buzz words. Its measuring rods would be performance, delivery, quality and cost. Its philosophy would be continuous progress through competition *and* collaboration. Its vision would be long-, not short-term. It would be democratic, voluntary, humane and lawful. In no way would it be a corporate state as presided over by Hitler, Mussolini, Franco or Salazar. Nor would it be 'Great Britain Limited', which would be too narrow a formula. It would be more like Roosevelt's New Deal, Adenauer's Germany, de Gaulle's France and post-war Japan. Margaret Thatcher's phrase a 'go-getter society' would describe a large part of it. It would be a new state of mind.

The social justification for the development state would be to satisfy people in work, to create wealth and to point the way for people to meet their obligations to each other and to those poorer than themselves. The objective would be to stop the endless slither and to catch up with other countries, which have recently gone ahead of us in wealth per head and standard of living. If you don't advance you are bound to fall back; you cannot stand still. We all agree that this is true.

The development state would be an exercise in co-operative management; seeking agreement where possible, but recognizing that when all is said and done, managers must manage, and manage better. This should operate throughout business, the public services and government at all levels. The keynotes of this management would be low overheads, value for money, continual improvement, keen competition in the market place

---

Trust Them to Tell the Truth?

Now I will read out a list of different types of people. For each, would you tell me whether you generally trust them to tell the truth of not?

	Tell Truth	Not	DK
Clergymen	85%	11%	4%
Doctors	82%	14%	4%
Teachers	79%	14%	7%
Judges	77%	18%	5%
Television News-Readers	63%	25%	12%
Police	61%	32%	7%
Ordinary Man/Woman in Street	57%	27%	16%
Civil Servants	25%	63%	12%
Business Leaders	25%	65%	10%
Journalists	19%	73%	8%
Trade Union Officials	18%	71%	11%
Politicians Generally	18%	75%	7%
Government Ministers	16%	74%	10%

MORI interviewed face-to-face a representative quota sample of 1,082 adults aged 18+ on 16 December 1983.

© MORI/Sunday Times, 1984

and collaboration everywhere else.

The development state could not come into existence if British management were to persist in its traditional technique – summed up in the phrase 'tell the buggers to do it!' That is becoming part of history. The British people came of age in the sixties and made significant discoveries about themselves. They no longer gave implicit trust to their leaders at work, in trade unions, in government, in politics, in journalism, or even in families. The gap between ideals and realities had become too great.

No one knows exactly why this happened, but the new attitude soaked through the entire Western world. Perhaps it was more money to spend, and television, with its ability to inject desire for goods straight into the bloodstream of the consumer. It may also have come from the ease of getting a pay rise by threatening to strike. Above all, employment seemed to be guaranteed, and if you lost one job, you could always get another. The failure of governments to solve problems had a lot to do with it – the failure of the American effort in Vietnam, in particular. The wooden-headedness of many bosses, in management and trade unions, locked into rule-of-thumb practices, refusing to listen to the voice of fresh experience at the sharp end, added to the confusion. Many saw the sign of the times in rock-'n'-roll music, unfettered satire and open sexuality, but most drew back from what seemed revolutionary or chaotic.

The 'pop' explosion of the sixties has lost much of its force with the passage of time and with its spread into all classes. But its essence remains – the British are not going to return to the old deferential world, nor will they work well in jobs which give them no chance to express intelligent opinion. No real advance will be made which does not recognize this.

This is bad news for traditionalists – for those who like hierarchies, bureaucracies and centralization and have inadequate professionalism. It is they who have come to see that Britain is ungovernable, which, in the old way, it certainly is. You can no longer manage by just issuing orders from your office. You can no longer get elected by relying on the old loyalties. You cannot teach by making your pupils learn irrelevant facts. No one is going to sacrifice his chance of a pay rise when he knows that the next man in another union will go for it regardless. As Professor Samuel Beer of Harvard writes of us, 'the self-defeating logic of short-run self-interest has won out . . . the outcome has been incoherence and paralysis . . .'*

We are now playing a new ball-game, and failure to understand it has caused authority much despair and a yearning for the older, easier, more respectful way of life. But this is no longer an option. We are witnessing another outburst of British energy, not so different from many others in the past. The British have a genius for designing, making, adapting and using new forms of work, sport, art, leisure, teaching, management and government over the whole range of life's activities.

The British of all sorts long for friendly, fair, communicative, professional management. They respond positively to 'small is beautiful'. Their loyalty to and pride in the enterprise or institution they work for are hidden assets of incalculable value to those who know how to uncover and develop them. The Falklands War was won by self-reliant men, non-commissioned and pilot officers in small units, responding to professional and trusted leadership. Civilians in peacetime cannot perform in exactly this way because Queen's Regulations are not there. But all good managers know how to produce a spurt, when needed, and many are learning how to involve their workforce in consistently better results – 'top down' leadership meeting, and fusing with, a 'shop floor up' movement. This is a master key to the development state.

In the recent national census two-and-a-half million people described themselves as managers, or employers: another two-and-a-half million as self-employed. On these few – not the 'upper ten' but the 'driving ten' – the future of Britain depends. The development state would seek to create a flexible, positive, creative link between them and government, workforce, share-holders, customers, schools and colleges. Unless management responds to the needs of the development state by moving quickly into new products, new processes, new markets and new industrial relations, the efforts of government will be, to use an old phrase, as 'farts in a colander'.

The management *of* anything *is* everything – Villiers's law.

Trade unions at national level, while they persist with their old-fashioned ideas and structures, would exclude themselves.

* S. Beer, *Britain Against Itself*, Harvard, 1982

Maybe they too will start again, recognizing that their original mission is largely fulfilled and that they need to find a new role. At local and plant level many trade-union officials do invaluable work, and it is this which should be built up and fitted into the development state.

The development state would not be a socialist state, but it would retain social security for the needy. Nor would it be a classical capitalist state based upon Adam Smith's theory that economic growth can safely be left to market forces only. Nor would it have much time for the modern Tory policy of 'doing good by stealth'. It would in fact be an organized capitalist state, based upon individual performance and the best use of capital. It would recognize the paramountcy of market forces, but it would nudge these in the direction of long-term development. Government would encourage, facilitate, steer and accelerate, but it would be private enterprise which, collaborating with government, workforce and others, took the risks, did the work, and reaped the rewards.

This development state would acknowledge the sad truth that Britain is no longer, if ever it was, a fully self-adjusting, self-correcting economy. The British disease, explored in later chapters, checks automatic complete recovery from recession and further development. Lack of skills, of entrepreneurs, of plentiful cheap capital, of innovation and research, combined with adversarial and uneducated attitudes, nips development in the bud before it flowers. Competitors overseas do not suffer so severely from this deadly complaint and they have gone ahead of Britain, picking up our markets abroad and even at home. This leaves Britain poorer, weaker and today dependent on North Sea oil, which has only a short life at the present high level of benefit. Unless we move forward now, we shall go down further later.

This is an extremely dangerous situation and a vast problem, which only a radical move, as into a development state, could hope to resolve. I dare to say that this threat could, unless we cope with it, grow into a greater danger to Britain than were the pretensions of Napoleon, the ambitions of the Kaiser or the campaigns of the demented Adolf Hitler.

Some may remember me at British Steel – a most difficult job. It remains difficult, even after the great efforts of my friends and successors there. The last thing I would wish to do is to add to those difficulties, so I do not refer much to BSC; naturally my time there did influence and educate me greatly but, as Kipling said, 'that is another story'.

I also exempt the British Steel managers from my general criticism of British management. They have been through the wringer several times and have emerged slimmed into a team which, before the coal strike of 1984, produced at some works more tonnes of steel per man than Germany, the European leader. This did not come easily and it is an example to the whole of British industry, part of which has, indeed, started out down the same hard road.

I write as I speak, in day-to-day language for people who, like me, want to help make things better, using the resources to hand. I have shamelessly plucked other men's flowers in backing my arguments and illustrating my themes, and I acknowledge this as I go. My own maturing thought has been influenced by Dr E.F. Schumacher's *Small is Beautiful*, by my friend Christian Stoffaes's *La Grande Menace Industrielle* (Paris, 1978), by Chalmers Johnson's *MITI and the Japanese Miracle* (Stanford, 1982), by Martin J. Wiener's *English Culture and the Decline of the Industrial Spirit 1850–1980*, by Ralf Dahrendorf's *On Britain* (BBC, 1982), by Sir Michael Edwardes's *Back from the Brink* (Collins, 1983) and by a series of penetrating surveys of British life carried out by Opinion Research & Communication between 1978 and 1983.

In this book 'Chancellor' means the British Chancellor of the Exchequer, '£' equals pounds sterling, 'Germany' is West Germany and 'national income' is the annual gross domestic product; other abbreviations are explained in the text.

I bow in gratitude to the many tutors, friends, businessmen, journalists, civil servants and politicians who for more than fifty years have kept me reading, thinking and talking about the subject of this book. Jane Francis suggested, and has never failed to find the raw material for it. Nick Brady steered me through the international economic comparisons. Paul Usher has most helpfully improved my script. Elizabeth Hennessy has rigorously edited the text. My assistants Sheila Larner and Marion Ford kept their heads when I was in danger of losing mine in the *paperasserie*. But above all I am grateful to my dear wife, without whose mixture of prodding and kindly tolerance it would never have got written.

Charles Villiers
Summer 1984

To the present and future managers of Britain, in whose hands the fate of Britain lies.

'Compete like hell in the market place, but collaborate everywhere else.'

1 The Manufacturing Disaster

Alfred Herbert was a great man, like many British industrialists of his generation. He died in 1957 at the age of ninety-one, still at daily work, still enjoying life, with £7 million in the bank, a knighthood and the knowledge that he had built, from nothing, the biggest and best-known machine tool business in the world, based in Edgwick, Coventry, England.

In the mid-sixties shares in Alfred Herbert were trading at around £18 each. Ten years later they were at $2\frac{1}{2}$p. In 1980 the business went into voluntary liquidation and in 1983 Alfred Herbert went into bankruptcy. The flagship of the British machine tool industry was broken up.

It began and ended in Coventry where, towards the end of the last century, Alfred Herbert made and repaired bicycles in a small firm, started with a little money his father had given him. He moved to Edgwick and made simple capstan lathes. He was a brilliant businessman. During the First World War his business expanded to become a huge concern, still on the Edgwick site. He became a very rich man and was appointed government controller of machine tools.

Alfred Herbert was an autocrat of the old industrial school. He could pick and motivate a team of junior managers, but he took all the decisions himself. He walked around his shop floor every day and would stop and ask a machinist for a cigarette. He was feared and respected. His company never became public in his lifetime and its balance sheet and profit and loss account were in fact his own personal accounts. In bad times he built for stock financed by his own money. As times improved he stood in the market as the only manufacturer who could deliver machine tools from stock. His product was the capstan lathe, but he stocked and sold all the best tools, British and foreign. His catalogue, two inches thick, was the Bible for engineers the world over.

There was no holding Alfred Herbert; even before the Second World War he was the biggest machine tool builder in the world. During the war he delivered 65,000 machine tools. The post-war boom carried him along, and when he died his companies and their products were pre-eminent throughout the world. Some years later a visitor reported that his widow still came to the factory every Thursday with fruit and preserves, home-made, for workers who had gone sick or were in difficulty.

On his death Colonel C.W. Clark became chairman at the age of sixty-six – as I write he is still alive. Colonel Clark had not been in charge of a company before. He is described as having installed himself comfortably on the first floor of the office block, directly on top of the managing director. The Colonel apparently 'radiated quiet confidence'. He had a splendid inheritance of market domination, technical skills and ample cash. He acquired several other machine tool companies. Failure to innovate was the weakness; after the Second World War the company traded on its reputation. The momentum was lost. Top management was old, new blood was not injected, the competition caught up. First the American firm Warner and Swazey came up with a more efficient and more accurate machine tool turret. Then the firm of Charles Churchill produced a new low-cost lathe. Profits faded and losses began, which were only occasionally stemmed. Cash melted away and bank borrowings mounted.

In 1966 Sir Richard Young became chairman. He immediately formed a joint company with Ingersoll to make special-purpose machine tool systems. In the same year Herbert acquired all the machine tool interests of the Birmingham Small Arms Company. But these extensions were to no avail, and by 1975 another £7 million had been lost.

In 1975 another top management team, with Walter Lees as managing director, took over. They found the factories 'over-large, run-down and a shabby mess'. They paid tribute to the way the workforce had behaved during this trauma.

What had happened? Many negative forces had coincided in Herbert from the mid-sixties on, and the management had not been strong enough to fight them off:

• The market for machine tools started to fall away, and never since has it achieved a substantial recovery. This left Alfred Herbert with too much capacity and too many employees.
• The forecasts of sales to sixty countries, based on many years of easy trading, proved much too optimistic, but surplus capacity and workforce were retained instead of being reduced.
• Inflation in the economy was raising costs in every department, but orders taken in earlier years were at fixed prices. These turned out to be unprofitable. Inefficiency in the factories prevented speedier production and the order book got further out of date. Profit and cash turned negative.
• New factories acquired after Alfred Herbert's death were run from the centre, and had no direction or control over orders taken. The centre became paralysed and could not form or implement new strategy.
• The machine tools produced by the business were still conventional and no match for a new generation of automatic machines.
• As orders were completed, usually at a loss, new orders became hard to obtain due to Herbert's high costs and lack of modernization.

The new management team were backed by the National Enterprise Board (NEB), which in 1975 bought up the share capital of Herbert for £1 million at 2½p per share, and injected £25 million of long-term finance. New men were brought in at every level – thirty new managers – and the whole business was tidied up. Herbert returned to profit in 1977, but again the market fell away and, as traditionally, Herbert manufactured for stock. Once again losses mounted and cash melted. By 1980 NEB had had enough. Herbert was put into voluntary liquidation. The factories were sold to any willing buyer, but another £57 million had been lost.

The next owners of the Edgwick factory tried to make a success of the range of new computerized numerically controlled (CNC) lathes, which they acquired with the factory from the liquidator. The new men, Ron Lynch and John Wright, young enterprising engineers, had made their way as dealers in second-hand plant. When they bought Edgwick they expanded their workforce from seventy-five to 780. They may have paid too much, but in 1981 they traded at a profit. They had a good product, but they hit terrible markets in Britain and America. Japanese machine tools of similar capacity appeared on the market at prices 25 per cent lower than those charged by 'the heirs of Alfred Herbert'. Once again the owners of Herbert built for stock. Once again the bankers called a halt, and a receiver in bankruptcy was appointed. The Japanese picked up the market share.*

Did liquidation come too soon or too late? Liquidation on Alfred Herbert's death would have been ideal. Others would then have continued his amazing achievement – but no one thought of that. Liquidation in 1966 would have been wise – it would not at that time have been too late, and a new generation of modern tools could have been created by others. In 1975 that new generation was designed, planned and financed and it was known that it would take five years to bring to market. The new tools were offered in 1980 and were well received but the NEB, under the Tories, was impatient of all government intervention and wanted out. That time liquidation may have come too soon. By 1983 bankruptcy was inevitable.

The moral of this tale is clear. By 1945 Alfred Herbert himself was nearly eighty years of age. It was natural that he should trade on his success and reputation. It was natural that his appetite for innovation should have slackened. It was impossible to remove him. It was inevitable that his business would later suffer from the lack of innovation and be overtaken by the competition.

What was not inevitable was the succession. Why was the 'quiet confidence' of Colonel Clark allowed to continue? Why did the 1966 management team not get into the real problems? Why was the 1975 management team chopped off by the liquidation in 1980? Why was the new 1980 team allowed by the financiers to build for stock? These are the questions that have to be asked about recent British management, industrial,

---

* *Management Today*, May 1982

The path to the graveyard: pitfalls of management. Reprinted from the
Financial Times, 8 March 1983

financial and governmental.

On the other side of the world the Japanese were unknown as machine tool exporters. Nevertheless, they saw an opportunity to apply their business skills to this industry. Before the British, the Germans or the Americans knew what was happening, the Japanese had got a substantial share in these markets. By 1980 they had half the American market for CNC lathes and over one third of the market in Britain and Germany. Their exports of machine tools have risen from £125 million in 1975 to £600 million in 1981. In Britain 52,000 employees in 1973 were reduced to 37,200 in 1982 and the companies are fighting for life in an industry 'perilously close to collapse'.*

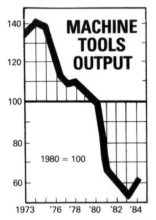

In 1984 there came a slight recovery as this chart from the *Financial Times* on 4 July 1984 shows. This has been helped by an excellent government aid scheme to enable small engineering companies to buy CNC machine tools. Orders at home and abroad have increased, but many British tool makers have now linked up with Japanese firms. Yamazaki is to invest £30m in an automated plant to build CNC machine tools in Britain. Import penetration of the UK market is still at the rate of 55 per cent.

A sad story, and a cautionary tale. But it does not stand alone, and much of it can be found elsewhere in Britain since the Second World War. Why in this country do we now have only the last remains of once thriving industries, such as motor-bikes, watches, sewing-machines, special steels, cameras, typewriters, chains, tyres, cutlery and lighters – to name only a few? Why have we seen such an enormous decline in ship-building, cars, steel, paper and chemicals? 'Sunset industries', you may say, but they are 'sunrise industries' in many other countries.

Britain in 1984 is emerging from absolute industrial decline – not only less growth than other countries, but in most of industry no growth at all; loss instead of growth. This is an

* *Financial Times*, 15 February 1983

extremely serious situation, and it confronts us with three options:

- to continue drifting along behind the competition to a deteriorating future;
- to move to a planned, quasi-Marxist economy;
- to make a successful turnaround and start to catch up with the competition.

The British show little desire to move to a Marxist economy; they would rather be more individualistic, with better opportunities to develop their talents. Some would, with a shrug of their shoulders, choose to continue to drift but most would go for a turnaround under trusted leadership, even if it meant new people, new methods, new ideas, new attitudes, new institutions. The move would take a mammoth and continuous effort by all the positive, progressive people in Britain. That would come from a move on through the welfare state, taking social security, democracy and individual liberty with us, into the development state – call it what you will. That is the option this book explores.

Britain has been declining compared with America and Germany for a hundred years, and compared with Japan, France and several other countries for the last twenty years. The great alibis – World Wars I and II, North Sea oil and the Falklands campaign – enabled us to convince ourselves and others that we were richer and more powerful than we really were. By the fourth year of the Second World War Britain was almost exhausted, and the Americans carried us. By the end of this century North Sea oil will be approaching exhaustion, and who will carry us then?

We must look this danger in the eye without excuses or cover-up. The 'as is' establishment dodges embarrassing facts with which it does not know how to cope. The facts are not difficult to grasp.

Look at what has happened to Britain's share of exports to world markets in manufactured goods. Twenty years ago our share in that market was 15 per cent – not very wonderful, but respectable and enough to keep our trade in reasonable balance. Today that share has fallen to 8 per cent – a fall which means the

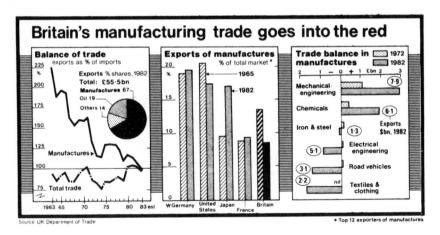

Britain's manufacturing trade goes into the red

Source: UK Department of Trade

* Top 12 exporters of manufactures

The *Economist*, 10 September 1983

loss of nearly one half of our share of world trade in manufactured goods, supposed to be our speciality. During the same period most other countries hung on to their share of that market. America and Germany lost a little, but Japan increased its share by an incredible 140 per cent. This is the acid test for any country, corporation, firm or person – if you persistently lose share of the markets you depend upon, you are in trouble. To lose nearly one half of export market share in our speciality in twenty years hurts like hell!

Now look at what happened to Britain's home trade. In almost every industry imports have increased their share of the British market since 1970. Only food and drink, coal and oil have resisted this trend. So – and note well – imports have increased their market share from 18 per cent to 28 per cent since 1970. This is a huge rise – over 50 per cent in thirteen years – and it is still growing. Other countries have also been hit in this way but Britain has suffered much more than any other, and one quarter of everything we buy in our shops is now imported.

Look now at the effect of that on our foreign trade. We cannot live without importing raw materials and food. Traditionally, that was paid for by exporting more manufactured goods to the rest of the world than the manufactures we imported. Only twenty years ago manufactured exports were twice the value of manufactured imports. That left a credit balance to pay for essential raw materials and food. But year by year that credit balance diminished; the volume of imported goods increased, exports fell back. In 1982 exports just managed to stay ahead. In 1983 imported manufactured goods exceeded the export of British-made goods for the first year ever recorded – and by over £2 billion. The trend has been that way, illustrated by the pictograph from the *Economist*. To turn that around will need a colossal effort.

North Sea oil and the 'invisible' earnings of the City of London and other services will be able for a time to pay for essential imported raw materials and goods. But note that North Sea oil is a wasting asset and the City is under increasing competition from New York and Tokyo, whose share of international lending is steadily increasing.

Unless powerful action is taken, the new debit balance on manufacturing account will remain. Britain will not be able to plug it, and that spells disaster. 'The real weakness is in the overseas sector.'* In the stately words of the Bank of England: 'Despite the recent pick-up, British non-oil exports probably grew less than world markets as a whole between 1982 and 1983 inclusive.'† Even the most optimistic CBI report showed imports continuing to grow faster than exports.‡ It is scarcely possible that the manufacturing account should remain at its disastrous 1983 level, when imports grew at 5 per cent and exports at only 0.5 per cent, but to turn this around is what Britain has to do.

North Sea oil is now at its peak production in Britain of 2.5 million barrels a day. In four years' time it will have dropped to 2.0 million barrels and in fifteen years (by the end of the century) to 1.2 million barrels.‡‡ That is a cut of more than one half of the peak rate. That will bring back the balance of payments problem which dogged us before North Sea oil came to our rescue. The trading benefit to Britain from that oil in 1983 was £17 billion.‡‡‡ How do we replace even one half of that

* Sam Brittan, *Financial Times*, 10 November 1983
† *Quarterly Bulletin*, March 1984
‡ *Financial Times*, 2 April 1984
‡‡ Report by Economist Intelligence Unit to Shell UK, April 1984
‡‡‡ Chairman of Shell UK, April 1984

without a complete business turnaround out of the industrial disaster?

What is more, until 1986 oil revenues flowing into the Exchequer will be around £11 billion a year. Then they will start to diminish rapidly; by 1989 these revenues will be down to £7 billion and falling fast. That will create a serious budget problem. If ever there was a wasting asset it is North Sea oil, and we are relying on it to pay for our essential imports of food and raw materials and to cover annual spending at home equivalent to, for example, the whole cost of public education. The combination of actual declining benefit from manufacture and prospective declining benefit from North Sea oil puts Britain, I have to say again, in an extremely dangerous position. We should all be aware of it, because it threatens the jobs and living standards of everyone in this country.

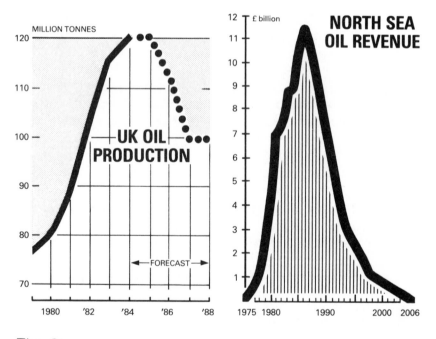

The *Observer*

The 'brown book' published in May 1984* indicates that the proven reserves of oil in the North Sea available to Britain have been somewhat underestimated, and that there are other 'undiscovered recoverable reserves'. Fine. So be it! But Chancellor Lawson said in April 1984: 'It is reasonable to expect that there will be some return to the traditional trade pattern of a surplus in manufacturing and invisibles to offset deficits in food, basic materials and eventually fuel.' Is that reasonable? The manufacturing surplus has declined steadily over the last twenty years. What sort of tradition is that? The Chancellor betrays the Treasury's ignorance of British manufacturing industry, and makes too light of the immensity of the manufacturer's and businessman's task.

These enormous losses of market share at home and abroad by British industry since the sixties have had a devastating effect upon employment. Professor Thirlwell of the University of Kent has calculated the actual results.† In 1966 employment in manufacturing was at a peak of 11.85 million people. Since then there has been a continuous fall, and by 1981 the total was 4 million fewer. There has not been a switch from manufacturing to service or other industries on a sufficient scale to take up the slack. The total workforce in Britain is still 26 million, as it was in 1966, but now 3 million are unemployed. The decline is not relative just to manufacturing, it is absolute, and this is a major disaster for Britain.

It is doubtful if we have yet seen the worst of this, and it is due to two unpleasant facts. First, British manufacturers have been uncompetitive in world markets; second, in our own home market we have increasingly preferred foreign-made goods to home-made products. The worse the foreign trade balance in any industry, the greater the decline in the number of people it employs. Compare this with the gains reported by the International Labour Organization‡ of 14.5 million jobs in America and nearly four million in Japan in the ten years to 1982. In addition, over the last ten years Australia, Italy, Finland, Greece, Ireland, Norway and Portugal have all increased

* *Developments of the Oil and Gas Resources of the UK*, HMSO, 1984
† *Lloyds Bank Review*, April 1982
‡ *Observer*, 29 April 1984

Employment in Manufacturing Industry 1960–1981 (Thousands)

Industry Order	1960	1966	1970	1974	June 1981	% Decline from Peak Year to June 1981
Food, Drink and Tobacco	816.4	861.7	890.5	766	632	29.0 (since 1970)
Coal and Petroleum Products	—	—	63.3	40	37	19.0 (since 1961)
Chemicals and Allied Industries	530.3	527.3	475.1	435	395	
Metal Manufacture	617.1	623.0	591.7	507	326	48.5 (since 1961)
Mechanical Engineering Instrument Engineering Electrical Engineering	2 048.9	2 376.9	2 283.2	1 980	1 530	35.6 (since 1966)
Shipbuilding and Marine Engineering	278.8	213.6	199.0	185	144	54.0 (since 1956)
Vehicles	919.8	853.2	842.4	792	636	31.0 (since 1960)
Metal Goods n.e.s.	546.0	599.0	639.9	582	428	33.1 (since 1970)
Textiles	901.8	810.8	716.0	585	364	67.0 (since 1951)
Leather, Leather Goods and Fur	63.5	60.0	54.0	43	32	60.0 (since 1951)
Clothing and Footwear	591.7	554.2	501.3	427	313	55.2 (since 1951)
Bricks, Pottery, Glass, Cement	339.3	364.9	340.8	301	216	40.8 (since 1966)
Timber, Furniture	292.9	319.0	299.8	283	227	30.4 (since 1968)
Paper, Printing and Publishing	603.0	650.9	654.9	589	493	24.7 (since 1970)
Other Manufacturing Industries	301.9	348.7	358.8	358	265	27.8 (since 1969)
Total Manufacturing	8 850.5	9 163.1	8 910.5	7 871	6 041	34.1 (since 1966)
Total of Production Industries[1]	11 456.5	11 852.1	11 086.3	9 895	7 843	33.8 (since 1966)

[1]Includes Mining and Quarrying, Construction, and Gas, Electricity and Water, in addition to manufacturing industry

Source: *Department of Employment Gazettes*, HMSO, London

their manufacturing populations. There have been losses in Germany, Spain, Sweden, Austria and France, but most of these losses have been made good elsewhere in their economies. Only in the Netherlands has the fall in manufacturing employment been on the same scale as in Britain.

It is not sensible to say that this loss of manufacturing industry does not matter. Manufactured exports were worth

Jobs: Gains and Losses

	1973	1982	%
	millions		
US	85.0	99.5	+11.7
Japan	52.6	56.4	+ 7.2
France	20.8	20.9	+ 0.8
Germany	26.4	25.1	− 4.8
UK	24.7	23.2	− 6.0

Source: *ILO Year Book*

three times our exports of oil in 1983. Industry is one of the main ways in which wealth per head is increased and the standard of living improved. Productivity, which is output per head in industry, is the chief source of increased wealth and if industry is shrunk the scope for national growth is thereby diminished. The wealth of a whole country is upgraded by successful industry. Someone has to make the things we use and if we don't, we must import, and how do we pay?

Nor can it be maintained that there was not enough demand in Britain to buy the products of British factories. In the seventies total spending rose by 20 per cent and consumer spending by 23 per cent. In 1980 and 1981, recession years, consumer demand did not fall back, and consumer spending actually rose in 1982 by 4 per cent and in 1983 by another 4 per cent: *so did imports.*

The products of British industry have not been good enough in quality, design, reliability, delivery, service and price to meet the existing demand at home and abroad; this demand has therefore been met by goods made in other countries. So, Britain has been in chronic trouble and has had heavily to restrain government and industrial spending; industry and public services had to cut back and make people redundant. This is the downward spiral in which this country is caught, and we will not escape unless we make a drastic effort to break out of it on a scale not so far contemplated.

Lest there be any doubts about this, look at the situation of three major British industries:

● First, cars and trucks: in 1972 we made 2.3 million, but in 1983 we made only 1.2 million. In 1972 we imported 20 per cent of our

Major Problem Areas
Products in which the trade balance has deteriorated
significantly in the past year include:

Product	£m[1]
Passenger cars	536
Commercial vehicles and parts	519
Chemicals	276
Construction equipment	226
Textiles	213
Aero engines and gas turbines	206
Piston engines	181
Scientific apparatus and photographic equipment	121
Electronic components	107
Agricultural equipment	100
Pumps and compressors	97

[1]Decline in trade balance in first eleven months of 1983 compared with
whole of 1982
Source: Overseas Trade Statistics of the UK, Department of Trade
Financial Times, 23 January 1984

new vehicles; in 1982 it was 55 per cent. In 1983 there was some
recovery but the industry is doubtful if that can be maintained,
and imports of all vehicles are still rising and exports falling.
The motor industry used to be Britain's biggest foreign exchange
earner. The *deficit* on this account in 1983 was £2 billion.

● Second, engineering, Britain's biggest industry: in the last ten
years new orders have fallen by 16 per cent in the home market
and by 30 per cent in export markets. Output has fallen during
these years by 33 per cent, and mechanical engineering was still
contracting in the first months of 1984. In other engineering
sectors the hoped-for recovery may be short-lived and the long-
term downward trend may not have been halted.

● Third, electronics, where Britain's hopes are high: the annual
world market for electronics is now £200 billion, rising to £450
billion in ten years. Britain's share is only 5 per cent and falling.
We shall soon be importing each year £2 billion more electronic
equipment than we export.

Why, oh why? Not for any one reason, but because of the total
effect of poor productivity of capital and labour, lack of profit
and of investment; interest, inflation and exchange rates too

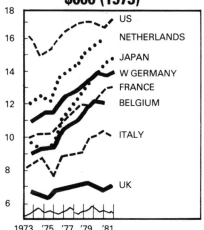

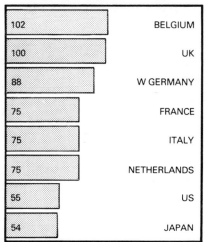

Source: National Institute

high; bad management, bad industrial relations, bad training – just not being good enough. All these factors have been moving in an unfavourable direction for years in many of our competitor countries too, but in Britain they have moved furthest.

Look at output per man – productivity. If we take Britain's labour productivity as a base line against which to compare the productivity of our competitors, we have been grinding away at the bottom of the big-country class. There was an upturn of productivity in the eighties, when a lot fewer people were making rather fewer goods, but by 1984 Britain was still trailing miles behind the international competition; they got the message, too!

Pay is an important element in productivity. Pay increases in the UK have been greater than the increases in all the competitor countries, except Belgium. In the ten years to 1980 pay in Britain increased by 346 per cent and productivity rose by only 25 per cent. The average wage increase in the competitor countries during that time was 190 per cent, but their productivity rose by 52 per cent.*

* *Economist*, 23 October 1982

The Medium-term Evolution of Business Investment
and Business Output, 1955–1979[1]

(average annual rates of growth, volume)

Country	1955–1965		1965–1973		1973–1979	
	Output	Investment	Output	Investment	Output	Investment
United States	3.2	4.6	3.8	3.8	2.3	1.9
Japan	10.2	16.4	11.2	16.1	4.2	2.2
Germany	5.5	6.9	4.1	4.4	2.1	3.2
France	5.5	7.9	5.7	8.5	3.0	–0.1
United Kingdom	3.1	5.4	2.7	3.1	0.5	1.3
excluding North Sea oil	—	—	—	—	–0.1	–0.1
Italy	5.8	3.9	5.6	7.5	2.5	0.7
Canada	5.1	5.2	5.6	5.2	3.3	4.3
Major seven countries[2]	5.3	7.7	5.6	7.0	2.7	1.9

[1] The terminal years of the 1955–1965 and 1965–1973 periods are not always cyclically comparable
[2] 1978 GNP/GDP weights and exchange rates
(Source: OECD)

On the competitiveness scoreboard of the twenty-two OECD* nations, prepared by the European Management Forum in Geneva, Britain had in 1982 dropped back from twelfth to thirteenth place. The CBI reported in January 1984 that 'we are still 20 per cent less competitive against our main rivals than in 1975'.† Could productivity and competitiveness be increased by further investment? There is undoubtedly a case for the positive effect of new investment on a scale which we have not seen in Britain for many years. Investment was considerable in the fifties and sixties. After the oil price rises in the seventies, the rate slowed down and even with the huge investment in North Sea oil, Britain could average only a small annual increase. Other countries also reduced their investment, because output was falling. The rise in oil and other energy prices absorbed revenue, which was not therefore available for spending on investment, output and employment.

* Organization for Economic Co-Operation & Development
† *Financial Times*, 1 February 1984

In recent years the growth of output has shrunk in all industrial countries, and investment with it. Sadly, the British record is the weakest among our main competitors and the growth of investment, without North Sea oil, slid into reverse – more capital written off than invested. The USA has four times our population and does not far outstrip us in investment per head. France and Germany are about our size and invest substantially more. Japan is twice our size, but has invested four times as much.

Investment would be at the very heart of the development state. Without saving there could be no investment and without investment no progress. Investment is the dynamo that drives a modern society. Manufacturing investment in Britain fell by another 5 per cent in 1983. The forecasts for 1984 vary from 3 per cent to 7 per cent increase. This would be the first increase for five years. Its purpose would seem to be to improve efficiency rather than to increase capacity. An improvement in investment would be the best hard evidence of the new start in manufacturing and of recovery but the deputy governor of the Bank of England commented, in February 1984, 'Current levels of investment are insufficient to support sustained expansion of the economy.'

A major deterrent to investment in Britain has been lack of profit. The real rate of return has been downward since the fifties, and in 1980 reached a low of 3 per cent earned by non-oil companies. Since 1973 the overall return on capital has not paid for its cost. Other countries have experienced heavy falls in profits, but the greatest fall has been in this country, where the lowest level of return on capital is recorded. There is now a sharp recovery in real profitability in British industry, but only back to the 1978 level, around 8 per cent. The need is for investment in manufacturing companies through shareholders and lenders taking longer views. That needs confidence that development rather than welfare is going to be the national theme. This would trigger the development state.

The productivity of invested capital in Britain is another unhappy story. It is found by dividing investment by the increase in value added – not an easy sum! What one can say is that the USA and France get twice as much output from their new investment as does Britain, and that Germany and Japan get

UK MANUFACTURING INVESTMENT
£ billion at 1975 prices
Seasonally adjusted quarterly data,
excluding leased assets
Source: Dept. Industry

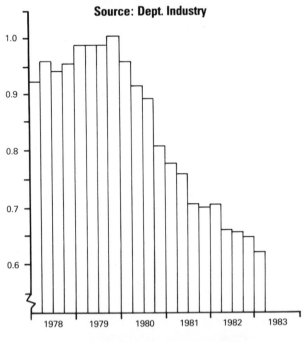

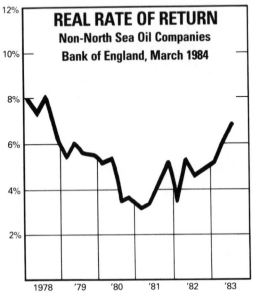

NON-FINANCIAL CORPORATIONS
NET RATES OF RETURN. Source: CBI

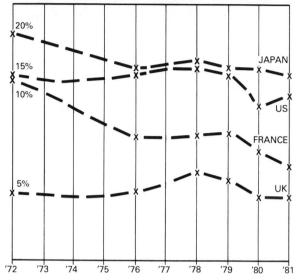

50 per cent more. Britain gets a very much smaller addition to output from its investment than is obtained by any of its main competitors. Britain's managers have failed to use industrial investment, in exactly the same way as they have underemployed their workforce. This is extremely bad news and gets right into the tired, weak, old heart of the matter.

In the remoteness of university studies, and even at some editors' desks, it is said that Britain has enough investment, that it would be better to invest overseas and get a better, safer return, and that at present levels of productivity British industry simply cannot afford new investment. That has an element of truth, on the basis of 'as is'. But we have to break out of 'as is'. The conditions in which much of the work is done in British manufacturing industry are a disgrace and a disincentive to starting again on a new industrial path. The technical changes now taking place make it essential to scrap and replace machinery on a great scale, if we are even to hang on to our present share of markets. If we are to recapture lost market share, which will be slow and difficult, we shall need further massive investment in plant, computer-aided for design and manufacture, and in new or rebuilt factories.

Why did we not do all this before? Why was British industry allowed to get into this decrepit state? We are not fools, or ignorant or evil people. Yet no other country has recently lost 50 per cent of its share of export markets, allowed imports to take 28 per cent of its home market, and lost four million jobs in manufacturing of which only one million have been absorbed elsewhere. Why are we at the bottom of the big-league tables of productivity and profitability? Why has British industry got less from its non-oil investment than the competition? Why are our unit costs the highest and our output per head the lowest? It is impossible to overlook the fact that in the income per head league Britain has dropped to eighteenth place, just below New Zealand, below the average of all the Common Market countries; indeed, for every three things we can buy the French can buy four.*

The inescapable conclusion is that there has been a massive failure of management at all levels in British industry and in all that bears upon it. Of course governments have failed to understand industry. Of course unions have been power-hungry with their 'snouts in the trough'. Of course public opinion has been hostile to business and to profits. Of course nationalization has been a flop. Of course many industries have been riddled with militant Trots or Marxists. Of course the overhead costs of government and the welfare state have been far higher than expected. Of course taxation of income and capital have been huge disincentives to investment and to risk-taking – one could go on for ever!

But at the end of the day the judgement has to be that the majority of British managers in business, in government and in the public services, including education, have been stuck too long in the old ways, have been too secretive and unco-operative and have been insufficiently tough and aggressive, lacking in professionalism and ignorant of the endless improvements taking place elsewhere.

John Harvey Jones, Chairman of Imperial Chemical Industries, said that his company had 'taken a disproportionate share of

* President Mitterrand, *The Times*, 22 March 1984

British management talent for a great many years and it has not turned in the performance that the talent should have achieved . . . if we have failed to perform – and we have – that says something about the leadership, the direction and the organization of these people . . . there are no bad troops; there are only bad leaders'.* Nevertheless, Britain is now moving into a new industrial atmosphere. British industry has been under siege for many years now. In the last four years it has been blitzed; there are gaping holes where once there were factories. Now there are a few new buildings and converted workshops starting again. The old industries have shrunk into their core. New industries are trying out their strength. Everybody is searching for new orders, but markets are too tough and competitive for most of British industry. Unemployed managers and men are to be found everywhere. In many plants workforce and managers plan together to survive by improving all their systems, processes and products.

In the light of the evidence it is clear that Britain has suffered a major manufacturing disaster. Many things have contributed to this, but old-style management has been the chief culprit. Recovery and a new start have begun, but they have a hell of a long way to go before Britain ceases to be dependent on the wasting North Sea oil. Some of the greatest old companies have made completely new starts, described in later chapters. Profits and cash have begun to accumulate once again – to the survivors the spoils! The CBI survey of 1,800 companies in March 1984 reported 40 per cent expecting to increase output. Output in manufacturing is, however, not yet back to the 1979 level and there is as yet only talk of investment for expansion and innovation. Where is 'more and better' going to come from, and how can it compete?

It is no good comparing present British performance with past British performance. We have to take daily account of what the competition overseas is up to. On that comparison there is no room for anything other than stark amazement, indeed horror, at the size of the task in front of us:

---

* *Director*, May 1983

Oh, England. Sick in head and sick in heart,
Sick in whole and every part,
And yet sicker thou art still
For thinking, that thou are not ill.

(Anonymous: Seventeenth century,
when England both collapsed and recovered.)*

* *Faber Book of Epigrams and Epitaphs*, edited by Geoffrey Gibson, 1977

2 Reluctant Industrialists

In March 1978 the magazine *Chief Executive*, working with the American Management Association, published a poll of chief executives of businesses in France, Germany, Italy and Scandinavia on why, in their opinion, British industry in recent years had experienced such a relatively low performance and slow growth. The bosses of 194 foreign firms took part; they covered most industries and all sizes of company. Most did business with British companies, and many were competitors. They showed no desire to write down or write off British management, but their views, whether right or wrong, are what they went by when making business decisions.

Nearly half thought that 'promotion to senior posts too often depends on family or social connections ... British managers are too conscious of social class to be able to motivate their workers ... they are too arrogant in their dealings with customers and suppliers in other countries'; only a quarter of the foreign chief executives thought that this was no longer the case.

One out of every two complained about 'broken delivery promises' and one in three complained of 'poor quality of goods and services'. Nearly half rated the performance of British managers as 'below average'. One half thought that British managers worked less hard than their European counterparts. Only one in ten thought that British managers were significantly better in any respect than their opposite numbers in Europe. Very few considered that the slow growth of British industry was primarily due to 'ineffective management'; most blamed labour and trade-union difficulties, low productivity and lack of investment. Nevertheless, 41 per cent saw no improvement in British management, 35 per cent saw a deterioration, and only 24 per cent thought that management had improved in recent years.

The European chief executives thought that British managers were better-educated generally, but much worse trained for management than themselves. British managers, they thought, had greater financial skills but little ability to communicate or motivate others; in respect of willingness and company loyalty they were about the same as themselves.

British goods were seen by the Europeans to be competitive in price but much worse in packaging, delivery, marketing and after-sales service. No change in British standards was seen by 60 per cent, but of the remainder more thought standards had fallen rather than risen. Labour problems in Britain were thought to be worse than in Europe by over half of the foreign chief executives.

Most of the blame for the failings of British management was put upon senior management, and in the view of the executives, here is the litany:

Too old to understand the complexities	58% agreed
Too weak to stand up to the trade unions	75% agreed
Too hesitant to take normal business risks	62% agreed
Too demoralized by industrial problems to give leadership	80% agreed
Too badly paid	70% agreed
Too handicapped without a second language	50% agreed

Finally, nearly half saw no change in the trend in British management; 40 per cent saw an improving trend; 12 per cent thought the trend was downwards. Failure to cope with labour problems was the main criticism. That, as I write, was only six years ago. In the same year the British Department of Industry analysed Britain's poor industrial performance. The conclusion was that the decline in UK competitiveness was not due to price but to design, reliability, delivery dates and after-sales service. It seemed that British firms were able to compete quite well in slow-growing markets, but less well in the fast-growing markets. British industry needed to attend particularly to research and development, which by comparison with the competition overseas was insufficient and badly directed.

These criticisms can be laid only at managements' door. It is not possible to shuffle them off on to government, unions, workforce, the exchange rate, the competition or anywhere else.

We do indeed have a management problem. We have to dig deep to find out why. Some of the reasons are suggested by Martin J. Wiener of the Department of History at Rice University in America, who concluded that the English businessmen's desire to become 'gentry' had led to a weakening of their competitive effort when compared with their counterparts in Germany, France, America and Japan.* Most people who have any knowledge of the English are aware of some strange aspects of 'Englishness'. It is gentlemanly, certainly, and it endorses fair play. But it is suspicious of change, of progress, of profit, of 'go-getters'; also of the whole industrial process. This, it suspects, covers exploitation of ordinary people by hard-faced men, making their fortunes at others' expense. This is a caricature, but it lives on in the imagination and to this day colours the English attitude towards industry.

This image gave rise to deep social undercurrents in nineteenth-century England, which tugged businessmen away from the noise and smell and trouble 'down at t'mill' and up the hill to a mansion, a garden, a park, sport, public schools for boys, governesses for girls, 'society', public life and perhaps, eventually, a title. In this way the Industrial Revolution and the modernization which should have accompanied it were blunted, absorbed into an older culture, slowed down and eventually halted, incomplete.

The landowners became capitalists and the businessmen became landowners and the blend was the English gentleman, whose imagined qualities have inspired much that is good throughout the world. They also inspired a detachment, an amateurishness, a semi-retired attitude to life, which in industry led step by step to our present poor performance. Industrial leadership was muffled and domesticated by what was seen as a more desirable, semi-aristocratic form of life, which flinched

* *English Culture and the Decline of the Industrial Spirit,* Cambridge University Press, 1980

from industrial and technical effectiveness.

C.P. Snow, in *The Masters*, says that 'nine English traditions out of ten date from the latter half of the nineteenth century'. Our thinking even today, whether we know it or not, is influenced by the views of Victorians such as John Stuart Mill, Arnold, Ruskin and Dickens. They were critical of the social revolution begun by industrialization, and this view became part of accepted English culture. The explosion of industrial energy, innovation and wealth was channelled, even before Queen Victoria was dead, into 'society', the Army, the Church, the City, India and the colonies, the gentry, the public schools and country life. There is little doubt that this contributed to a dramatic decline of English fortunes in an increasingly competitive world.

The professionals, however – lawyers, doctors, civil servants, professors, writers and, later, accountants and scientists – were not seduced and absorbed in the same way as successful businessmen. This professional middle class came to have immense influence, but it detached itself from business and claimed that its expertise and integrity put it above haggling in the market place. It is these professionals who today are most trusted and respected by the British people generally. They have, however, now become numbered among top people, sharing in their education, their love of country and sport, their self-confidence and their hesitation about change. In times of crisis it is the professionals, among whom many industrial managers must be included, who have held the country together because of their interest, their discipline, their loyalty and their deep conservatism. If there is to be a new start in Britain it is the professionals, in support of the entrepreneurs, who will have to help it to happen.

The first Industrial Revolution was a genuinely spontaneous event. The use of coal for steam power, iron for steel, and machines for spinning cotton, wool and silk revolutionized the way people worked, lived and thought. It was the engineers, Watt, Arkwright and Stephenson, whose ingenuity triggered this extraordinary happening, which changed the life of the world. When Stephenson died in 1859 he was buried in Westminster Abbey and the route was lined with silent crowds. All work ceased, all shipping lay silent in his home county of

Tyne, Wear and Tees. 'Never again,' it was said, 'would a British engineer command so much esteem and affection; never again would the profession stand so high.' Isambard Kingdom Brunel, who designed the steamships and much else, died in the same year. Thereafter, Wiener believes, public admiration for material progress began to wane and currents of thought started to flow in another direction, away from the full development of the Industrial Revolution and away from the new industrial bourgeoisie. The modernization of attitudes, techniques and performance, as a continuing element in English life, was checked and never regained its early momentum.

Many things caused this change of direction, but none more than the rise of the public schools. Eton has had its 500th anniversary, Winchester has celebrated its 600th birthday. It was, however, in the nineteenth century that the public schools expanded and flowered. They perpetuated a system which distinguished the gentry from the business and technical class – the class which in truth was responsible for Britain's reputation in the world, and anyway paid for everything by creating the wealth. At the public schools the classics were taught as an essential part of a liberal education. Science was for long ignored as vulgar and utilitarian, serving industry and commerce, which were 'not quite nice' in upper-class estimation. Business was associated with working with one's hands and earning money direct, rather than through rents, interest and dividends. The philosophy of the public schools was summed up by the headmaster of Uppingham in 1864: 'The object of a great school is mental and bodily training in the best way, apart from immediate gain.' The result was imitation of the leisured gentry, at the expense of the modern role of a professional expert.

The sons of many businessmen entered the public schools, but few businessmen emerged. The public school leavers became the social and political elite, filled with a great desire to maintain stability and order but with little urge to increase individual or national wealth. The grammar schools, the secondary schools, Oxbridge and finally many of the new 'redbrick' universities got set in the same path and found it difficult to get out of the rut.

The poets and novelists, philosophers and moralists were all against acquisitive, competitive society and by the end of the nineteenth century the established culture had put economic growth and material progress down – 'in their place', as it was said. That position was limited and comfortable, but it was deteriorating quite fast. Other industrialized countries had a strong, virile, technical business class which, having failed to penetrate the aristocracy, formed its own coherent business society. These foreign business leaders were by no means vulgar, money-grabbing philistines. They were and are highly educated, moral, patriotic, committed technical or professional people, just as the British were at the beginning of their Industrial Revolution, and as they are now becoming once again.

By the turn of the last century a critical view of the English Industrial Revolution was being taken by Toynbee, Kipling, Chesterton and Belloc, the leading writers. They all disdained and degraded the revolution, which they held was about manufacture and greed and should be exchanged for a society concerned with distribution and the quality of life. The same theme shone through the *English Saga* of Arthur Bryant and Trevelyan's *English Social History*, published in 1944; 250,000 copies of the former and 400,000 copies of the latter were sold. What was the culture of a public which only forty years ago bought 650,000 copies of books by the most famous authors of the day, describing Britain as having 'lost its soul and sense of purpose in the Industrial Revolution'? Even Keynes, who saved capitalism in the thirties and forties, as his biographer Roy Harrod points out, 'found something unsatisfactory in the quest for gain as such, and came to hope that an economic system might be evolved in which it was curtailed'.

Toryism instinctively disliked commercialism, materialism and profiteering, although it has certainly become a business-man's party. Joseph Chamberlain offered, in Wiener's words, 'an activist, urban, industrial version of conservatism that promoted economic reform. He called for making economic resurgence the central aim of politics.' His call was rejected. Stanley Baldwin was not interested in the fearsome economic problems of the thirties so much as in the preservation of Parliament and the moderation of the British character. Winston Churchill was not so different. His view of history was nostalgic and heroic and he had little time for business, industry or even economics.

Rab Butler and Quintin Hogg were committed to agriculture rather than industry and they distanced themselves from industrial capitalism. Harold Macmillan understood industry better than all other prime ministers before him. Indeed, he was criticized for the materialistic implications of his phrase 'You've never had it so good'. Edward Heath had been a banker, but he had little feel for industry. Margaret Thatcher, using her instinct for small business, saw industry's failings and squeezed them mercilessly.

Labour politicians always had a yearning for the Tudor 'Merrie England', before the Industrial Revolution had introduced greed and materialism and taken the place of rural England. Ernest Bevin, the Transport Union leader, was keen to improve industry in Britain but he disliked the 'crude, noisy, boastful materialism' of America. Clement Attlee, like Bevin, thought the American unions were much too materialistic in their aims. Stafford Cripps was a Socialist, zealous in raising production in wartime, but he felt thereafter that the economic problem had been solved. Anthony Crosland, Labour's last philosopher, agreed that the programme for economic growth should increasingly be overshadowed by 'social policies'. Harold Wilson and James Callaghan, like Ted Heath and, later, Margaret Thatcher, moved in a different and more realistic direction.

It took a very rugged individualist to swim against this strong tide. Most businessmen swam with it and, as Wiener found, they limited their quest for expansion, productivity and profit. This did not, however, apply to the financial and commercial community in and around London. To be in trade was on the borderline, but to be a banker was all right. The City of London attracted many of the best brains in Britain, which goes a long way towards explaining why today our financial services are not only our best industry, but probably the best in the world. 'The City' is clear proof of British capacity to apply and concentrate energies successfully in activities which are considered gentlemanly. It is also proof that these energies are capable of profound change. If any part of Britain is starting again, as I write it is in the turmoil and upheaval now taking place in the City of London.

The City, however, turned aside from investing in home

industries in order to browse upon the richer pastures of
financing overseas trade and raising loans for governments and
enterprises overseas. The leading professions followed the
bankers, the merchants, the shipowners and the insurers in the
same direction. It is hard to explain this split between finance
and industry in Britain, but it has had serious and far-reaching
consequences. The Macmillan Committee, reporting in 1931,
found that there was a gap in the financing of industry. Fifty
years later the Wilson Committee found the same thing.
Bankers live by handling the current accounts of industry,
provided overdrafts are well secured, but the long-term lenders
have worked on the rule of thumb that it is unwise to make
much investment in the industrial, manufacturing North.
Those attitudes are slowly breaking down, but they are deep-
rooted and have been a damaging part of the widespread
hostility to industry in Britain. Industrialists are touchy about
this and Wiener quotes one who burst out in exasperation,
'behind all the public exhortation to industrial growth, industry
is a leper'.

Efforts to direct education towards industry in Britain have
not so far had much success. In 1977 *Encounter* commented
how, in Victorian times, 'the Empire needed a large, confident
and fairly conventional class of administrators, whereas the
economy seemed to be taking care of itself. This situation
reversed itself a century later. As the Empire disappeared and
the economy lagged, the need to reform the curriculum and
destroy its unworldly bias arose – and was missed.' Much later
the *New Statesman*'s education correspondent was saying that
the engineer's low status was 'at the heart of our industrial
problem'. In 1976 Prime Minister Callaghan complained that
'many of our best students have no desire to join industry'.

Recently more and more boys from the public schools have
been going into business, and they have taken the concept of
gentlemanly behaviour with them. The educated amateur from
public school and Oxbridge – together with his manager, the
practical man from a secondary school, polytechnic or factory
bench – is running British industry today. These amateurs are,
thinks Wiener, full of a vague but persistent belief that some
things are indeed more important than profits and that business
is a rather distasteful way of acquiring the wherewithal to

conduct real life, and to develop the values which they consider to be truly important. This is devastating, but can we deny that Wiener has pointed an American finger at a continuing British belief? We do indeed have a gentlemanly economy which works well in agriculture, in banking and the other financial services at which Britain excels, but which has put up an inadequate performance in many sectors of industry. The attempt to combine manufacturing industry and services with the leisurely lifestyle of the English gentleman has failed, and should be universally abandoned. This has already happened in some, but not yet most of our industrial companies and the acceleration of this process should become a major plank of educational and industrial reform.

The quality of British management was seen to be a national problem soon after the Second World War. Both major political parties were, however, hesitant about tackling it. They did not know what could be done to improve it. Indeed, part of Tory thinking has been that the market in some wonderful way produces good managers and eliminates bad ones. This elimination takes a long time!

An independent study of management was made by Political and Economic Planning in 1964, financed by the Nuffield Foundation.* Six industries were investigated, forty-seven firms participated, and long individual interviews with managers and works conveners took place. The managers were measured by their thrust. The judgement of the report was that for every ten thrusting managers, there were fourteen who were sleepy or neutral. Not an encouraging result! The real flavour of 'them and us' came through strongly. It is the backdrop for today's performance.

There was confusion among managers. 'Some people tell me that all you have to do is to make money for the shareholders. I think you provide a service and a livelihood to a number of people,' said one. 'The thing that occupies my life is keeping the profit and the return on investment constantly before us,' said another.

Few managers mentioned productivity as their objective. Management training was not much appreciated. 'It was a

* PEP, *Thrusters and Sleepers*, George Allen & Unwin, 1965

haphazard business, people were promoted off the shop floor and they took all the decisions as they appeared best. Now we are in the middle of a changeover to a more scientific approach.' Many firms said that they were too busy to let anyone go on an outside course, or too poor to afford it. 'We haven't been successful, because of the inertia and resistance to anything non-traditional, but I think I've persuaded the managing director that we need a higher calibre of management.'

Management attitudes were constipated. 'Nobody looks after the plant like you look after your own. This is brought out by foster mothers!' To search for managers from other firms was thought by many to be unethical; 'we shouldn't like them to do it to us and so we shall not do it to them'. Many firms were not prepared to shift managers who had not fulfilled early promise or who had been wrongly appointed in the first place. 'Attempts have always been made to avoid hurting people and it is not very wise to adopt sweeping changes.'

Growth was not considered essential. 'We're doing very nicely, thank you, and I don't know why I have to worry my guts about all these ventures. Why should I try to increase my sales by spending a lot of money overseas?' But what about professionalism? 'We're suffering from the end of a long family era, when it was a question of son succeeding father, whether he was good at the job or not. My feeling is we've got to bring new people in and pay them.' 'We're moving from the traditional family-controlled firm with rather old-fashioned ideas on payments and methods into a professionally controlled engineering company.'

In managing men the problem was seen to be the need to reduce wastage due to absenteeism, high turnover of labour and shoddy workmanship. 'The good old British working men as usual stand by each other. Whether they are right or wrong they always take sides against the management.' A thrusting manager said: 'I think to get good labour relations inside the company the main thing is easy access to shop-floor problems and consultation and a man knowing that if he doesn't get satisfaction he can appeal.' A more general view was expressed by a manager in one of the older industries: 'The union is very militant here, but the things they are asking for are reasonable – more money, more work, more duties for their men, so that their union can become larger.'

Over pay, typical managers' views were: 'The men only work for what they can get. The reason that men no longer work hard is that they have no incentive, but exactly how to apply it is difficult to say; there has to be some equivalent established, so that a man has got to produce something for what he earns.'

The difference between staff and shop-floor workers loomed large. 'We have no pension schemes for the man on the shop floor, but our old servants do get a little pension. For the staff we have a proper pension scheme.' 'I think there ought to be a more equal treatment all round, but it will take a hell of a long time to do it.' 'You have' (a convener said) 'a magnificent office over there and you've got prehistoric lavatories here in the factory; if you put your foot on the pedal you get water squirting up your trouser leg.' 'They say we are all in it together, but in times of redundancy when our workpeople have to go down the drive, how many staff or supervisors go with them? None!'

Communication and joint consultation aroused mixed feelings. A personnel manager said about management, 'If they do not explain carefully what they are going to do and why, people will arrive at their own conclusions, which are likely to be the wrong ones.' A convenor said:

We know what is going on. Whether they're telling us the full story or not, I can't say. Whether they're telling the truth – you don't know. It's no good a gentleman sitting there and telling us that everything is bad and gloomy, that men are being paid off, and then a week later, as happened on one occasion, a 25 per cent dividend is announced. It doesn't lead to a good feeling between management and men.

Nearly half of the firms in the survey had no system of communication. Some had tried, but given up. A manager said, 'We had one or two hot-heads nominated to the Works Committee. It was getting a bit out of hand – they were telling us what to do.' Other managers had had more success: 'The amount of time lost now through stoppages is practically nil. It did occur a few years ago, but now we've developed a form of consultation and we go deeply into any point before taking serious action. We lose very little time now.' An operative said, 'I don't say we've reached utopia by any means, but I think in the time we've done remarkably well: you must have the full confidence of your top management. They must lay all their cards on the table, otherwise the whole scheme breaks down. Our management have tried to do that from the start.'

There were wide differences in method and results. The thrusting managers contrived to make their workforce an asset by encouragement, training and creating confidence. Other managers allowed relations to deteriorate and they came up against bitter resistance by trade unions, or a high absentee rate and a general apathy towards work. The survey found nothing to contradict the saying that 'management gets the shop stewards it deserves'. The responsibility for improving the situation was seen to lie with management. The gap between the best firms and the rest was glaring. It still is.

Industrial life in Britain became much more competitive in the last twenty years, and management changed too, but not as fast and far as the situation demanded. In 1981 a report on British industry was made by a group from the University of Uppsala in Sweden with others from business schools in France, Germany, Italy and Britain. They questioned almost 1,000 marketing and purchasing executives in 300 companies in Europe about the performance of British suppliers, as seen by their European customers. There were, sadly, many of the same old criticisms which have dogged Britain for so long.

The reputation of British marketing for technical and commercial competence was reasonably high, but British companies seemed reluctant to keep foreign customers informed of new product development or to go in for joint development with their customers. British suppliers were the least 'international' of all the European countries when it came to product standards. All the European buyers agreed that British suppliers have a lower standard of quality control than any other European country and that they do, in fact, often fall below acceptable standards. Two out of three of European buyers agreed that in speed, punctuality and reliability of delivery the British gave the worst service. British suppliers were regarded by European buyers as unwilling to establish a local service operation, and were slow to handle complaints.

The European buyers emphasized that the British representatives they met were fully aware of their failings, but their companies did not seem to have the willingness or ability to correct them. Labour difficulties and changes in policy as governments alternated were thought to be the main reason for this. One in four European buyers was unhappy at having to buy from British companies and would switch to another supplier given the opportunity.

A new factor began to emerge from this survey – neglect of the British home market. European customers found British salesmen very keen to get new business, but British customers reported that British salesmen found them of less importance than customers overseas, and took them for granted. Indeed, British buyers appeared to have a low regard for British suppliers as to product development, compliance with international standards, delivery and quality. British buyers were particularly critical of the technical competence of British suppliers. This is strong evidence that a gap exists between what is being demanded and what is supplied on the home market. It is also an explanation of the fact that in recent years imports have come flooding into the country at a greater rate than ever before.

British buyers understand the problems of their British suppliers and probably share them, but they are now fully alive to the better delivery, reliability and quality of many European products. There is a real danger that British suppliers, while chasing overseas business, will lose out in their own back yard and that the import flood will continue.

What of British production management? A survey of Britain and Germany was made by Professor Hutton and P.A. Lawrence of the University of Southampton, and the results were published in July 1980. They examined the view that 'production management tends to be neglected by top management and staffed by "old faithfuls" with poor career prospects . . . production is above all the function which the ambitious executive will avoid.' They found that in this country production has a low status and is poorly paid, promotion is slow and production managers are seen to be immobile and disadvantaged by long hours, cramped offices, noise and the sharp end of industrial relations problems. In Britain they found that this was 'drearily well-known', in Germany 'the suggestions were preposterous'. The Germans were certainly better educated and trained in engineering and none wanted to leave production; over 25 per cent of British production managers wanted to get out of it. Nevertheless, the authors of this report found no evidence in Britain of low morale or failing motivation in management, and they were impressed with the 'commitment, sense of purpose, and determination to get things done, whatever the obstacles, exhibited by the British production managers'.

Germans, they found, proceeded in a stable, orderly and predictable way, but the British were often hectic, relying on tenacity and resourcefulness – almost a Dunkirk spirit, a heroic battling against odds. The British were continually coping with shortages, breakdowns and bottlenecks, with more fires to be fought and crises to be handled than in Germany. All too often in Britain supplies or parts do not come on time, or the wrong components turn up, or the right part turns out to be defective. Often a list of 'desperately and urgently needed parts' has to be prepared every day. British managers have become extremely skilled at substituting, cannibalizing and rescheduling. There is a lot of stress in production, and this has an adverse effect on quality and delivery.

Breakdowns in plant and machinery, even with new machines, were found to occur far more frequently in Britain than in Germany, and British managers sometimes take a perverse pride in the age and dilapidation of the machinery which they somehow manage to keep going. In Germany plant is newer and breakdowns are infrequent. When they do occur an outside repair man is quickly on the scene with professional maintenance skill. British production managers think that they have been let down so often by others in the past that they must check everything personally, but in German companies the production manager expects perfection from all about him and reacts violently if he does not get it. British managers exhibit precisely those strengths required by the weakness of the system in which they work.

British industrial relations are better, Hutton and Lawrence found, than the British public believes them to be and better, they say, than they are represented by the media. The trouble is the cumulative effect of strikes and stoppages. No company is an island: all suffer from the effects of past or present stoppages somewhere else, and it is this which causes the delays in delivery and faults in quality. Nevertheless, British managers everywhere showed signs of tightening up on punctuality, attendance and discipline among their workers and of being prepared politely to say 'no' to demands by workers' representatives. Time spent by British managers on industrial relations still far exceeds time so spent in Germany. Many British production managers have succeeded in rising above the 'them and us' attitude and have gained the trust of the workforce through their evident integrity.

Some British production plants are just as successful as those in Germany, and they have much in common. Firstly, many are housed in newer and better-looking premises, better laid out and with newer plant. Secondly, in such plants the production managers have a more perfectionist stance: everything has to be right and if it is not, there is trouble. Thirdly, a lot of effort is put into getting small things right, and bad performance is censured loud and clear. Fourthly, a clear system is regularly used for control and diagnosis. Fifthly, arm's-length management is absent – directors are on the shop floor, the managing director watches a first run, chief executives discuss product changes. Sixthly, there is a strong desire to anticipate problems of design, training, succession, updating plant, improving systems, stock control and visiting suppliers. The philosophy is simple: 'Take trouble to see everything is OK now and do what is needed to see that it stays that way.'

Should there be more graduates in production management? Hutton and Lawrence found a strong body of opinion that production managers should 'work their way up' and that they should come from the ranks of people of ability who are not attracted to higher education. It is held to be difficult for graduates to reach the skills and know-how level of people who have had years of workshop experience, and difficult for them to cope with the shop-floor culture. The graduate suffers from a credibility gap in the eyes of the workforce, even if he can avoid arrogance, ambition and impracticality. Higher education does imply some privilege and superiority, and many managers think: 'No college boys here, we're all grafters.'

But this is traditional thinking and harmful to a new start in British industry, which should now be concerned with new technology and white collars on the shop floor. If there were

more graduates on the shop floor it would be more difficult to
say that production is a second-best career. We should agree
with Hutton and Lawrence that there should be more movement
between production and other functions. Brain and brawn
should move around and get more mixed up together in an
increasingly technological world, and training should be
designed to stimulate this. This should lead to better order and
planning, making the 'future accessible to the designs of
the present'.

For many years British industrial managers and workforce
have seemed crushed by the weight of their inadequacies, of
which they are constantly reminded. This has increased their
scepticism about enthusiasm of any kind. The media have
encouraged this same downbeat attitude to their readers and
viewers. But the British would like to be more positive, as was
discovered by a Gallup study in late 1981 for the European
Value Study Group. The British are happy at work and take
more pride in it than do the other nations in Europe. They are
very patriotic and the majority would fight for their country.
Nevertheless, they are hard to lead and manage because they are
extremely prone to the feeling that they are being exploited or
discriminated against. They respond to 'one out, all out' in
factories before they know why.

My own view is that most British people are suspicious of
politicians, national trade-union leaders, company chairmen,
'do-gooders', the City, and the gentry. They trust committed,
professional, classless, considerate people who do well and offer
a prospect of success. They have come to feel that people from
outside Britain, especially from North America and the old
Dominions, have got something to teach us about management.
They do not know much about Europe, but feel hostile to it.
Their awareness of Japan is only just beginning.

The attitude of the British workforce to their managers varies
directly with the quality of management. There is no evidence
that the British, with good management, are a truculent,
bolshie, idle, unmanageable lot. In fact the British like to be well
managed and to have confidence in their bosses, and they
respond to people who know what to do. They will gladly work
well for friendly managers who treat them as individuals, who
tell them what is happening and what is likely to happen, who

act fairly without dithering and who do their work in a professional way, with the habit of success. It is not much to ask.

The gentlemanly approach has impeded aggressive improvement of design, processes, products, sales and industrial relations. The shrewd money managers in the City of London have turned aside from the reluctant managers of British industry, not believing them to be winners. Shop stewards and trade unions have seen that a reluctant manager is a soft touch and that they can get him on the run. Reluctant managers are an endangered species, which ought not to be protected. Fortunately, a new breed of managers is now coming up – not yet plentiful enough in supply, but they have started to set the pace. They may well have their eye on a Buckingham Palace Investiture, and all stations en route, but they gaze with much greater intensity on the performance and morale of their shop floors or office staff. They know that unless the 'bottom line' of their accounts shows a plus, they are not being competitive and are unlikely to be long for this world. They recognize the British attachment to 'small is beautiful' and they divide their operations into the smallest possible operating units. Thank heaven, they are on their way, as can be seen in later chapters, but they need to be encouraged and to collaborate with other skilled people. That goes for all business managers and for the managers of the public services, including the civil service, and for our schools and colleges. It would be a main drive of the development state, which at no point could tolerate leisurely, amateur, gentlemanly, timid, isolated, uncompetitive, reluctant management.

'We are none of us gentlemen any more.'
(Fowler's *Dictionary of Modern English Usage*;
2nd edition)

3 The Weinstock Story

Our philosophy of personal responsibility makes it completely unnecessary for you to spend time at meetings of subsidiary boards or of standing committees . . . all standing committees are by this direction disbanded, and subsidiary boards will not need to meet again . . .

That was Arnold Weinstock (now Lord Weinstock) since 1963 Managing Director of the General Electric Company (GEC), to the managers of English Electric (EE) on 29 November 1968. Starting again with a vengeance!

I tell this story because it shows how even in the grandest British companies the post-war record was a saga of disappointment and failure, due to old style and wrong systems of management. It was the arrival of Weinstock upon the scene which showed how this could be changed. He did not borrow American consultants' ideas; indeed, he reversed many of them. He worked out for himself, with the help of Kenneth Bond,* his inseparable business colleague, what was needed to make British business profitable and then he did it, irrespective . . . and it worked. This was the start of a new management explosion, badly needed in Britain. Weinstock has been the hinge between the old and the new, between the hopeless and the hopeful.

The history of GEC, the acquisition of Amalgamated Electrical Industries (AEI) in 1967 and the merger with EE in 1968 have

* Sir Kenneth Bond, Deputy Managing Director of GEC since 1966

been brilliantly described by Robert Jones and Oliver Marriott.* The memoirs of Lord Chandos† and Joseph Latham‡ tell part of the AEI side of the story. Recent years are covered by the annual reports, and I have had long talks with Weinstock. The story is still alive in my mind, because I was managing director of the Industrial Reorganization Corporation (IRC) at the time of the EE merger and vividly remember several crucial meetings. These have been neatly described by Professor Sir Douglas Hague and Geoffrey Wilkinson.‡‡

GEC will soon celebrate its centenary. It was founded in 1886 when Gustav Byng‡‡‡ and a fellow-Jewish Bavarian, Hugo Hirst,‡‡‡‡ registered in London the General Electric Apparatus Company. The name was changed in 1889 to the General Electric Company, and it had a capital of £30,000. Byng had money, Hirst had none, but they were joined by yet another Bavarian, Max Railing,‡‡‡‡‡ who insisted that Hirst be enabled to take up part of the capital. Hirst was a genius, but for the next twenty-five years he quarrelled continuously with Byng. Fortunately, he – a flamboyant expansionist – found in Railing his perfect partner: cool, analytical, financial. Hirst and Railing ran GEC until their deaths in 1943 and 1942 respectively. Railing never lost his guttural German accent, or his love of careful, detailed, dedicated work. Hirst bought a big house in Berkshire, became an elder statesman and liked to advise prime ministers. He went to the office every day until his death. It was said by a colleague, Tom Kerr, that without Hirst GEC would have remained a small electrical shop, but without Railing it would have gone bankrupt.

GEC's opportunity came as it was starting, when the electric lamp patents of Edison and Swan expired. Its fortune was built upon the manufacture of electric lamps at a time when the use of electricity was spreading all over the world. Its first prospectus in 1901 said that 'GEC carried on its business in almost every

* *Anatomy of a Merger*, Cape, 1970
† Oliver Lyttelton, later Lord Chandos, Chairman of AEI 1945–51 and 1964–8
‡ Sir Joseph Latham, Deputy Chairman of AEI 1964–8
‡‡ *The IRC. An Experiment in Intervention*, Allen & Unwin, 1983
‡‡‡ Gustave Bingswanger, founder of GEC
‡‡‡‡ Lord Hirst, Managing Director and then Chairman of GEC, 1906–43
‡‡‡‡‡ Max Railing, Deputy Chairman of GEC, died 1942

civilized country'. The profits that year were £70,000, the employees numbered 3,000 and the factory was on a forty-two-acre site at Witton, near Birmingham.

Acquisition of the Osram lamp company brought GEC nearly level with its British rivals, British Thompson Houston (BTH), which was owned by General Electric (GE) of America, and British Westinghouse, which became Metrovick, owned by Vickers. BTH and Metrovick were strong powerful companies who fought GEC and fought each other, even when they were later merged together in AEI. Cartels and rings were organized to diminish the cut-throat worldwide competition, but these collapsed when the Second World War broke out and the anti-trust legislation was introduced in America.

Hirst was determined to make GEC the greatest British electrical company. His slogan was 'everything electrical'. During the First World War GEC made shells and cables, too – and a great deal of money! Hirst was one of the accepted leaders of British industry. He became 'gentrified' to some extent, but he always had Max Railing to keep him at business. They had married sisters. They were extremely pro-British. Hirst had family ambitions within GEC, but his son died in 1919 of 'flu, after surviving an active service war, and his grandson was killed in action in 1941. He had intended that Railing should succeed him, but Railing died first. Hirst then laid down that he should be succeeded as chairman and chief executive of GEC by Harry Railing,* Max's brother, a brilliant engineer, and after him by his son-in-law Leslie Gamage,† son of the owner of the famous Holborn store.

Up to 1943, the year of Hirst's death, all had gone well for GEC. Hirst was nearly eighty when he died – still in harness. Harry Railing was sixty-three when he took over and Leslie Gamage was seventy when he became chairman. These successors never got on together and Gamage was always losing his temper. As the cartels broke up, the cosy world to which these men had become accustomed was changing. Their colleagues, too, were old and inadequate. Jones and Marriott say that 'competitors considered the fire had gone out of GEC's

---

* Sir Harry Railing, Chairman of GEC 1943–57
† Sir Leslie Gamage, Chairman of GEC 1957–60

belly'. It was an inbred, indecisive organization. The post-war consumer boom carried them along, but by the mid-fifties profit margins were slipping. In 1957 Harry Railing, aged seventy-nine, stood down. Leslie Gamage took over a very big company, with sales of over £100 million, but profits were slumping and borrowings from City financial institutions rising.

The crisis came in 1959. Arnold Lindley* was made vice-chairman, but when it came to renewing a large issue of GEC loan stock the mighty Prudential Assurance, the leading City institution, signalled that it would not renew more than half its participation. That was a fearful slap in the face for GEC, and there was no hiding it. Gamage lost his temper. Management consultants were brought in to report on the organization. Gamage was pushed out. Lindley became chairman, and he knew he had to look for talent outside GEC. In 1960 GEC took over Radio and Allied Holdings, owned by Sobell† but run by Arnold Weinstock.

Bad top management had brought a great company down almost to its knees. The succession had been wrong. Old age and family were allowed to play too important a part. Organization was not understood and was therefore faulty. Finance became top-heavy and was not supported by profits. The influence of the City was brought to bear decisively, but too late. This situation goes on repeating itself elsewhere in British industry, despite all the warnings and experience.

The AEI story has a different beginning, but the same ending. In 1926 Gerard Swope, President of GE of America, which already owned BTH, tried to bring all the leading British lamp-making companies together 'to the general advantage of the trade'. He got Metrovick from Vickers, but Hirst defeated him over GEC and he lost interest in EE, which he thought was a hopeless case. Swope failed to bring together the British electrical companies. Forty years later Weinstock succeeded.

In 1929 GE owned both BTH and Metrovick. These two GE subsidiaries were then brought together under a holding company, AEI. They were, however, amalgamated only in name and their long-standing rivalry was continued until Weinstock's

---

* Sir Arnold Lindley, Chairman of GEC 1961–3
† Sir Michael Sobell, Chairman of Radio and Allied Holdings

day by what were called the Barons of Rugby (BTH) and Trafford Park (Metrovick).

The first chairman of AEI was Felix Pole,* formerly chairman of the Great Western Railway. He completely failed to rationalize the common manufacturing interests of BTH and Metrovick. These companies continued to go about their own business to the irritation of their customers, the detriment of AEI and the considerable damage of Britain. For example, both companies were researching into jet engines without telling the other! Neither had the strength to go it alone. BTH worked with Frank Whittle† and the Americans cashed in on his invention. Metrovick persevered, but after the war sold out to the Bristol Aeroplane Company. The business characteristics were secretiveness, conservatism and timidity, overriding the natural British genius for invention.

In 1945 Pole was sixty-eight and going blind; he had been the wrong man for AEI. He was succeeded by Oliver Lyttelton, later Lord Chandos, a member of Churchill's War Cabinet, where he held many important posts with success. At AEI, he felt, 'my professional qualifications were useful. My role was to organize the company on modern lines.' Pole had complained that it was impossible to rationalize while the two companies were doing badly, in the slump of the thirties. Lyttelton found it was impossible to rationalize in the forties because they were doing so well! By the time Lyttelton returned to politics to join Churchill's last administration in 1951, little had changed.

In 1953 GE sold its shares in AEI. The reason was the long anti-trust case against GE in America. GE's shares in AEI were offered to the other shareholders in AEI, but the offer was a flop and 70 per cent were left with the underwriters. The *Daily Express* yelled: 'a shameful case of pocket before patriotism'. Nevertheless, AEI was now free of American control. Lyttelton came back to the chair, as Lord Chandos. Expansion was in the air and the prospects looked good. Chandos reigned at AEI for nine years, until 1963. He was a natural spokesman for AEI and for British industry. He was big in every way. 'To stand still is to die,' he said; he was clever, experienced, grand, respected in the

* Sir Felix Pole, Chairman of AEI 1929–45
† Sir Frank Whittle, inventor of the jet engine

City, but arrogant with professional people – engineers in particular. He did not know how the intentions of top management could be made effective on the shop floor. One day, when we sat next to each other at an insurance company board meeting, I asked him how he did it. He replied, 'I tell the buggers to do it.' This was a classic in its day and age of British management.

For five years Chandos expanded AEI on money borrowed in the City; for the next four years he was wondering how to service that debt. By 1960 he was writing to Eric Ball, the managing director of BTH, 'Where do we go from here? I am at a loss.' He dominated the whole group and could have drawn it all together, as Weinstock did later, but he did not know how. In nine years there were four reorganizations of the management structure. None of them was successful. All the introspection and analysis failed because there wasn't enough determination to change and improve. Great economy campaigns fizzled out; there was no major surgery. In those Chandos years sales doubled and profits were halved. Earnings available for ordinary shareholders fell from 55 per cent to 8.7 per cent.

The old rivalry within AEI was still at work: 'trespass on my parish and I'll set the dogs on you'. On top of this was over-capacity in the industry, and open criticism of management. As Sir Joseph Latham said, 'Every reorganization was a challenge to what Chandos had done.' Chandos retired in 1963 and 'Mike' Wheeler* from Guest Keen & Nettlefold became chairman. Latham became vice-chairman. George Walker, director of central services at AEI, wrote '. . . everyone scrapping and snarling for his own ends'. The situation of AEI at that time was very bad – it was to get worse.

For nearly four years, to 9 November 1967, when Weinstock took over, Wheeler remained chairman of AEI and Latham vice-chairman. Latham was made chief executive on 1 January 1967. The four non-executive directors of AEI made these appointments; of these directors three were 'City' and one was an industrialist. The appointments were wrong. Wheeler was never the man for the job; he was a salesman, cheerful, optimistic and popular, but with no cutting edge. Latham was

* Sir Charles Wheeler, Chairman of AEI 1963–7

careful, cautious, analytical, financial – always a number two man. Wheeler was often away. Latham was not a man of action but in a tight corner, with care and determination, he made an impressive effort.

AEI in these years exhibited 'the paralysis of analysis'. Only in 1965 were finance and marketing directors appointed to the AEI board. They came from outside AEI, but do not seem to have made an impact. Profits picked up somewhat, but the old sacred cows were neither nourished nor dispensed with. AEI reports were full of 'proposals are in hand', 'arrangements have been made' and 'much remains to be done'. The 1966 profits, which had been forecast at £13.5 million, came out at £9.2 million. The first half-year of 1967 produced only £3.7 million of profit. That was the signal for Weinstock to move, and on 28 September 1967 GEC offered cash and shares worth £120 million for the AEI capital.

Conversations with Latham about a merger with GEC had been going on since 12 July, but he said he had not received a 'specific proposal'. Indeed he had not, but IRC and others were 'feeling him out', and found him hostile. When GEC's bid became public there was a flurry of activity in AEI. Shares in subsidiaries and properties were sold off; AEI made optimistic profit forecasts of £10 million, £15 million and £20 million for the next three years and volunteered Lord Beeching, of British Rail fame, as chairman. A great lobbying for shares took place, but Weinstock and Lord Aldington (then chairman of GEC) had the edge and on 9 November they announced that they had over 50 per cent of the AEI ordinary shares. Latham then advised all AEI shareholders to accept the GEC offer. 'In the face of AEI performance,' he said, 'it was not possible to defeat a bid made by a company with a better profit record.'

The management flaws in AEI were different from those of the old GEC. What was the point of merging BTH and Metrovick if the advantages of putting the two companies together were not taken? If this is not done instantly in a merger, it becomes harder and harder as the years go by and eventually requires a trauma, such as in the end AEI suffered. Perhaps Gerard Swope had just been indulging in 'dreams of glory' and the hope of reinstating the lamp ring. Whatever the reason, the failure to rationalize was disastrous. Another remarkable failure was the appointment to the chair of so many wrong people – Pole, Lyttelton and Wheeler were all the wrong men at the wrong time in that job. One must suspect that the job description was never thought through. The non-executive directors must carry the blame for that.

The final flaw in the system is exposed by the fact that AEI's profits turned down in 1956, and stayed at a low level for ten years, despite rising sales and capital employed, before effective action was taken. Even then change was not originated by the internal management, the shareholders, or the financial institutions, except the Prudential. Corrective action, Weinstock's bid, might not have happened if there had not been an IRC and a radical merchant banker* ready to suggest and support violent action. 'Gentrification' is very deep-rooted – too many 'good chaps' still around at the top. The Americans are sharper and say 'nice guys come last'.

English Electric had been formed in 1919 with a capital of £5m, which made it then the biggest British electrical company. The purpose was to amalgamate and rationalize a mixed bag of electrical companies. The directors came from railways and shipbuilding; they never made a success of the newer electrical industry. In 1930 the merchant bankers, Lazards, made a financial investigation and others looked at the technology. Lazards raised more money and the Edmundsons electricity generating group found more business. George Nelson† came over from Metrovick at Trafford Park as managing director. He saved and made English Electric. He became a great British industrial leader and died in 1962, still at the helm, having been president of all the professional engineering institutions and of the Federation of British Industries.

Nelson was autocratic, irascible, tenacious and a great engineer, but he would allow no executive except his son to sit on the main board. He imported a number of distinguished outsiders to the board-room, but none that would challenge him. He was not for having any nonsense of that sort and kept the seat warm for his son George, affectionately known as 'half Nelson'.

---

* Kenneth Keith of Hill Samuel, later Lord Keith, Chairman of Rolls Royce
† Lord Nelson, Chairman and Managing Director of EE 1930–62

Nelson took over a company with heavy losses. EE shares stood below their par value. There was much over-capacity in the industry. By the 1960s EE had a turnover of £200 million and earned more profit than either GEC or AEI. Nelson got the Southern Railway contract for electrical equipment in 1934 – the only main-line surface electrification project. He built Hampden and Halifax bombers. By 1945 EE had 30,000 employees and had built 3,000 bombers and 4,500 aircraft engines. After the war he built no fewer than 1,400 Canberras, the first jet-propelled bombers. He also built, for the London Midland and Scottish Railway, the first main-line diesel-electric locomotive, but he had to wait until 1955 to get the first big order for them! He bought up Marconi to get into radio communications. He tried to buy up Siemens but failed, and he lost out to Thorn and to GEC in TV, but he spent heavily on research and had no fewer than 2,000 young people in training. His achievements were immense.

Young George Nelson* became chairman and chief executive of EE when his father died in 1962. He was an excellent businessman diplomat, but he had neither the time nor the ruthlessness to do all that was needed in EE. He was always much influenced by his father's work but, whereas Lord Nelson had been a co-operator within the rings and cartels, George Nelson had to be a competitor with no protection. Maybe George had been 'gentrified'; certainly he did not get angry, nor was he conceited. He became and remained totally loyal to Weinstock in serving the GEC group. In 1983 he handed over the chairmanship to Lord Carrington.

On 22 July 1968 a conversation took place which I remember well. Nelson and Weinstock had been discussing with IRC the rationalization of their mutual turbo-generator business, and they both came to IRC to meet Frank Kearton† and myself. When the talk was over Weinstock said to us, 'I would like a word with you.' We said goodbye to Nelson and moved next door with Weinstock, who at once said, 'We are playing around with details . . . GEC is now ready to take over the whole of EE, and with their assets and facilities on the chess-board we can play a

---

* Lord Nelson, Chairman of EE and then GEC, 1962–83
† Lord Kearton, Chairman of Courtaulds, the IRC and later BNOC

much bigger and more successful game.' Kearton and I knew
how well Weinstock had remade AEI. We looked at each other
and said, 'OK.'

Then out of the blue, on 21 August 1968, came a bid by
Plessey* for EE, worth £260 million. Plessey was smaller, but had
nearly the same profits and less debt that EE. Nelson said, 'We
don't want Plessey's help.' Wedgwood-Benn, then Minister of
Technology, said, 'This is one the market should not decide.'
From 26 August Nelson and Weinstock were talking, and on
26 September Plessey backed down tactfully in a statement
made by their merchant bankers, Warburg.† In the end EE shareholders got one third of the ordinary capital of the joint GEC/
AEI/EE company and the prospects of better profitability. GEC
had increased its capital by 140 per cent by these acquisitions,
but its sales had gone up by 373 per cent. Good for Weinstock!

Looking back at English Electric you could, of course, argue
that Nelson should not have kept the seat warm for his son
George, but leaders have done this since time began and it
sometimes works. In this case it worked up to the point when it
could work no more, and then there was change. George Nelson,
like many others before and since, saw the merit of a more
trenchant management style than he could muster himself. He
knew what his father had been able to do and what Weinstock
was doing, and he decided to go with Weinstock. He was right,
and the City and the EE directors were right to go along too.

English Electric thus came into the GEC fold in a much less
painful way than AEI. Indeed, at their board meeting which
approved the merger, after Poole‡ of Lazards had recommended
it, there was only one hand raised in dissent – the hand of the
Marconi man, I think. As representative of IRC, I was sitting
next to George Nelson. There was sadness in the air and
resignation to the inevitable. Aldington stood down to make
room for George Nelson, as the new chairman of GEC and there
was minimal fuss and bother. We had had a crisis with Anthony
Crosland, President of the Board of Trade, about whether he
would refer the merger to the Monopolies Commission. IRC

* The Plessey Company, Chairman Sir John Clarke
† S.G. Warburg & Co., Chairman Sir Siegmund Warburg
‡ Lord Poole, Chairman of the Conservative Party and later of Lazard Bros,
Merchant Bankers

made a strong pitch for no referral, on the grounds that it would disturb and disorganize two great exporting companies for many months. All the civil servants present took the opposite view and urged referral. It was a great relief when Crosland ended the meeting with 'I settle for the IRC'.

The IRC report of 1969 said: 'the problem is to shift sub-standard top management before it is too late'; that was the lesson learned from the real-life stories of the three great old British electrical companies. The IRC report of the previous year had stated: 'The merger of the GEC with EE in September 1968 created one of the strongest groups in the world ... IRC advised government that such a merger would produce wide and increasing benefits for the economy and give impetus to further constructive reorganization.'

That judgement was based upon reams of industrial analysis, but the strongest drive was the ability of Arnold Weinstock – proved in GEC's earlier acquisition of AEI – to manage, inspire and control large numbers of other managers, carrying out a complicated series of related actions and options. As we now know, fifteen years later, Weinstock has been successful and has set standards and established techniques which today are followed in other good British businesses. There is an old Latin tag, *ad hominem*, meaning 'to the man', and there is no doubt that the decisions leading to the creation of the modern GEC were 'to the man', and the man was Weinstock.

Weinstock is an enigma, indeed a riddle wrapped in an enigma. He has so many springs of action and thought, constantly interweaving, complicated by his modesty and then suddenly by a touch of real arrogance, that he has defeated analysis. He is a rare phenomenon: youngest son out of the large family of an immigrant Polish tailor, he has built a huge industrial empire and a fortune. He has been awarded a knighthood and a peerage; his horses have won many races, including the Derby. He knows the music of Mozart better than most professionals, but he can't play a note. His home and gardens are perfections of taste and care, his children are brilliant, he adores his wife. His advice and support are sought by prime ministers, economists, businessmen and social reformers. Even the great German combine AEG sought his help. He did, indeed, originate a method and style of industrial

Lord Weinstock: an eye for 'all the details, every angle', also for spotting managerial talent in the workforce. 'The shop floor is every bit as suitable as a business school.' The *Director*, January 1984

management which he started to perfect in 1954, when he went to work with his father-in-law Michael Sobell.

Weinstock is exceptionally clever and clear-sighted. He is highly numerate and has an instinct for margins of any sort. It is not clear how much he owes to education at school and the University of London, where he gained a degree in statistics. He was called up and drafted to the Admiralty in 1944; there he came under the strong personality of Sir James MacKay, who influenced him greatly. Probably the seeds of his genius started to sprout in 1947 when he went to work for Lewis Scott, a property man. He worked with him for seven years, doing deals and making money.

Weinstock developed a flair for money business, but he says he found he was by nature idle and had to force himself to work. Nevertheless he remains motivated by Old Testament principles; about everything he does he cares passionately . . . and this caring he has transmitted to his managers.

He married Netta, the daughter of Michael Sobell, in 1949 when he was twenty-five and never looked back. Sobell had a small business, Sobell Industries, making radio and television sets. In 1954 he sold out to Electrical and Musical Instruments (EMI) and took in exchange cash and a factory in the Rhondda Valley of South Wales. Sobell was then sixty-three, but he wanted to go on giving employment to the people who had worked with him before and he asked his son-in-law, Weinstock, if he would like to 'come in with the boys'. So Weinstock joined Sobell at a small salary and with no special brief. He learned from Sobell, who was a talented salesman; from Banner and Gould, the production and commercial managers, and from Vesely, a brilliant émigré Czech engineer.

By 1955 Weinstock was running the business, then called 'Radio and Allied' (R & A), and the annual turnover was up to £4m. He laid out the production and purchasing programmes. He spent a day each week in the laboratory and two or three days a fortnight on the factory floor. Every Monday all the managers had to sit with him from 5.30 p.m. until all the outstanding questions and programmes had been reviewed and corrective action agreed. This used to take four or five hours at the beginning, but as everyone learned that in a self-contained business any problem is everyone's problem, the meetings got shorter and then less frequent.

An essential element in Weinstock's success has been his business partnership with Kenneth Bond, which began in 1956. Bond had been auditor to EMI, with whom Sobell had many dealings, and his clever, practical, detailed, commercial outlook has provided Weinstock with the perfect sparring partner and financial controller. The door between their two rooms is seldom closed. They have deep respect for each other's capacity, they do not queer each other's pitch, they have grown and flourished together.

In 1956, on his way to the factory in South Wales, Weinstock found himself driving past the MacMichael factory at Slough.

MacMichael was a small independent company and its shares were quoted on the Stock Exchange; Weinstock got it for £345,000. It was his baptism of corporate fire. Bond investigated and reported favourably. Warburg, the merchant banker, advised against the purchase, but finally acted on behalf of Weinstock. Williams and Deacons bank offered a standby credit but then, as now, Weinstock had enough cash to pay up in full on settlement day. By 1958 R & A had become a public company, forecasting profits of £1m. The public held 26 per cent of the shares, the remainder were held in family trusts.

For some years John James of Broadmead, a distributor of radio and TV sets, had been a great friend of Sobell and he came to admire Weinstock's business capacity. James believed that Weinstock could run a big company, and he introduced him to Harry Moore of merchant bankers Philip Hill. Moore took Weinstock to see Lindley, recently appointed chairman and managing director of GEC, and his deputy Tom Kerr. It was Kerr and the auditor, George Touche, who saw the value of R & A and of Weinstock and in 1960 GEC bought R & A for £5m, three times more than its value three years before.

In 1960 Weinstock was thirty-six. He had been a small businessman and had had a lot of success in only a few years by building up a family company. He was now to be pitchforked into one of the biggest industrial situations in Britain. He and Sobell joined the board of GEC, since they were among its largest shareholders. Weinstock joined the management committee. The committee was a shambles; Weinstock could not bear it and left. In 1962 Weinstock was invited to come back as managing director; he accepted on condition that Bond took over the whole of the finances. Lord Aldington became chairman. At that time the annual turnover was £90m. Twenty years later it was fifty times greater.

Within four years GEC had been turned round. Weinstock did not feel that he was starting anew; it was a continuous process of change. He says he 'just went in and dealt with a whole series of things. The rabbit warren at Kingsway was sold and was replaced by a minute headquarters in Stanhope Gate. The masses of indigestible paper work were reduced, as there was no point in paying for unusable information.' Bond knew more about big organizations than did Weinstock and between them they got away from the old 'functional' basis of management into 'profit centres', and they set up indices of performance, whether better or worse. They sent David Powell, an accountant they hired from EE, to study what GE and Texas Instruments were doing in America. Powell described the differences and this enabled Weinstock to evolve the system of precise reporting, which concentrated attention on the core of the business.

Weinstock and Bond then set up their famous control system. First and foremost there was a cash report every day. Firms do not go bust for lack of profit but for lack of cash and Weinstock seems to have a terror about this, which accounts for GEC's cash mountain. They imposed ratios for margins on sales, for the velocity of turnover of stock and debtors and sales per head. They monitored the volume of sales and the monthly cumulative balance sheet, showing the capital employed in each area of the business. By 1967 GEC's turnover had risen to £200m and its profits to £18m and the time had come for Weinstock to move, towards AEI and EE.

Weinstock is not gregarious and he did not compare his systems with those of other companies. For some years he had simply been concerned with putting right what he calls the 'improprieties' in GEC. He felt critical of what he saw in British management, but he had not realized the general malaise which was causing so much to go wrong. He believed very much in a Spartan regime for managers and fought against the excessive privileges managers like to give themselves. He concentrated on the management of managers. He tried to establish a moral basis of competent managers. He did not himself enjoy the grind of going through 120 profit centre reports number by number, line by line, each month. He found his work was mainly grind and only a small percentage was flair, but the system devised by him and Bond put paid to 'management by surprise'.

Aldington was Weinstock's first chairman at GEC and he made way for Nelson, which greatly eased the EE merger, and in 1983 Nelson made way for Carrington* as GEC Chairman. Weinstock just worked and learned. Some of the old managers have gone. Those who stayed and those who joined them are

* Lord Carrington, formerly Foreign Secretary, Chairman of GEC 1983–4, now Secretary General of NATO

better, they act more responsibly and are paid more. The system is now codified and this stage of management revolution is completed. There are 120 companies in the group, of which eighty employ more than 500 people each. Perhaps Powell's report on the vital statistics of GE and Texas Instruments in America was the key to it all, but Weinstock manages now in the systematic way he and Bond have evolved. This is management 'by exception' and 'pulling at the pieces of wool sticking out of the knitting which show something is wrong'.

Weinstock has moved GEC into the United States, where he has found all the old management problems cropping up again. It looked good at first, but as he pulled at the wool he found the weaknesses – optimistic contracts, neglect of detail, and the need to replace managers. He had again to get to the bottom of what was wrong and apply his famous ratios and management system.

Today GEC is Britain's largest company. Its turnover is more than £5½ thousand million a year and some 200,000 people are employed worldwide. GEC's exports from the UK are worth more than £1,000 million annually. Its profits before tax in 1983 were £670 million and there was £1.3 billion in cash at banks. The group has over one hundred principal subsidiary companies, a third of them overseas. It is one of the largest, richest and most powerful manufacturing companies in the world. It manufactures all the new technologies – electronics, automation, space and defence systems, radar, satellites, computers, System X telephone exchanges, microwave radio, viewdata systems, liquid crystal display facilities, integrated circuits and microprocessor controls for a great range of purposes. It makes cables containing optical fibres, domestic appliances, microprocessor-controlled, and arms for robots with doubled-speed working. Weinstock dryly commented recently, 'Another reasonably successful year . . .'

Was it all worth it? Weinstock wishes that he had had another talent and career which would have avoided the awful problems he has had to face. He is still not satisfied; standards are not yet high enough. He never worries about the fact that people watch everything he does. He is a pessimist and his main motivation is fear of failure. He knows he can 'influence things', but he distrusts success. He says, 'What is a good result? There will be better or worse reasons for it.'

Weinstock has all the time been pushing out the frontiers of his capacity and he does not think he has missed many big opportunities. He has no hesitation about the rightness of his decision to go into GEC or to acquire AEI and EE. 'Otherwise,' he says, 'they would have sunk.' He remains pragmatic about size; perhaps at heart he is still a small businessman. He is not impressed with people who try to dominate their managers. He tries to encourage. 'What counts most,' he says, 'is the relationships between people who run the business several layers down. They must not compete with each other's egos, they must serve the customers.'

He is agnostic about whether GEC should be broken up into smaller companies. Tax arrangements would probably not yet permit that without damage to shareholders. He would encourage management 'buy-backs' in any part of the group where the technology is simple, but he likes to keep the complicated technologies to work at himself. If he has a secret formula for success it is to make a business coherent and properly accountable with a very small central overhead.

Weinstock is now mature, but still energetic: he is at the midpoint of *si jeunesse savait, si vieillesse pouvait*. He sees some, like the philosopher Isaiah Berlin, as cleverer than himself. He admired Lazell, who built up Beechams. He thinks a lot of William Waldegrave, now an MP, who worked in his office with him. He admires his son Simon, a banker, who looks after the family horse-racing and -breeding interests, and his daughter Susan, who has chosen 'Housing by public authorities' as her PhD thesis. Top of his list is Tom Paine, who ran the NASA programme which put man on the moon.

Brains he finds useful for storing, scanning and collecting information. Business qualities are integrity, humanity and above all flair. Out of that comes judgement and getting people to follow, which is leadership, and that leads to power. You cannot, he says, teach this. All you can do is create an environment of success – always expecting expectations to go wrong, so as to be ready to put them right.

There are, nevertheless, questions about the GEC which need answering. Why, for example, it is necessary to have such a huge cash mountain – £1.5 billion, as I write. Is the interest on deposit the best that can be earned on it? Weinstock clearly sees that what got GEC, AEI and EE into trouble was too much borrowing, too little profit, not enough cash. He has learned that lesson. Big contracts do go wrong, new activities are expensive to fund and nurse. Research is very costly and much of it never comes back. Recessions can be long and painful for over-extended companies. Weinstock is just not going to get over-extended.

'Besides,' says Weinstock, 'GEC is investing all the time as fast as it can find things to do.' GEC is seeking product development continuously throughout its huge product family. Acquisitions of good well-managed companies are too expensive. Acquisitions of good, but badly managed companies take an enormous amount of management time. 'We make the best use of the cash that we can,' Weinstock says. 'We don't have to invest, just because we have cash . . . if we were short of cash for a project we would borrow it.' Nevertheless, in May 1984 he said: 'A part of cash resources is being set aside to form a specialized activity . . . to assist managements of companies in which it takes a stake, to improve their performance to the general benefit.' Is this a real change of strategy, a redeployment of the cash mountain, or a bit of PR? Probably something of all three. The government's industrial privatization programme, now in full swing, may tempt Weinstock to make another major move. But fear of failure after so much success must be a restraining factor. Weinstock will move only at his own time and speed.

It has been asked why Weinstock has not gone in for the mass production of integrated circuits – the 'chips' which go into all electronic devices. These are imported into Britain in enormous volume and contribute to the deficit on the electronics account of the British balance of payments. GEC makes all the specialized integrated circuits it needs for its own purposes and it makes 'industry standards', but Weinstock does not believe in making 'commodities'. He likes to design, assemble, test and market but, he says, manufacture should be done by those who do it cheapest and best, whether in America, Germany or Japan. Weinstock is very much aware of the threat from Japan. He believes that Britain can meet it, but only by continually leapfrogging, by pioneering, as in the fifth-generation micro-processor or computer, which will calculate much faster than anything seen so far. In that project in its predevelopment stage, when there will be government funding, GEC will work with other companies at home and abroad. Weinstock is at the leading edge.

Who will succeed Weinstock? What happens if he is run over by a bus? That is his nightmare. Perhaps that is why he is health-conscious. He is, and he knows himself to be, unique, ahead of the field, making the running for industrial Britain. He will soon be sixty, an age at which many would be starting to think of retirement. He has seen the succession problem proving fatal in other great companies. Could son Simon cope? Not yet, certainly; perhaps one day. Kenneth Bond, like Max Railing, loves the figures and the detail. Which of the thrusting managers Weinstock has brought on could stride up into the top job? How would the non-executive directors, men of wide experience, choose his successor? Weinstock knows that his successor will run GEC differently; the next man will do it his own way. Perhaps he will de-merge, break up Weinstock's creation ... perhaps he will re-merge internationally ... that will depend on what seems best to do at the time . . . and the non-executive directors will have a lot to say about it.

What comes out of the Weinstock story, as out of all good management stories, is that

● with the best management even the worst situations can be turned around,
● the British *can* manage very big companies, organized in small units,
● Britain needs managers who
    mind deeply about the results of what they do,
    care about how people do their work,
    take endless trouble about details and numbers,
    insist upon quality and improvement and innovation,
    care about winning,
    infect others, so that they care, too.
● collaboration with government can lead to great success.

Stories like these show that progressive management can win the battle against 'couldn't care less' – that insidious symptom of decline. Old-style managers either have to start again or make way for others who can.

4 Starting Again

Weinstock, thank heaven, does not stand entirely alone! Other enterprising managers have done great things, and some of these are described later in this chapter. Before that, however, see how British management faces its work and views its chances of success, as Thatcher Two unfolds.

During Thatcher One the world recession, the high cost of money, the ridiculous fluctuation in the value of the pound (up to £ = $2.46 in 1980 and down to £ = $1.30 in 1984) have made business life more difficult than at any time in the last fifty years. The rate of company liquidations trebled, manufacturing output fell to its lowest level for fifteen years. Profits, excluding those from North Sea oil, fell by 40 per cent, manufacturing investment likewise. Unemployment has never been so high, the unions have never been so unpopular and management has not been so battered since the 1930s.

This has been shock treatment for British business, but there have been pluses too. Inflation came down from 20 per cent to 5 per cent. The take-home pay of senior, but not of junior management was considerably improved by tax reduction. Productivity rose sharply and it is easier to be competitive with a lower value for the pound. Apart from the Scargill factor, there has been much less 'buggeration' by trade unions, due to high unemployment and diminishment by government. Working together and flexibility on the shop floor have improved. Something has been done to help small businesses start up and expand. There is undoubtedly a new spirit of enterprise, collaboration, hope and confidence that Britain is capable of considerable recovery.

There can be no doubt in 1984 that, as expected, recovery from that deep depression is under way. How far it will go without relapse will depend on how far management will overcome the strains which have aborted full recovery in the recent past.

A new start has in fact begun, but it is still hesitant. It should be nurtured and accelerated before it is killed off by the British disease, which should now be tackled and treated at source. The symptoms of the British disease are:

Truancy and failure in education.
Lack of engineers and technicians.
Old-fashioned design in products and processes.
Absenteeism from work ... couldn't care less! ... Why bother?
Poor productivity, quality, delivery and service.
Over-manning and demand for wages in excess of productivity.
Uncompetitive costs.
Loss of markets.

These symptoms prevent Britain from being a completely self-adjusting economy. We do not fully bounce back after recession, and our recoveries fizzle out before full advantage has been taken. Only management in all its forms, encouraged by government and a new public understanding, can reverse that disastrous trend. That would be a prime function of the development state.

How does management in Britain view its prospects? A recent comprehensive and detailed survey* found British managers generally buoyant about their own and their companies' future. Ninety per cent felt they had begun to tackle core problems and had become 'leaner, fitter, more confident and better equipped to design, make and sell products to the world'. That is the good news. The bad news is that low profits and fierce international price competition were holding them back from 'great success' in both home and foreign markets. Many companies have to sell at very low margins or even at a loss to keep hold on a market. More than half the managers questioned found this the most serious issue because it impeded new, necessary investment.

* *British Management and the Recession*, ORC October 1983

Another report* found British managers highly realistic, with the prime objective of cutting costs by raising productivity by the use of the new technologies. Senior managers were seen to be going for a bigger slice of existing markets rather than experimenting with new products in new markets. The big needs were better management information, savings in energy use and some form of professional/technical education – not business schools. A further report† found that management resistance to wage claims is likely to weaken as the economy picks up and that the assertion of managers' 'right to manage' is likely to provoke unnecessary industrial conflict. A survey of European managers‡ found 70 per cent optimistic about their own and their companies' prospects, but one in two were unsure about political and economic trends in Europe. More than half looked to economic growth and new technology to improve their quality of life; nearly all are 'determined to do things better' but, but, but . . .

• Listen to Ian Nussey, an IBM man, also deputy chairman of the Cabinet Office ACARD:** 'Because Britain failed to develop technology we enter the eighties trailing 30 per cent behind the world's front runners for competitiveness. Governments have been aware of this lethal threat to our manufacturing existence for years but have been unable to communicate the extent of this threat.'††

• Listen to Geoffrey Holland, director of the Manpower Services Commission, 'British employers see industrial training as a do-gooding Welfare Service', and to the Institute of Manpower Studies, 'Young people on apprenticeship in Britain have fallen from 100,000 four years ago to 40,000 in 1984'.

It has become clear that managements worldwide have improved, or have tried to improve, the performance of their

* *The Chief Executive and His Outlook*, Heidrick & Struggles, October 1983
† *Industrial Relations Opinion Survey*, EPIC, May 1983
‡*Chief Executive* and Management Centre Europe, September 1983
** Advisory Council for Applied Research & Development
†† *Chief Executive*, October 1983

organizations simply to survive. No country should think that it has scored a resounding advantage over others. All have improved. As we have seen, Britain was lagging behind the competition when the recession began. There is not much evidence to show that the lag has been greatly reduced. Those reports give no grounds for complacency, rather for anxiety that the competition may go on drawing ahead of Britain. Nevertheless, a bull point has been scored. British managers have shown a new willingness to change – by and large – and that is now backed by some confidence that this can lead to greater success. The new start does now have a chance of catching on country-wide, of spreading a new dynamic infection rather than the old British disease, and of drawing level with the competition.

The new business philosophy was described by Sir Alex Jarratt, Chairman of Reed International, speaking in 1982 of corporate renewal or 'back to basics'. He had spotted Britain's 'massive deterioration in ability to compete overseas and in the home market'. He had also spotted how for many years Britain had been able to mask this ... avoid risk and confrontation ... buy up the competition ... ignore the gross under-employment and over-manning ... believe that inflation would bail Britain out . . . So, expand, diversify, go overseas, go anywhere, do anything and hope you will somewhere, somehow find the management to cope with the resulting problems.

By the eighties, British managers could no longer believe in eternal growth and the ready availability of money to finance it. Jarratt said of his own company:

> We had to settle down to re-establish, from scratch as it were, future business objectives. We had to withdraw from activities no longer relevant to mainstream business and where the costs and risks were higher than any possible contribution. We had to reduce our debt and foreign currency exposure. We had to concentrate on where we had high skills and sustainable profits. We had to optimize earnings to benefit shareholders. The immediate result was not INvestment but DIvestment – selling off and closures. Keep your head down, grow an extra skin and get on with the job!

That was the philosophy behind the sale of the *Daily Mirror* to Robert Maxwell for £113 million in 1984.

Jarratt achieved a rapid turnaround at Reed because he identified and supported the mainstream, well-managed businesses which recovered their confidence when available cash was invested in them. He made major changes in top management, he developed a more open, consensus style of management at board level and he improved communication between management and workforce. He also made major improvements in strategic, business and financial planning and reporting. Jarratt regards planning as 'A tool to be used with all the other inputs a manager brings to bear in making judgements. Planning is an attitude of mind, of thinking forward in an ordered way and not being dominated by everyday events. The ambition is to be "surprise-free" – the reality is less than this, but remarkably superior to the information with which we set out to reconstruct.'

Jarratt spoke of deindustrialization as an alarm call and a threat to our wealth and employment base. He concluded that we must operate what we have more effectively and create conditions in which new industrial activities can be added in. He called for

● no letting up on hard-nosed approach in judging our companies and organizations;
● investment in key activities even though the going is rough, because we believe they have a future;
● growth of new businesses. Renewal demands more than making the best of what we have got.

Government, said Jarratt (previously a distinguished civil servant) cannot instigate, so renewal is something companies have to start to do for themselves. That means that managers must have deep knowledge, a capacity to motivate people to change, an ability to disappoint as well as to encourage and – what they have always needed – the realization that uncertainty is what markets are about. Jarratt made this policy successful and Reed's profits have risen steadily.

The following stories from my case book show how other companies have made a new start. They show the different ways in which success can come, and how hard and deep is the surgery needed.

Babcock

Babcock is a grand old British company, established in 1891 at
Renfrew near Glasgow to make steam boilers. The first directors
were Charles A. Knight, an American, and James Herman
Rosenthal, the English-born son of a German father and an
English mother. Rosenthal changed his name to Kemnal in the
First World War. He was knighted for his and Babcock's part in
the war effort and reigned at Babcock (then called Babcock &
Wilcox) from its foundation until he died in 1927. He was the
complete industrial autocrat, and for many years he was the
only man at Babcock allowed to travel to London. His board-
room colleagues included Sir William Arrol, whose firm built
the first Forth Bridge, and Sir Andrew Stewart, the founder of
Stewart & Lloyds, the tube makers.

This tradition continued in spirit, but with diminishing
effect, until 1970. Occasionally chairmen or specialists were
brought in from the outside world, but Babcock was run by
practical men, promoted from the shop floor, with little academic
or formal training. They were extremely good at making boilers
for steam-raising in the traditional way. They were conservative,
tough and fair, but unwilling to change their methods. They did
not think much about bottom-line profits, they just made
excellent boilers. In wartime they also made tanks and
ammunition.

In 1970, however, a series of loss-making contracts forced a
change. Babcock had by then become a multinational group
with subsidiaries or shareholdings in America, Canada, South
Africa, Germany, France, Spain, Australia and Japan. Few power
stations in the world were put up for which Babcock did not
tender, but the traditional methods of production and the
autocratic tradition at the top could not take the strain of
continuous and what was often considered 'unfair' international
competition.

In the late sixties, the advanced gas-cooled reactor programme
of nuclear power stations forced Babcock to absorb a new
technique without which they could not stay long in the
nuclear business. At Renfrew some young engineers borrowed
ideas from American Babcock and set up an industrial
engineering department. This introduced the most modern

methods of production, welding, value engineering and procurement, with a strong influence upon design. At the same time the
top management at Renfrew was swept away and replaced by a
firm of consultants. This was proposed by Sir Iain Stewart, who
was also responsible for the 'Fairfield experiment' in shipbuilding
on the Clyde. New men also came in at the headquarters in
London, led as chairman by Sir John King, later to be given a
peerage as chairman of British Airways. Existing talents were
released and encouraged, finances were overhauled and corporate
policies were changed. Within two years Renfrew was
transformed. The consultants were released and men from the
industrial engineering department formed a team of thirty
trained professional 'in-house' managers.

The strength of this production team at Renfrew, led by Alan
Smith, lay in the fact that they had all worked together for some
years, and that they all had a Higher National Certificate of
Education or better; they had the mental discipline to take in
new ideas. Further, they had all worked on the shop floor and
earned the trust of the workforce. They had learned at night
school, but always in their own time. Babcock had helped to pay
for extended university courses, often over three years, but
never in company time. So far, so good, but . . .

The management/workforce relationship in Renfrew at the
end of the sixties was conflict. There was rebellion and criticism
about everything, especially rates of pay and overtime, which
the shop stewards regarded as their right to fix. The consultants
scrapped all the varying rates throughout the works and
established a flat day-rate payment with no bonuses; for some
years this system held. Then in 1974 the oil explosion in and
around the North Sea created an unimaginable demand for
welders and at Babcock they were there for the plucking. In that
year Babcock lost 275 of its 300 regular welders, so by
agreement with the unions it put up the day rate for welders.
Neither managers, unions nor workforce expected the protest
which followed, but in 1975 the works were closed by a long,
bitter strike.

By the following year Babcock at Renfrew was almost on its
knees. At the eleventh hour, to avoid closure, the entire
workforce came together to work out a survival plan. In the next
year one third of the workforce was made redundant, but the

works got the contract to build the power station at Drax. In 1978 the Renfrew management put up a plan to rebuild and re-equip the works at a cost of £20m, some of which came from company funds and some from government grants. The workforce endorsed the plan after it had been put to invited audiences of the whole workforce – twenty-five at a time – in a forty-minute video. A thousand questions were asked. A second long video answering the questions was made, with a famous BBC programme presenter interviewing the managers, shop stewards and workforce. At last all the unions at Renfrew agreed to combine to talk regularly with management in a series of joint councils directed towards attitude change. This new technique is now being widely used in industrial relations in Britain.

The steering committee of this system is chaired by the managing director. Reporting to it are twenty-four planning committees, which define the action taken by employee action groups, which in turn report to a co-ordinating group, which reports back to the steering committee. Already a thousand of Babcock's three thousand employees at Renfrew have participated, and the essential feedback to top management has been achieved. Japanese 'Quality Circles' (described in a later chapter) have been modified to suit British requirements. Babcock has instituted a team approach, in which teams meet under their foreman weekly for ten or twenty minutes and plan improvements. Almost at once the sacred 'eight welds per shift' were increased to fourteen. All parties benefit from these short, sharp, regular meetings. There is much of Japan in Babcock, following careful study of the joint company, Babcock-Hitachi.

The main investment plan has been completed, giving Renfrew the most advanced boiler-maker capacity in the world. Most of the machine tools are computer-numerically-controlled; the machining centre, costing £3m, was imported from Germany. Welding, an essential feature in boiler-making, has been deeply researched. Computer-aided planning, design and manufacture covers half of all Renfrew's work, much of it transmitted by Telecom from the designers in London. Of the middle managers a third use keyboards themselves; of the new intake of young managers 100 per cent use keyboards.

So Renfrew changed its image and its attitude as well as

establishing a new reputation for quality and delivery on time. It still had to reduce its unit costs to the lowest international level. The factory rebuild saved 7 per cent of costs, increased, by consultation with the workforce in 1980, to 10 per cent. This increased further in 1982 to 17 per cent and reached a 25 per cent cost reduction by the end of 1983. It is a never-ending process which implies fewer unskilled workpeople but greater use of electronics, which requires more skilled workers.

All this change and improvement at Renfrew would be short-lived if it did not have a beneficial effect on the bottom line of the profit and loss account and show an improvement of the cash flow into the balance sheet. By 1977 the heavy losses of the past years had been eliminated and Renfrew was on a rising profit trend. But great success comes only from endless improvement, and by 1984 Babcock needed to spend another £30m on bending and rolling huge steel plates into heavy-pressure vessels. Once again the main board agreed to find and spend the money, if it could be justified by a further leap in productivity. The shop stewards of the boiler-makers and shipbuilders have to lug their members out of the world of turners and fitters into a variety of new engineering skills and tasks. Foremen and operators will have to do their own maintenance and repair. The Japanese model has been studied. The workforce, their representatives and Babcock are contemplating all this in Japanese style. As they look around, they see the good results of major investment in the past, they praise management for being ready to back them in the future and they have learned that big changes are needed to stay alive in an intensely competitive world.

Babcock nearly went under in 1976, but management and men saw the danger. They acted quickly, making some mistakes, but with continuous improvement overall. There were key men available, within and without, to get the start-again process moving, but it has to be kept moving. This is the industrial echo of Sir Winston Churchill's reminder, 'The price of freedom is eternal vigilance'. But for Babcock, as for others, survival is not enough. Babcock has to grow and that means the endless search for new markets to satisfy.

Davy

'In 1969 Davy Ashmore, as the company was then called, touched gloves with the Dark Angel' – so wrote its chairman years later. The accounts for 1969 record that 'a loss of £2.9 million arose from provisions of £11.4 million for loss on a contract with Continental Oil (UK) at Immingham'. The company had run out of profit and cash and top management, all at the same time. Further, it was very largely pinned into contract work in Britain in industries which were threatened with decline, such as those needing rolling mills, forging presses, processing lines and finishing equipment at the very heavy end of industry. At Davy's Sheffield works the company was losing £5,000 a day.

IRC reported in 1969: 'A severe overrun on a major contract threatened Davy Ashmore, a leader in both process and steel works plant, with unfortunate consequences for the UK in both sectors. IRC sponsored arrangements to bridge this crisis and remained in close touch with the company; a substantial part of the short-term finance was swiftly repaid.' New management, new policies and new cash were injected. Buckley, later Sir John Buckley, became managing director. As so often, the influence of one man triggered new efforts by many others.

By 1970 Davy was back in profit and by 1973 the profit was £2.8 million – a record for the company – then in its 143rd year of operation. Buckley's policy was risky, but logical. Davy's strengths lay in technical expertise in engineering and in constructing plants for the steel, non-ferrous, chemical, oil and gas industries. Davy decided, under its new leadership, to update its techniques (moving from town gas to North Sea gas, for example) and to move into the field of major international plant construction contracts, where Britain was sadly under-represented. Whatever did not fit into the new pattern was sold and cash was thus raised to pay off the 1969 borrowings. The company scoured the world in the search for new companies to acquire as a base for its projected international role. While fighting for life on the home front, Davy sought its future in new fields overseas.

By 1970 Davy had paid off its debts and had cash in the bank, and its great Darnall engineering works at Sheffield were being converted to higher technology. The new industrial countries wanted the new plants, but they also wanted to use their own growing engineering capacity. Davy got contracts by encouraging the use of local capacity. It shipped from Darnall only the most sophisticated high-value parts, such as pieces weighing up to 350 tons each which would operate with extremely high precision. Darnall is now the largest and best-equipped works of its type in Europe.

As the home base became secure, international action was pursued with greater confidence. Partners in Germany and USA were sought; by 1973 Bamag and Zimmer, then Zieren in Germany, followed by Wellman-Lord and Olsen Engineering in America, had joined the Davy Group. The companies joined Davy by agreement and of their own volition. The organizations were harmonized, processes were pooled, project management was shared out within the group and a continual interchange of technical know-how and people began to stimulate the whole enterprise.

The biggest step was taken when the McKee Corporation of USA approached Davy with merger proposals. This amalgamation was completed in 1979 and virtually doubled the size of the group, which now employs assets totalling £145 million – ten times the level of twenty years before. From a bankrupt, home-trade, heavy engineering contractor in 1969 Davy had become, ten years later, one of the six largest engineering and construction companies in the world, actively competing for the biggest international contracts and offering a wider range of technologies than any other comparable organization.

Davy McKee, as all its engineering and construction companies throughout the world are now known, is building in forty countries. It is the main contractor for key parts of the steel works being built in central Brazil. This project has a potential of ten million tons per annum, which is not much less than the total British steel production in recent years. It is building the world's biggest polyester plant in China. Half the modern methanol plants in the world, using natural gas which would otherwise be wasted, have been built by Davy McKee. In Korea it is the technical co-ordinator for a copper smelter costing $180 million. In the Arabian Gulf it has built the world's largest oil recovery project at a cost of $900 million; each day

500,000 barrels of sea-water are injected to boost the oil recovery rate and extend the life of the field. Clean air, pharmaceuticals, the search for new fuels and the latest technology – mainly computerized – for rolling mills, continuous casting and many non-ferrous processes are all part of the Davy McKee expertise.

Big investment has been needed for all this – £12 million in 1980 – and the risks of a big contract going wrong are high. Orders on hand in 1982 were worth £2 billion and the turnover in that year was nearly £1 billion. Most of that was overseas, but exports from Britain were worth £185 million. Employees worldwide totalled 17,000, of whom half were in Britain.

The choice of the right policies, the appointment of the right people, taking the right risks and selecting the best partners at home and abroad are the job of top management, and in the case of Davy this hauled the company up by its bootstraps. But vigorous, expert middle management is also necessary and all employees in Davy are 'put in the picture', as Field-Marshal Montgomery used to say. Perhaps the secret of Davy's extra-ordinary start-again case was that John Buckley fostered the spirit that welcomes change as the best provider of opportunity. When he retired from Davy, Buckley said, 'In times like this you toughen your resolve. This gives a new impetus and opportunity to sharpen companies.' He was 'very optimistic about Britain. We have come through the fire and there is a new spirit.'

The collapse of international investment in 1982 brought trouble to Davy once more. Profits were halved, orders disappeared and a change of direction became essential – out of steel and chemicals into electronics and other new technologies. Davy is again in the eye of the storm and in a high-risk phase, but the management has developed the habit of change and knows, in Jarratt's words, that 'uncertainty is what markets are about'.

Ferranti

There had been trouble brewing in Ferranti for years. The genius of the founder, Sebastian, and his son Vincent, who made the first electric transformer, had been transmitted to his grandsons, but not in the same guise of inventor/businessman which had enabled the former generations to stride ahead earlier this century. Vincent had retired from active business in 1963, but his shadow still loomed large and his influence over the next generation remained formidable. He did not care for change.

By the summer of 1974 profits at Ferranti had vanished. Borrowings were £20m against total assets of £25m and the bankers were saying 'no more'. The Wilson government was in the toils of inflation and early in 1975 prices on the Stock Exchange crashed. Ferranti, despite its important defence contracts, was tottering and in May the Department of Industry subscribed half its new capital and made a substantial loan; all this was later taken over by the National Enterprise Board.

By September Derek Alun-Jones, manager of Burmah Oil's industrial group, had been recruited as managing director and Sebastian Ferranti, grandson of the founder, gave up day-to-day management, remaining non-executive chairman. Alun-Jones faced a task that tested him to the full. Company policy had been what the Ferranti family could be persuaded to do. There were many departments, but little formal management. The accounts each month showed a profit or loss, much like those of a high-street shop. The board was preoccupied with donations to charity, congratulations on awards and suchlike. Investment was difficult because for years there had not been enough cash in the till to pay much more than the wages and other unavoidable costs. The family still held a majority of the shares, and the situation could best be described as management by omission. It had been an exercise in the shareholders' right to ruin their business.

To a professional manager the diagnosis was not hard to make; most of the managers on the staff and in the factories knew what ought to be done, and that involved changing the old order and breaking the power of the centre. The old Ferranti structure was highly centralized in the men at head office, who had access to the top. The chairman had also been chief executive and managing director; he had a life of many interests and was not in his office or in his factories continuously, which was what the crisis management needed. The structure was, if anything, 'functional'; maintenance was, for example, a head office responsibility, employing 600 people. Alun-Jones initiated management by profit centres run by six managing directors in the field, keeping a small head office of 100 staff. He adopted modern management accounting and a high degree of decentralization, with two planning sessions a year for all senior staff. An elaborate system for communicating with the highly unionized workforce was set up, as were productivity-linked remuneration schemes. The workforce came in on the side of management and the stage was set for change.

The results were magical. 1974/5 was break even. In the next year pre-tax profits were £4m; most of this was due to an unexpected bonanza in Canada but never mind, morale went through the roof. Thereafter, the profits rolled in and up year after year. The borrowings were paid off and investment was made in the very latest plant. The old transformer business was run down and a new microchip was introduced – a world leader. Equal status for both staff and workforce was achieved on the basis of comparable pension benefits. Ferranti once more took the lead among inventors – and among businessmen.

The start-again process at Ferranti began with the break-up of the centre and the liberation of the profit centres, but it did not encourage unilateral declarations of independence. The operating divisions were made more formally accountable, the split of central overhead was more strongly enforced. Invention was carefully monitored to avoid overlap. In fact the feudal barons, who used to run Ferranti, welcomed a strong boss in Alun-Jones, a professional to whom they could respond as professionals – no more reluctant industrialists.

The electronic component division at Oldham in Manchester became Ferranti Electronics and a physicist and engineer, Alan Shepherd, previously a university lecturer, became its managing director. In the early seventies the components, which were mainly semiconductor chips and transistors based on silicon, accounted for a total annual turnover of about £1m. In 1982 the turnover was £36m, this despite a massive decrease in the price of each chip. Chips called Uncommitted Logic Arrays (ULAs), with, for example, 64,000 components on a quarter-inch square surface, are sold for £7 each. Chips like these are used in industry, in domestic appliances, cameras, communications and defence. In each of the last ten years there has been a major increase in the activity of Ferranti Electronics. Although turnover doubled and redoubled and profits increased greatly, it was only after nine years that enough cash to finance expansion could be generated. The British share of the world market in electronic components has for long been stuck at 3 per cent, but Ferranti's share of its speciality, ULAs, is 30 per cent.

This progress was possible only because the old transformer business was run down and no longer soaked away the company's scarce cash. The struggle to keep transformers going against the trend was ruining the whole concern. The first fruits of the start-again in management was a build-up of cash to support new products. Electric component products were aimed at Ferranti's existing main industrial customers. The components had to make use of Ferranti's existing expertise. Ferranti looked out for markets where the great American competitors were not and where they were not likely to be. Ferranti sought to be complementary to the Americans and carved out a niche for itself. In the Sinclair personal computer, Ferranti designed one ULA to take the place of fourteen chips made by other manufacturers. There is a ULA at the heart of a Leica camera and of Telecom's private telephone exchange system. There are now thirty main types of ULA.

The new stable financial base permitted not only the development of ULAs but also investment in three American component companies, one in Silicon Valley in California and two in San Diego. There everyone knows everyone else and there is a huge trade in ideas as technicians talk with each other. Even financial information is much more easily available than in Britain; progress is so fast that results are soon overtaken. Ferranti also makes computers, mainly for defence systems, instruments for control of energy, aircraft, weapons, submarines and telecommunications, and heavy engineering products. Since the start-again group turnover has trebled, annual profits have risen from zero to £25m, borrowings have disappeared, new investment has gone up from nil to £25m.

The new Chairman, Basil de Ferranti, and Managing Director Alun-Jones reported in June 1982: 'The last remaining traces of government intervention disappeared when dealings began in the shares previously owned by government . . . this was the signal of our emergence from the difficulties of the past into a major independent electronics and defence company.' The new shareholders are delighted with the results of their investment in a real start-again company.

These stories of famous British companies show what is being done to start again, out of the reluctant industrialism of the past. They have been savagely shortened to illustrate only the main themes of this book, but they do show what can be and has been done to stave off disaster. They are positive, hopeful stories and must raise the question – if these can do it, why not others, too?

I have to point out that in each of the cases quoted above there has been an extensive and beneficial relationship with government. Babcock depends upon government contracts to build power stations. At a vital moment in its life it came under heavy pressure from IRC to change its top management: this was done and produced almost miraculous results. Davy was saved in 1969 with government money and management change. Ferranti was saved by the Department of Industry in 1975 in the same way. There is nothing wrong or extraordinary about this. All modern states do it. The question is, is it done well or badly? Is it done to save artificial jobs or to save essential products and processes? Is government motivated politically or industrially? The development state would need to put uppermost the industrial factor which creates real, lasting jobs.

The start-again process in British big business has followed a consistent pattern. First there is a restlessness felt by managers below the top but senior enough to constitute a challenge. Then the top moves over, not without a struggle, and makes way for the new man, leading a team. The team then spots the real trouble and puts in a task force to identify what should be done – close or invest. It then decides whether to recommend the plan of the task force. If it does, the top man has to carry his board of directors with him and raise the money for the inevitable investment. With the money in hand the team sets the timetable and a detailed operating plan, involving the workforce at all stages. Jobs may be lost in this process, but investment benefits those who remain. Success depends upon how realistic the plan turns out to be and how good the managers are at carrying it out. At the beginning and at the end management is the most important factor. There is no conceivable substitute for it.

The role of government is to encourage in a collaborative way the start of this process, to steer its general direction and, if required, to facilitate and accelerate progress with advice, money and procurement orders. That is one of the jobs of government in the development state. The next stage is to make and do more and better. That is where the new jobs come from: old companies expand, because they have become competitive, and new companies start up, because they can see new opportunities. New investment programmes are the only source of real new jobs.

Starting again on the ground in Britain has made some progress, but not enough, so far, to bring about a national turnaround. The changing attitudes of British management are a good sign, but the change must be followed up, or it will prove another false dawn. The few have been magnificent, the many have been poor. The British capital/manager/workforce system is imperfect. It is too slow in shedding duds at the top end, and too timid in encouraging the starlets further down the line, too preoccupied to plan for the longer term and too adversarial all round.

'We catch a glimpse of the light and then seek out darkness.'
(Clyde F. Crews, *Fundamental Things Apply*)

5 The Management of Change

The case-book stories about improvement in big business get at the heart of management. There is nothing that government, workforce, unions or customers can do to improve matters if management refuses to perform well. There is no doubt that Britain has suffered from poor management, not only in business but in government and in the public services. It is hard for Britain to recapture enterprise and efficiency after long years of an exaggerated welfare mentality. The enterprising development state, even more than the bureaucratic welfare state, would depend above all upon management, and on the management of change all depends.

Management in this country threw away in the first eighty years of this century almost all the advantages built up in the previous century, which in world terms was Britain's century. British managers have been through a period of insensitivity and arrogance with customers, of neglect of innovation and of distance from the workforce – in a word, complacency. What is now certain is that a revival of management skills in a thoughtful and co-operative form is essential, to re-establish Britain as an international winner, to cope with the new technologies and the long grind of getting people back to work.

A hundred years ago an American, Frederick W. Taylor, started to observe and study 'work'. He called his studies 'scientific management'. He analysed manual work, and identified and arranged operations in a logical sequence. His analysis of shovelling sand proved that that the size and shape of the shovel, the length of the handle, the amount of sand lifted, the

position and size of the container were all of vital importance.
All these details had to be scientifically worked out. In this way
the life of a working man could become less tedious and work
less harmful to health.

From this came industrial engineering, mass-production and
techniques such as critical path analysis, all of which boosted
the cult of the manager. A trained manager is supposed to know
all he needs to know, and all he has to do is to work everything
out carefully in detail and then see that the workforce carry out
the instructions precisely. If things go wrong it is not the
manager's fault but the operator's, for being careless or lazy or
clumsy, or whatever.

That was not Taylor's intention at all; he wanted to make life
easier for the uneducated, unskilled labourer. What has
happened is very different and lies at the root of most British
management – or mismanagement – thinking. The mistaken
cult of the manager has directly led to the neglect of the shop
floor and to the rise of the unions and shop stewards. The
sequence has usually been that the brilliant individual manager
strode to the top, with sovereign powers while he lasted. He led
the team, which took its style and pace from him as the source of
power and promotion. To unseat him when he got past his best
was difficult. Lesser managers who were successful and
challenged him were switched to new and more difficult
situations. The danger of this was seen by shrewder bosses in
Britain, who divided their business empires into profit or cost
centres, each with its own promotion ladder and success or
failure record. This worked better, but because of the continuing
cult of the manager it was still not normal to get the workforce
to co-operate in the improvement of quality and competitiveness
where this was most needed. The problem remains – how to
combine industrial leadership with industrial collaboration
all round?

If Britain is to get all-round improvement, the management of
managers has to be brought out of its hiding place. How do we
find, appoint, control and, when the time comes, remove top
managers? There must come a time when their energies are
exhausted, their vision blurred, their appetite for leadership
sated, or when their attitude to subordinates has become either
timid or contemptuous.

There are few successful activities run by a committee when change is coming fast. The record is that improved performance comes when a single individual takes the bit between his or her teeth, takes the strain and leads a team. These are the people who will provide the drive for Britain's new start. If they do not come forward in sufficient numbers and quality we shall not be able to arrest and reverse decline. Each manager has a job to do, which perhaps no one else can do. When it is done there has to be change, so that another can take the lead in the next phase. There are no safe, lifetime, unchanging jobs in management.

The financial institutions – pension funds, life assurance companies and investment trusts – have formed an Investment Protection Committee to look after their interests in companies, which are usually a substantial slice of the voting capital, and loans as well. But in any contested situation they are heavily lobbied and may not act together. Besides, they are money-men with little knowledge of industrial management and of what to do when that has gone wrong. They did little about Woolworth's lingering decline. They took five years to act firmly and force the appointment of a new chief executive in the case of the failing Rank Organization. They did not tackle AEI's long years of falling profit. The Prudential Assurance is the best of City institutions at promoting change. So far not many of the others have helped to get the duds shifted – more's the pity!

It is not a question of whether the boards and managements of public companies are public-spirited or ethical. It is whether they are sufficiently aggressive, competitive and efficient in investment or sale of the assets and processes and products or services for which they are responsible. Boards and management can easily become a self-absorbed hierarchy, resisting change, clinging to the familiar, the cosy, the unstirred and unstirring way of life.

I have heard this myself. 'Well, Sir Thomas, now that you have reached the magnificent age of ninety years, the board would like to know if you wish to be appointed for another three-year term.' 'If that is your wish, chairman,' said Sir Thomas, 'I should be delighted to continue. Thank you very much.' A traditional story, but one with a grain of truth, is of the chairman who, before any major decisions, opened the centre drawer of his desk, looked down and shut the drawer quickly. On his retirement his colleagues looked into the centre drawer and found a note in the old chairman's handwriting: 'Liabilities in the balance sheet are on the side nearest the window.'

It is not legitimate to say that if the shareholders do not look after their own property, the rest of us should mind our own business. The Ferranti story established that. But shareholders need a rallying point if they are to exert their undoubted rights and power. How do they throw out a board which may have avoided bankruptcy, but which has failed to make good use of the assets under its management?

We come back to the problem, identified by the IRC in 1969, of how to remove sub-standard top management before it is too late. Seeking an answer to this problem in 1982, the Bank of England, the CBI and a number of senior City institutions came up with a possible solution. They decided to promote the old idea of non-executive directors (NEDs) on company boards through a small organization (PRONED), to 'strengthen the capability of boards to perform their task of directing British industry with advantage to shareholders, employees and customers, by enlarging the appointment of non-executive directors and by the selection of persons of suitable calibre and qualifications'. A quarter of the companies in *The Times* top thousand had NEDs on their boards in 1979, and the number has since gone higher. The first specific task of the NED, according to PRONED, is 'advising the chairman on succession in top management, particularly in respect of the chairmanship itself and the office of chief executive'. So far, so good! But how is the poor NED, who with any other NEDs on the board is likely to be in the minority, to get into a strong enough position to get a chairman, past his best but still tenacious, to pay attention to what may well be unpalatable advice? Unless the NEDs have some sort of power base, they will be shot down. Palace revolutions are difficult to organize and liable to backfire dangerously. A NED who started to intrigue with other directors behind his chairman's back is very likely to become a casualty, because to executive directors the chairman, while he is there, is the source of their advancement.

American business, which is less tolerant of inadequate management, has devised the audit committee of the board with a majority of non-executive members, independent of executive management, 'to review financial information, the company's internal control and administration and to liaise with the company's external auditors'. The appointment of an audit committee is a condition of listing a company's shares on the New York Stock Exchange.

There has also arisen, first in Canada, then in America, and now in Britain, the practice of calling for a Value for Money (VFM) audit of any particular activity of a company or local or public authority, or department of government. Such an audit needs precise terms of reference as to the boundaries of its inquiry. Once focused upon an area, however, it can search out if anything has gone wrong, why it went wrong, whose fault it was, if alternative methods were proposed or tried and recommend what should be done to get value for money in future. VFM audit can be done by the regular auditors, or by another firm of auditors, or by consultants with specific qualifications. Such an audit can be commissioned and received by the audit committee of a board or of any organization, public or private. This is one of the sticks of dynamite needed to explode Britain into the development state. A long fuse has already been lit.

No respectable and efficient company or public authority need be frightened by this, but many will resent intrusion into their business and a lack of trust in their administration. Knowledge is power and audit committees of non-executive directors, with the knowledge that Value for Money audits give them, would have the power base from which to urge changes which may be needed at the top.

The management of managers has a dark side which few penetrate, but many suspect. It is a dangerous, cruel minefield for the naïve or unwary, but therein lurks the source of much British failure. We can put the problem in the 'Out' tray marked 'Too Difficult', or we can simply make the establishment of audit committees a condition of Stock Exchange quotation, as they are in New York. Once established, there is no reason why audit committees should not call for Value for Money audits where they suspect inefficiency, waste or lack of competitive power, and advise on the necessary corrective action. If nothing happens, and as a last resort, they could report to shareholders direct – and that would put the cat among the pigeons!

Audit committees in private companies are another matter.

The accountants, lawyers and bankers to these companies should press their clients to follow the advice of PRONED and appoint good businessmen as non-executive directors. Pressure for change can be applied more easily in private than in public; besides, pressure for change by customers bears more directly upon the results of smaller companies.

Audit committees and VFM audits should also be part of the control system in central and local authorities, in the world of public health, education and welfare and in all the public corporations supplying our communications, transport, energy and water and in our nationalized industries.

The setting up of a new Audit Commission is a strong new intervention by Thatcher One into the affairs of local government. The new Commission selects the auditors of local authorities from the leading private sector firms of chartered accountants. The Audit Commission not only selects but also briefs and pays the newly appointed auditors, who also have the capacity to conduct Value for Money audits. A new broom, indeed! This is a sensitive spot in Britain's anatomy and rubbing it arouses irritated and hostile reaction, but government and those determined to get a breakthrough in British performance cannot neglect top management as a prime subject for change and improvement.

Another deplorable feature of British management is the lack of technical ability and qualification in a highly technological time and place. Improvement here is quite essential if Britain is to catch up with the competition.

Sir Charles Carter, President of the British Association in 1982, concluded that one of the many constraints which have limited British performance has been that 'our efficiency in using science is sub-standard. We have applied too much scarce, high ability to pure research and too little to effective practice. We do, indeed, spend 2 per cent of national income on research and development, but in this we are too ambitious, too theoretical and insufficiently hard-headed.' Carter's criticism of British management is based on the fact that in 1981, in British manufacturing establishments employing more than twenty people, two thirds did not use computers or microprocessors in any process or product. Of that lamentable figure, some saw no scope for this technology and others saw scope but had done nothing about it, although they thought that competitors overseas were using microprocessors and they themselves were lagging far behind.* An update of this study in 1983 showed an improvement, but microelectronics were still applied to only 7 per cent of all British products and to processes in only 18 per cent of British factories.

Carter's view is that the successful use of science flows from the quality of management. 'Managers,' he says, 'need not be qualified scientists, but they must be able to make sensible judgements on what the experts recommend to them. Somewhere the progressive firm needs a leading personality with the breadth of experience to make judgements covering all aspects of an organization, and the readiness to face facts as they are.' Carter's verdict is that the successful use of science has been

'Many people fail to assess (accurately or at all) their competitive position either in emerging technologies or in existing ones' *Financial Times*, 2 March 1984

* Policy Studies Institute, 1981 and 1983

obstructed in Britain by 'sloppy analysis, facts ignored, decisions evaded or fudged'. The start-again process has to cope with this monumental problem. The case histories in an earlier chapter all involved a greater use of scientific methods. The trouble starts early, in our educational system. This is a hard nut to crack and is examined in a later chapter. Britain's future managers do not need to be specialists in biology, chemistry or physics; what they need is a basic knowledge of science-made-easy so they can start to develop the attitude known in Germany as *technik*.

Young people are enormously interested in technology. The problem is that teachers are scarce and school curricula are overloaded with a profusion of worthy, but unproductive options. Our schools seem to be obsessed with high-minded concepts which bore young people to death – and truancy. Instead of being taught science in a practical way to fit them for practical jobs, pupils get served up with a lot of unrelated stuff which they refuse to digest. Our young are in the consumer society, whether we like it or not, and they want to perform and to consume. We should contribute mightily to their future happiness in work if we built up a *technik* mentality – the basis of the development state.

By the intelligent use of information technology in all aspects of work, managers can now summon all the information they want at a tap on a keyboard. Managers must be able to use keyboards. It is calculated that only 10 per cent of managers in Britain have learnt to use keyboards; in America the proportion is 60 per cent and in Japan 90 per cent. If we are to move into the development state a new generation of managers will have to appear, all of whom will have used keyboards since school. Through them the whole range of information technology will come into play. It is a management tool of immense importance and an essential part of the technological future.

The official Labour Force Survey for 1981 showed that in Britain two-and-a-half million people (of whom 500,000 are women) class themselves as employers or managers. Of these less than 10 per cent have university degrees. Of male managers only a quarter passed 'A' or 'O' levels or got a Certificate of Secondary Education and only one fifth did an apprenticeship. A quarter of male managers and a third of female managers have no qualifications at all. Of professional institutions, only 320,000 members are university graduates. Throughout the entire working population only 6.6 per cent of men have university degrees – 34 per cent have no qualifications at all. In Britain there are 15,000 professional engineers graduating each year compared with 30,000 in France and 70,000 in both America and Japan.

This is appalling! In competitor countries such as Germany, France, Belgium, Holland, Japan and America it would be unthinkable. Not only British industry but Britain as a whole is uneducated and untrained, and most of those who are educated and trained are unprepared for wealth-creating work. An immense effort will be needed to change this situation and catch up with the competition. The development state would need to give the highest priority to the improvement of education and of *technik*.

Another priority for British management should be wider co-operation with other companies and organizations, with local communities, colleges and schools, with its own customers and workforce and with government. British management tends to 'squirrel' things and ideas, take them home and store them up for another day. The British are homogeneous, one race in times of crisis, when threatened or cheated, but at other times we keep ourselves to ourselves. In an island of mixed races and cultures, powerful ambitions and early industrialization this was, perhaps, inevitable. Today it is absurd.

If we are to develop our assets, the adversary attitude is quite simply unhelpful. Today we are a set of small tribes in an offshore island, trying to scratch a living in a hard and unforgiving world. In a development state we would rediscover our native genius, develop sophisticated, well-designed, top-quality products, using the latest technology, and deliver on the dot. No sane person believes that we can do this by beavering away for ever in isolation in our own back yard.

It is good news, as reported by MITI* in October 1982, that twenty industrial co-operation projects between Britain and Japan are in the pipeline. The industries concerned are computers, telecommunications, robots, machine tools and

* Ministry of International Trade and Industry, Japan

bioengineering. MITI indicated that the respective governments were acting as matchmakers, not as principals to the agreements. BL already has an agreement with Honda, as GEC has with Nippon Electric, ICL with Fujitsu and Thorn-EMI with Victor, and there are many others. What is important for Britain is that these deals are not limited to licences, but enable the British partners to develop their own home-brewed technology. This would continue to develop even if the Japanese licence ran out, or was for any reason cancelled.

What is needed is a climate of co-operation in research, combined with intense competition in the market place. That is a more subtle idea than we have widely used so far, but it is the sign of a mature industrial state.

Nowhere does Britain need co-operation more than on the shop floors of our factories and offices, on the construction sites and in most of the public services. The new practice of management includes the necessity to get employee co-operation, because without it the manager will not be able to deliver his quota as scheduled, or better. The adversary attitude, which makes the life of managers and managed so unrewarding, is what the management of change has to defuse.

The initiative lies with management, but the fact is that the interests of both managers and managed are the same. Both want to keep their workplace open. Both want their product or service to be in demand, so that their earnings will be secure. Both want to earn a margin of profit or be successful so that the workplace can attract further investment, bringing more security, more reward and more satisfaction. Both have an interest in the longer term.

It is at this point that rapport gets lost. Most shop-floor and public service workers feel that their managers don't come clean about money and that there is more in the kitty, which should come to them but in fact does not. This suspicion, it must be said, has had good grounds in the past and it will die hard. There are at least three obvious ways in which managers could improve their relations with the shop floor.

The first element is a more constructive approach in the build-up of foremen, supervisors and junior management – the men and women who link management to the workforce. A chain breaks at its weakest link and when the industrial chain breaks, it breaks at that point. For some unexplained reason British industrial management in the fifties and sixties started to make more use of shop stewards than foremen, or first-line supervisors, when communicating with the workforce – as if the unions could run the business for them! Shop stewards are, of course, trained by the TUC to promote trade unionism and for most of them the union comes first. By using the stewards to communicate, management raised the importance of the shop steward and diminished the influence of the foreman and the supervisor. The authority of management on the shop floor was undermined. Foremen need training, briefing, trust and the reward to go with these responsibilities. They have their equivalent in the Forces, where it is recognized that without excellent performance there can be no success.

The second point about the shop floor was made by Norman Tebbit when he was Secretary of State for Employment. Tebbit has earned a reputation for union-bashing, but he said:

> Above all, ... tell them about the affairs of your own firm ... educate your workforce ... I don't see how you can expect someone to work in a vacuum, making things at lower cost every day, unless he knows why he is doing it, where the things go, what affects the demand for them and whether the Germans are out-performing us.*

This is good advice and it reinforces the third point – the advice of the Industrial Society – that unless managers explain their decisions and policies direct, the workforce will inevitably seek explanation elsewhere. The company grapevine seldom gets it quite right, and endless misunderstandings result.

There is now wide acceptance that the relations between management and employees are changing. In 1980 the Institute of Directors said: 'There is an increasing body of evidence to show that companies which seek to involve employees . . . which help them to identify with the company . . . which communicate information about the company and which seek to consult employees before decisions are taken, achieve harmonious employee relations and high levels of productivity.'

* *Director*, September 1982

The British Institute of Management spoke of 'new management techniques with an increasing emphasis on participation and involvement'.

The breakthrough, however, came following a suggestion first made by the Industrial Society in 1974. In October 1982 a clause was introduced by government into the Employment Bill, then being debated in Parliament, that every director's annual report, in respect of companies employing 250 people or more in Britain should from 1 January 1984 contain a statement describing the action taken to introduce, maintain or develop arrangements aimed at:

• providing employees with information directly concerning them;
• regular consultation with employees, or their representatives, so that their views can be taken into account in making decisions likely to affect their interests;
• encouraging the involvement of employees in the company's performance through an employee share scheme.

This clause, incorporated in the Companies Act, was a giant step forward. It is also an example of how things get done in Britain – lobbying by determined people who know what they are talking about and are prepared to persevere over many years.

It has to be admitted, however, that many British managers still do not in their hearts want to consult their workforce; it still goes against the grain. Nevertheless, in 1981 a CBI survey found that the majority of managers thought they got benefit from employee involvement through greater realism in pay bargaining, improved morale, fewer disputes and acceptance of new technology. These are substantial gains, but there are not many managers who want to hear the views of their workforce or believe that workers can contribute useful ideas about efficiency or productivity.

When all the excuses have been made and the experience gained, a general directive will be needed to bring the performance of the laggard companies up to the average. We need three years' experience of the new clause quoted above, and then it should become mandatory on all companies to take the steps about which they have now only to report. Like so many other fiercely opposed improvements in Britain, when it is finally adopted the verdict will be 'why did we not do this before?'

It is to improvement in quality of the products and services offered by British industry that the workforce can make a positive, measurable contribution. That is certainly the experience in Japan and in a number of American and European companies. In Britain we are still at the experimental stage.

Good quality was Britain's hallmark from the Industrial Revolution through to the sixties. 'Made in Britain' was proudly stamped on our products and helped to sell them all over the world. Pride in work, craftsmanship, the understanding of customers, the need to maintain a good reputation and keeping the firm going were motives driving the board-room and most of the shop floor. At the same period there was only one phrase to describe Japanese products, and that was 'cheap and shoddy'. During the sixties and seventies these positions were reversed. The quality of Japanese goods became outstanding and they were no longer cheap; the quality and value of British goods deteriorated and they were no longer competitive. British managers realized that due to poor design, workmanship, delivery, finish and service they were slowly losing their markets. These faults proved hard to correct, so managers clung to being competitive in price, as the one trump on which to trade. This turned out to be a disaster, because it ate into profits and thus diminished investment: it weakened the market position and lowered morale. By the eighties poor quality, high wages, low price and a high rate of exchange had become major influences in widespread factory closure and mass unemployment.

A furore about quality was started by Prime Minister Thatcher. The British Standards Institution has entered a new collaborative agreement with government. The Department of Trade and Industry is launching quality campaigns. A register of companies which satisfy quality assurance criteria will be published. But a weighty report from ACARD says, 'Institutional arrangements to improve quality in Britain are fragmented and effort can easily be wasted through duplication or conflict.' This is just what is happening. On the other side of the world, Japan in the early fifties was striving to recover from the devastation of their country in the Second World War. Japanese leaders saw the need to get away from cheap and shoddy and establish a reputation for high quality. They realized that their managers must be retrained and they invited two Americans, Edward Deming and Joseph Juran, to advise them. The national award for quality in Japan, first made in 1950, is still called the Deming Prize. Juran wrote his best-selling *Quality Control Handbook* in 1950 and in 1982 he was still lecturing in Japan on this theme, that 'quality control is an integral part of management, rather than a specialist adjunct to it'.

The Japanese government and business leaders worked together, offering prizes and introducing legislation to promote highly sophisticated methods of quality control, to retrain top management, and to establish the Union of Japanese Scientists and Engineers and the Japanese Standards Association. Companies started in-house training in quality, courses were offered on the radio and booklets about quality control were sold on the news-stands. As a result of many years of effort, Juran says, 'the Japanese became the best-trained managers on earth in quality, and they were able to make improvements in product design and in the manufacturing process year after year after year.* How was it done? By co-operation!

There is a long tradition of co-operation in Japan, but after the total failure of the militarists in the Second World War relationships had to be remade on a different basis – democratic, peaceful, market-influenced and capitalist-organized – but always on the footing that the recovery of Japan had national priority. Japanese managers were directed by conscious effort to the improvement of quality in everything they did. Japanese people were continuously bombarded with the cult of quality in the media, at work and in schools. There then emerged in Japan the practice of setting up, in places of work, quality control systems, now known as 'Quality Circles'.

A Quality Circle is:

A small group of people, usually between three and twelve in number, who meet together regularly on a voluntary basis for about one hour per week in paid time, usually under the

---

* Quoted by Christopher Lorenz in the *Financial Times*, 3 February 1981

Quality circle six in prize share-out

Surrounded by British made washing machines and cookers, Chairman Ian MacGregor shakes the hand of Alan Brinkworth watched by the other five circle members including circle leader Bob Guildford, plant engineer, (fourth right) and works manager Mike Wakeman (left).

Steelnews, 19 May 1983. This QC at the Bromford Works of British Steel's Tube Division won a prize for redesigning a lathe, which saved over £12,000. Ian MacGregor said, 'Almost everyone can think of a better way of doing things, if they really put their minds to it.'

leadership of their own Supervisor, and are trained to identify, analyse and solve some of the problems in their work, make recommendations to their Manager, and, where possible, implement the solutions themselves.*

Carefully prepared, organized and followed up, the workforce can in this way become involved as never before. Given time, support and persistence, the method has yielded extraordinary results. This is where 'top down', which is essential, meets 'shop

* Definition by David Hutchins, a leading consultant on QCs in Britain

floor up', which can contribute a great deal to the minute detail of the cost and quality of production and service.

In Japan there are now said to be more than ten million people involved in QCs. Japan measures defects in parts per thousand, the West in parts per hundred. In steel, ships, cars, motor-cycles, radios, TVs, videos, computers, cameras and much else the Japanese now sell on quality as well as on price. It is the West which is now running scared as Christopher Lorenz wrote in the *Financial Times*, February 1981.

The West is now starting to imitate the Japanese in quality; as Juran says, 'There is no alarm signal that alerts a top manager as much as the inability to sell his product.' Ford, in their 'after Japan' policy, tried to introduce QCs in Europe, but could not get agreement. Better results have been achieved by Westinghouse, Lockheed, International Telephone and Telegraph, General Motors and General Electric. In all, about 250 companies in America have started QCs. In Britain there are QCs in Marks & Spencer, BL, BSC, Chloride, Mullard, Rolls-Royce, Wedgwood and others – over 100 companies in 1983 – and the first seminar on QCs in this country had been held only three years before.

QCs are not an instant magic wand. Professor Sasaki of Sophia University, Tokyo has warned that many QCs in Japan have collapsed: 'almost always management is behind the failures, either through too little interest or too much'. Nevertheless, the Japanese example is stunning. It is true that Japanese are more naturally group-minded and co-operative than the British. British managers still tend to believe that they can cajole those who work for them into better performance solely by the use of penalties or financial incentives – carrot and stick – and instruction rather than involvement.

This management reaction has been felt in Japan as well. The president of Fuji Xerox found he was suffering from an upstart competitor, Ricoh: 'After an initial period of shock, hurt pride and shattered arrogance came a cold realization that unless we did better, and very quickly . . . we would cease to exist.' His action included a new product 'surpassing all the accepted standards of quality cost and delivery, which has been a smash success'. His method included regular provision to the workforce of accurate information about the company's situation, close co-operation with lower levels of management, and QCs allied to 'aggressive use of shop-floor suggestion schemes'.

Quality Circles will succeed only where management is already in tune with some sort of shop-floor participation. In Britain we move slowly, but the idea has been established and in one form or another it will catch on. A tutor at GEC College of Management at Rugby says, 'The signs are that Quality Circles will continue to grow from strength to strength, but I don't think they will ever be as widespread as they are in Japan.' Why not, for heaven's sake?! I prefer the comment in a letter to the editor of *Management Today*: 'We are witnessing real people in a working environment, adapting, modifying and refining a Japanese technique into an extremely valuable British concept.'

In Britain we are obsessed with short-term results, but the management of change requires a longer term view. Government wants results from its policies while in office, but this is not long enough to develop new industries, new markets, new technologies, new relationships. Industry always has the nagging fear that the next government will reverse it all. The nationalization, then denationalization, then renationalization and finally the preservation of unwanted plant in the British Steel Corporation is an awful example of this. In the private sector, demands of investors for ever-higher dividends can be a tyranny. This hinders new investment, to bring results several years hence. There is always the risk of a hostile takeover in midstream. There is the constant movement of managers from one job to another within an organization, each wanting to see positive results attributable to his own efforts. He goes for maximum short-term returns – why pursue long-term investment which may be inherited by another manager, who will deny responsibility if the investment goes wrong and take the credit if it goes right?

How can we manage economic development and change as a priority that will involve, if it is to be effective, collaboration on a wide scale? For this Britain needs market-plus-organization, that is to say, organized capitalism. The state's role in this is to encourage, facilitate, steer into the longer term and accelerate. The company's role is to collaborate wherever possible and then to compete vigorously in the market place. We have in fact already started to make use of this technique in Britain. We should now work it up to be much more widely applied. The real world is not about intervene or don't intervene, it is about how to collaborate in a great number of in-between positions. Our need is to develop all our assets in the face of much monopoly at home and intense competition from abroad, and we should use the levers nearest to hand, to the extent required to get results. This means combining the enterprise of the private sector with the strength of the state.

We should not be deflected from this by remembrance of things past. It is true that there was no government intervention at the time of the first industrial revolution; perhaps things would have turned out better if there had been. But today all governments intervene or regulate or collaborate to improve industry – some in subtle and some in less subtle ways! We do this in Britain, but we do not do it well. British governments have inclined towards large, extravagant and prestigious projects, which usually fail. Don't I know! The need is for continuous, trustful, well-researched collaboration between government and management to secure niches, parts of a worldwide market. The British have always been sceptical. They like to stay close to what is familiar. The new start is still tentative and could easily be stifled by high interest rates, or choked to death by taxation, or frightened away by over-regulation, or just plain turned off by lack of encouragement.

It is tempting to think that Britain has a self-adjusting economy which, guided by the hidden hand of market forces, will correct all the old faults and deliver the improvement automatically. Perhaps in the days of Adam Smith, two hundred years ago when everything was different, that was so. It is certainly not so today. The flaws will persist and the decline will continue unless government plays its central and essential part in the correction required to reverse the decline by stimulating the management of change.

A sentiment attributed to Nigel Lawson, as he became Chancellor, sums it up: 'in a competitive society you have to force people to adapt, rather than just hoping that they will respond'.*

* *Sunday Times Business News*, 19 June 1983

6 'Them and Us'

Former German Chancellor Helmut Schmidt is quoted as saying to Harold Wilson in 1975, 'as long as you maintain that damned class-ridden society of yours, you will never get out of your mess'.

'The upper class is relaxed, the middle class is acquiescent and the working class is passive.' That is the view of Ralf Dahrendorf in his book *On Britain*, published by the BBC in 1982. Dahrendorf is a distinguished German academic, now Director of the London School of Economics. He calls himself a devoted, but not uncritical friend of Britain. He goes on:

> this is not the stuff from which disruption is made. Yet cohesion requires more. It requires a glue which binds social groups together ... Non violence, not using one's elbows, but queueing, protecting the integrity of others by being kind to them – all the civic virtues for which Britain has been so widely acclaimed – belong to the same story ... There were no institutions to bring about this result; it simply happened, as if people had discovered for themselves that this was the most civilized way to live ... Unfortunately queueing meant simply that one never got what one wanted.

One further quote, this time from Arthur Marwick,* Professor of History at the Open University: 'Managerial attitudes have been too much related to maintaining the outward symbols of an upper-class status and too little towards managing efficiently

* *British Society Since 1945*, Pelican, 1982

... the British working class has more and more concerned itself
with maintaining the status quo, than with the higher
productivity, through which alone higher living standards
could be attained.'

These observers are experienced and acute. But what should the
British now do about the class problem? My judgement is that if
Britain is to move on to the development state it will be
essential to improve this fault by moving quite rapidly 'with
the grain'.

Britain and France are still class-ridden industrial countries.
Scandinavia, Germany, the Benelux countries, Austria, America
and Canada are relatively clear of it. Japan was the most class-
conscious of all, but in order to recover, develop and succeed
Japan moved and has now reached a point where over 90 per cent
of the population consider themselves to be, and behave as,
middle-class.

Britain is divided not only into three classes, with infinite
gradations in each, but into North and South, black and white,
unemployed and employed and, lastly, into those who manage
and those who are managed. It is the depth of the last division
which is unique to Britain. This is the division that damages us
most. It holds the key to improvement and the key is turning in
the lock.

I am indebted to Opinion Research and Communication for
access to their research studies. ORC determined to find out
what workers thought about profit, because the earning and
share-out of profit is the greatest bone of contention. Their
evidence comes from adults all over Britain, in full-time
employment by organizations employing more than 500 people
– small business and self-employed excluded. Date: September
1982.

Most workers have two views about profit, which are
contradictory. The first is:

I am in favour of good profits. They are necessary for
investment in plant and machinery, better working conditions
and more pay. Profits protect jobs and without profits there is
a danger of bankruptcy, closure, redundancy and bad working
conditions.

But workers also say, in the next breath:

> Profits go to the wrong people. They go mainly to the
> shareholders, directors, the government . . . and workers get
> the least benefit from company profits. It will make little or
> no difference to me whether my employer makes good or poor
> profits.

How do you explain that? The British worker is not stupid,
devious or revolutionary. Somehow two conflicting ideas have
got firmly lodged in the mind. It seems that the old, traditional
trade-union teaching about profits conflicts with the facts of
modern industrial life, as seen by a worker; although the two
views cannot be reconciled, both are retained. The resulting
mental confusion will not be cleared up by the unions, who are
also confused on this. It is only intelligent modern management
which will be able to convey to workers a clear understanding of
the nature, need and destination of profit.

When asked if profits are a good or bad thing, nine out of ten
workers, from managers to unskilled, thought profits were a
good thing. When asked the meaning of profit, most came up
with a reasonable working definition. 'Added value' was greatly
confused with Value Added Tax and few workers, or managers
for that matter, understood the phrase.

ORC probed further. 'What do you think happens to the
profits?' Most workers thought that profits were used for
investment or paid to government in tax or to shareholders in
dividends. This correct answer was clearly given by the majority.
A few said 'managers pocket them' and a number of unskilled
workers said 'don't know'. Ignorance grows considerably when
'profit before tax' or 'profit after tax' is spoken of. Few understood
the meaning of 'retained profit'. Understanding was higher
where workers participated in an incentive scheme. What is
sinister is that only six out of ten in the managerial or
supervisory grades understood these terms. No wonder the
profit story does not get correctly down to the shop floor!

Workers were then asked what the results of poor profits
would be; they almost all replied loss of jobs, or closure, or less
investment, or short-time working or lower wages. Fair enough,
but, but, but – and here's the rub – one half of the British

workforce in larger companies don't know and don't care what
profit their company makes. They are indifferent, and the
indifference is almost as great in the managerial and clerical
staff as on the shop floor. When asked why, they replied 'it
doesn't affect me' or 'workers would get no benefit'. They
believe, overwhelmingly that

• benefits from profits go mostly to shareholders, managers,
bosses, directors or owners, and that workers benefit least;
• good profits in good times will go to 'them' and not 'us' and in
bad times it is workers who will suffer most and bosses less so. If
the company is doing well workers won't benefit; only one in
two thought they would benefit from higher profits;
• profits do affect prospects and job security but they probably
won't affect me and my job so WHY BOTHER?

That might seem to sum it up, but another factor emerged.
Clearly some workers had a better understanding than others.
Those who understood more worked in what might be called a
'one-family' type of company with reasonable communications,
some joint consultation and a bonus or incentive scheme.
Those who understood less worked in a 'them and us' style of
company where the communications were bad and there was no
joint consultation or incentive scheme. I call the one-family
type of company the 'progressive company' and the them and us
company an 'old-style company'.
   Managers and staff were more inclined to think that they
worked for progressive-style companies than the manual workers,
of whom six out of ten thought they worked for old-style
companies. Nevertheless, it is probably fair to conclude that

• less than one half of the bigger British companies have started
to move from the old to the progressive style of management;
• only one half of all those who work in bigger companies are
interested in the profits; the others do not believe that profits
will affect them.

The bigger companies have not convinced their workers that
company results matter to them personally.
   As might be expected, in progressive companies the workforce

is more profit-minded than in the old-style companies. What is depressing is that even in the best case fewer than half the workers think that profits make a difference to them. In the worst cases seven out of ten are indifferent to their company's profit. Deep down, the shop-floor worker believes that 'the benefits of profit are for somebody else, so why should I bother'.

Workers are overwhelmingly in favour of incentive schemes. Fewer than one worker in ten thought they were a bad idea. Nevertheless, one third of the bigger British companies have no bonus or incentive or profit-sharing scheme.

Methods of communication between management and workforce take many forms. In old-style companies most meetings are addressed by union officials. In progressive companies most are addressed by managers; these meetings are widely used, as are noticeboards, videos, company newspapers and leaflets in the pay-packets. What workers like most are meetings addressed by departmental heads. What they like very much, but do not get much of, is a senior manager walking round the shop floor, talking at random to workers as he goes. Briefing groups, Quality Circles, regular reports and works councils are no substitute for these contacts. They are the marks of the progressive company.

The outstanding fact is that workers have a great hunger for information about the company they work in, and want to be taken into the confidence of their departmental boss. What they are rarely told, and what they badly want to know, is what are the chances of redundancies in the future and why did management make certain big decisions, which affect everyone. Only one half of the workforce think they are getting this information.

More information about profit and losses is strongly desired by employees, despite the indifference factor. This desire is felt by twice as many people in the old-style companies as in the progressive companies. The same thing is true about hours of work and working conditions. Even in the progressive companies there are many who do not feel informed about wages and salaries, changes in the pension scheme and future redundancies. In the old-style companies there are many more. When it comes to knowing about the reasons for big decisions, affecting the whole company, more than half the workers in progressive companies do feel informed; in old-style companies only a third.

In progressive companies two thirds of the workforce said communications were good. In old-style companies two thirds said communications were bad. In Britain, with a manufacturing disaster on its hands, this is a disgrace.

After communication comes involvement. In about half of all British companies employing more than 500 people there is, it seems, no works council, joint committee or any joint consultation machinery. It may not be as bad as that, but if workers don't know whether such arrangements exist they cannot be very effective. Workers who do not have joint consultation would like to have it. Overall 60 per cent of manual workers think that joint consultation is a good idea; 20 per cent think it is a bad idea and 20 per cent 'don't know'. Most (70 per cent) who do have it think it works well or fairly well, keeping workers informed and telling management of problems, grievances and requests and dealing with health and safety. Not many workers think that works councils should negotiate problems with management or deal with pay claims, redundancies or short-time working.

Workers are not usually involved in decisions about the introduction of new machinery or short-time working, but most said they were asked how the work could be done more efficiently. In all companies workers feel that such machinery for joint consultation as does exist should be strengthened and that where it does not exist, it should be introduced.

Workers were asked: 'Does management treat you as an equal?' In progressive companies seven out of ten workers said 'yes'. In old-style companies nearly seven out of ten said 'no'. How about that, in Britain in 1982?

Workers were asked if they were told of major changes or news about the company before the public. In old-style companies nearly seven out of ten said 'no'. In the progressive companies more than six out of ten said 'yes'.

'Does everyone get the same holidays?' In the old-style companies only three out of ten said 'yes'. In the progressive companies five out of ten said 'yes'.

Finally workers were asked: 'What are the main weaknesses in the company where you work?' In progressive companies with good communications only 16 per cent thought that management was the greatest fault, but in companies with bad communications nearly half replied 'management'.

It pays management to communicate in many ways – no one way is good enough. If managements do not treat workers as responsible human beings, workers will not behave that way and will withdraw any natural enthusiasm or goodwill. If there is no clearly explained incentive scheme, workers will not become involved with profits and will become indifferent to the purpose of their work. If there is no machinery for consultation, the shop floor will believe what it wants to believe and probably get it wrong. Management will lose the advantage of early warning of trouble on the shop floor and of suggestions for improvement, which are often valid. The initiative for improvement is with management.

The question of worker directors is as old as the idea of nationalization. As I write it has gone into limbo, but it will not go away. In British Steel there had been worker directors in the divisions since 1966. I introduced six employees from steel works in different parts of the country to the main board. I wanted to follow the successful operation of supervisory boards in Germany and the BSC board was addressed by Herman Abs, chairman of many German supervisory boards. In British Steel the chief executive's committee became the equivalent of the German management board – the *Vorstand*.

The six employees on the British Steel board had a terrible time. They had to watch the closure of eleven steel works and the redundancy of two thirds of the workforce. They had to learn a new terminology, face entirely different problems and return to explain these to their colleagues at the workplace. This was extremely painful for them, but none resigned. One, during the long steel strike, even moved from picket line to board-room and back again.

The employee board members would always consult together before a board meeting. Nevertheless, they did not always take the same stance and they developed a line of thought and action related more to the problems of where each one worked than to the national policy of their unions. The union officers tried to keep a tight grip on them, but this was not always successful. The experiment could not be called a complete success, but it was not a failure. I do not believe that we are ready for worker directors everywhere in Britain. The Germans came to it in reconstruction after defeat in war. They have now had thirty years of experience, backed up by a comprehensive legal system. Britain is miles away from that position. The circumstances in which the BSC experiment began were unusual. I do not expect to see it widely repeated in the immediate future.

In an interview as he retired Sir Douglas Wass, Permanent Secretary at the Treasury for nine years to 1983, said: 'The improvement in shop-floor behaviour, due to fear and anxiety, is much greater than, I think, could have been secured by more co-operative methods.' Maybe, but the problems of 'why bother' and 'doesn't affect me' remain and will resurface as the economy picks up, unless they are resolved with a positive and progressive answer. Fear and anxiety do not excuse British management from the need to get the best possible performance on the shop floor; this will come from communication, involvement and some form of participation. The test is, does your workforce see the advantage *to them* of your company's rising profit, and the danger of falling profit?

There are in Britain today two styles of company management. One is new and good – open and participative. The other is old and bad – secretive and adversarial. Unfortunately, there are at least as many of the bad as there are of the new good style. This is changing, but there is not much time and the development state would need to accelerate the move to the new style and not leave it to market forces, whatever that may mean. Britain needs an explicit, progressive policy to combat 'them and us' on the shop and office floors. Fortunately, the move away from the secretive and adversarial style is gathering momentum and progressive companies are moving with the grain. The process should be accelerated along the lines of the recent amendment to the Companies Act, requiring directors each year to report progress in their industrial relations.

Let Bob Ramsay, President of the Institute of Personnel Management, have the last word (October 1983): 'People on the shop floor are reacting differently, but they are not thinking differently. Labour's approach to work and efficiency and customers, and all the rest of it, is still a long way down the road.'

7 The Unions

Trade unions in Britain have a long, strong tap-root down into history and their attitudes and purposes have not changed much with the years. What has changed is the lifestyle of the membership. They are no longer the *lumpenproletariat* of Marx's day. The silent majority own or are buying their homes and contents on mortgage or hire purchase; they have at least one car per family and holiday commitments; through TV they are adopting 'middle-middle' habits and tastes – as the BL car worker said, 'I have a Volvo, too'. In the general election of 1983 less than 40 per cent of the total trade-union membership voted Labour.

All this has left old-style union leaders, their organizations and rule-books high and dry. Unions and members are no longer the same thing. British working people are not going to be pushed around by bosses or unions; they want a say in what happens – hence the importance of the secret ballot in choosing leaders and deciding whether to strike. The union organizations are now at a watershed. They have to decide

• whether to collaborate in the new, technical, bourgeois Britain, the new start and something like a development state
or
• whether to persist in the old historic ways and run an enormous risk of 'including themselves out'.

This question is of absorbing interest. I am indebted to Robert Currie* and Sir Denis Barnes† for much of the history.

* *Industrial Politics*, OUP, 1979
† Barnes and Reed, *Government and Trade Unions*, Heinemann, 1980

The first trade unionists and the unions they formed were intensely individualistic. Jeremy Bentham, the English philosopher, greatly influenced the early years of the nineteenth century with his recommendation to pursue 'the greatest good for the greatest number'. So did John Stuart Mill, the English economist with his 'great principle of political economy, that individuals are the best judge of their own interest. So *laissez-faire* should be the general practice: every departure from it, unless required by some great good, is a certain evil.' British trade unionism, which was in its infancy at this time, was, and has been ever since, deeply influenced by individualism and *laissez-faire*. This is the philosophy of the market place, where everything, including labour, should be sold at the highest possible price.

In Britain unions, just as much as companies, still have *laissez-faire* in mind when they go back to fundamentals. The right thing to do, they believe, is to defend or further their interests, either alone or with others who share those interests. When interests clash, as they inevitably do, each should press his own, even at the expense of others. This led George Howell, MP (also a bricklayer) to write, in 1891: 'No one need feel surprise that the workman has but one aim, namely screwing out of the employer the largest possible . . . wages for the least possible quantity of work.' Trade unionists from the beginning did not have the new Jerusalem in mind nearly as much as the next wage claim.

The unions were shaken to the core by the Taff Vale case, where the judge ruled that the Amalgamated Society of Railway Servants should pay damages to the Railway Company for causing a strike. A tremendous campaign to reverse the judge's decision followed and it resulted in the Trade Disputes Act of 1906, which gave to organized labour immunities under the law greater than those enjoyed by any other group of people in Britain. It also confirmed the unions in their extreme conservative, *laissez-faire* attitude, since any change in their status, as they saw it, could only be for the worse. And so the immunities remained until modified, but not revoked, by Norman Tebbit's employment legislation in 1982.

From this position the trade-union movement, despite some reservations of the membership, was inevitably drawn into party politics. It played a large part in forming the Labour Party, which it saw as a sort of trade union, to further its interests in Parliament. It was, however, clear from the start that the trade-union purpose was not to reorganize Britain on a collective or Marxist basis, but to redistribute wealth within a *laissez-faire* society. The policy, as always, was quite simply to raise wages. Later this came to be joined to the Labour Party's policy of public ownership of economic power, although many trade unionists objected to that because they wanted to resist the power of the state, by whomsoever exercised.

By the end of the First World War there were eight million trade-union members – 45 per cent of the workforce – and the Labour Party polled 2.4 million votes, 22.2 per cent of the poll. Labour adopted a formula, at the suggestion of Sidney Webb, 'to secure for the producers by hand or by brain the full fruits of their industry and the most equitable distribution thereof, upon the basis of the common ownership of the means of production and the best obtainable system of popular administration and control of each industry or service'. For the Fabians and the Liberals in the Labour Party this was a great political objective, but to most trade unionists it was simply a means of squeezing more money out of industry.

A great test came in May 1926 after a report by a Royal Commission headed by Herbert Samuel, one of the Liberal leaders, which recommended nationalization of coal royalties, joint pit committees and profit-sharing schemes, but rejected special subsidies for miners' pay and nationalization of the mines. The TUC supported the miners' case and for nine days one-and-a-half million workers (11 per cent of the male work-force) struck; this came to be called the 'General Strike'. The strike failed and has so far never been repeated on such a scale. It caused trade-union leaders and members to rethink their social and economic ideas, and most of them went back to 'each man for himself'. Ernest Bevin, the transport union leader, conceded that 'the industrial leader has every day of his life to deal with the facts as they are'.

The trade-union movement opposed all the economy measures proposed in the last days of Ramsay MacDonald's Labour government in 1931 and by the National Government which followed. The unions maintained that the poorest citizens were being asked to carry the heaviest burdens and that the depression would be deepened by reducing domestic demand. They pressed for increased taxation and suspension of interest payments on the national debt. A decade of bitter disunity in the Labour movement followed. Webb, who supported MacDonald, said, 'the General Council [of the TUC] are pigs; they won't agree to any cuts'. The president of the engineers' union, however, declared: 'Labour . . . should recognize our importance, as the creator, financiers, and backbone of the political movement . . . the trade unions must be in control.'

The threat from Nazi Germany grew, but in 1936 the TUC voted to resist all attempts to introduce industrial or military conscription in Britain, because this was seen to threaten the absolute independence of the trade-union movement. A conference of trade-union officials resolved that conscription was a means to undermine British democracy and open the way for an attack on the unions.

Nationalization was, however, adopted as a major policy to cover coal, iron and steel, electricity and cotton, provided always that the industries were independent of government and that the trade unions would somehow control their day-to-day affairs. Herbert Morrison, then Labour's leader of the London County Council and later the 'father' of nationalization saw the dilemma and advised, 'it would be better, if you want a trade union fighting policy, that your officials should not see too much of the other side, but have a free hand to bargain'. The TUC agreed with Morrison and included in all their nationalization schemes the right to strike and the right to lock out.

The 1939 Trade Union Congress opened at Bridlington the day after Britain declared war on Nazi Germany. Of the 490 delegates able to be present, only two dissented from the resolution pledging full support to the war effort. As the war effort grew the economy was carefully controlled to avoid profiteering, and unions were able to improve the conditions of their members. The trade-union movement co-operated wholeheartedly with the government during the war. At the instigation of Bevin, then Churchill's Labour Minister, joint production committees were set up, and these increased greatly in number when Hitler attacked Russia in July 1941.

In 1945 Attlee's government changed, for better or for worse, the way the British thought and behaved – welfare took the place of self-help. The priorities of the trade-union movement were then first, to improve wages, hours and conditions; second, to maintain full employment; and third, to ensure that the need should be recognized for workpeople to have a share in the control of industry. Organized labour wanted the industrial reorganization to be redistributive, not revolutionary. It wanted conditions which would create permanent labour shortages, ideal for the use of trade-union power. It wanted increased government spending, financed by taxes on capital and higher incomes. It wanted a nationalization policy which would neither sack employees nor resist wage claims. It remained sceptical of workers' control which would compromise, distract and confuse trade unions. It wanted provision to be made for the interests of workpeople to be represented on the governing board of each nationalized industry. Under the Attlee government unemployment never exceeded 1.2 per cent, earnings rose by 48 per cent; the cost of living by 35 per cent and the Gross National Product by 46 per cent. The number of people involved in stoppages during 1950 was down to 269,000. The unions were very strong during this period. They co-operated with government, even over wage control, and during the government's last two years they had to put up with the fact that wage increases rose no faster than prices.

The Conservative government of 1951 continued most of Attlee's policies for the economy. The Conservatives maintained all the links with the unions, and a union leader in 1960 boasted: 'No Minister refuses to hear our views or take them into account . . . we now operate machinery for regular consultation . . . our influence is powerful and continuous . . . we look upon it as part of the process of collective bargaining and we have had a good education in that.' The unions were industrializing government! They claimed that they had exercised 'commendable restraint' and that low wages meant low investment and low productivity. Above all, they disliked the restraint upon their freedom which an incomes policy implied. Frank Cousins, the transport workers' leader and later a cabinet minister, made the classic comment: 'In a period of freedom for all, we are part of all.'

During the long Conservative rule from 1951 to 1964 the unions ceased to be frightened by the threat of mass unemployment. They began to dissociate themselves from the Labour Party and to emphasize their 'freedom to differ from any and every political party'. The miners' leader, Will Lawther, speaking at the Labour Party conference in 1952, said, 'You have no mandate and even if you had the unions would not accept it.' The characteristics of trade unionism remained innate conservatism, rugged individualism and 'I'm all right Jack!'

By the end of the fifties the unions were having to face a new situation. 'The rich are distinctly less rich and the poor are much less poor. When the wrongs were so manifest,' wrote Anthony Crosland, 'we all knew what to do . . . but now the certainty and simplicity are gone.' Pre-war socialist discussion had become obsolete. 'Traditional capitalism,' said Crosland, 'has been reformed almost out of existence.'

The unions agreed with Professor Clegg, a Labour thinker and wages expert, who said, 'The trade unions are to be industry's permanent opposition, an opposition which can never become a government, and collective bargaining is the means to industrial democracy . . . for this purpose it is difficult to see how the unions could be too strong.'

A great change came over the fortunes of Britain in 1964. The period when you could sell anything had come to an end. British industrial weaknesses began to be exposed and the struggle for survival began. It was the year Conservative rule ended and Harold Wilson came in with a call for a new start. He called Britain 'the sick man of Europe, in need of a national revival'. He foresaw 'a socialist-inspired scientific and technological revolution'. 'There will be no place in it,' he said, 'for restrictive practices.' And Roy Jenkins, then Chancellor, said, 'There is bound to be a degree of moderation in wage demands.' This was emphatically not what the trade unions wanted to hear.

In these circumstances it was not surprising that a New Left should have arisen, championing the human utopian revolutionary elements of the old socialist tradition. Its first members were young intellectuals. They had been shocked by the Russian invasion of Hungary and they hated communism. They loathed the thought of nuclear war and so they were anti-American. They were dispirited about Britain, following the débâcle at Suez. They became Maoists and 'Trots'. They were educated, intelligent and full of moral revulsion; they were also libertarian, which was new among socialists. Their revolt was due, they claimed, to the private control of public resources, inseparable from the existing order, which should be abolished.

The New Left were critical of British unions, but they were at pains to cover it up. 'If only the unions would understand that nationalization has broader, more social functions', and 'the unions must seek a new political destiny', and 'the power to compel remains with the organized workers, but the intellectual way may bring them . . . a sense of their own strength and political life'.

But the New Left has been submerged by the Militant Tendency, which took over the Labour Party Young Socialist movement in 1970. Militant is a Trotskyite movement, propagating Marxism, but opposed to Stalinism and to today's leadership in Russia. It plots on a secret centralist cell basis to spread a Marxist worldwide revolution by 'entryism', that is covert penetration of other socialist organizations. Michael Crick, in *Militant* (Faber & Faber 1984), estimates that Militant now has 5,000 members, spends over £1 million a year and has two MPs, David Nellist (Coventry SE) and Terry Fields (Liverpool, Broadgreen). On 23 February 1983 the five members of Militant's editorial board were summoned by the National Executive Committee of the Labour Party and expelled. This is unlikely to be the end of the story.

Militant became a threat to trade unions in Britain only in 1978. Even today, as Crick says, 'Militant is still relatively weak in the union movement; its public meeting at the 1983 TUC Conference attracted only eighty people . . . the only union it controls fully is the small bakers' union . . . Militant's small successes have often occurred when a union has been involved in industrial action and has been unsuccessful.' The National Union of Mineworkers (NUM) had better look to its moat; its leadership is Stalinist, rather than Trotskyite.

If trade unions chose to shrug off the New Left, they could not so easily dispose of the problems of productivity and incomes, which each successive British government was forced by the facts of life to tackle. This started with the idea of planning, which had been part of the War Cabinet's programme for post-war reconstruction and was continued by Attlee. It came to a head with George Brown's National Plan in 1965. He was

Minister of a new Department of Economic Affairs, which was to transform Britain. Due, however, to trade-union pressure, he had to make a significant disclaimer. 'We are not proposing, nor will I ever take a hand in, legislation to prevent wage negotiations taking place.' George Woodcock of the TUC made the comment, '... you might say, "we will have ... a tight control of labour". I would not like it and I do not think it would work anyhow.' The unions, deep in their individualistic, *laissez-faire*, free-for-all jungle, were not going to have planning from Labour or Conservative governments. Len Murray* of the TUC later said, 'the only long-term incomes policy we are interested in is ... MORE'. At the same time Joe Gormley, the miners' leader, said, 'Who are they as a government to say what should be the wages of men who work on the coal face five days a week? Who are they to lay down the law in this democratic society we have?'

The National Economic Development Council, set up by the Tories in 1962, was shunned by trade unions till the pay pause then in force was ended. The unions vetoed the National Incomes Commission set up at the same time, and it never got off the ground. In 1964 the Prices and Incomes Board was created by Harold Wilson, and this had some effect in introducing a bargain, based on higher wages for increased productivity, but the union response was that any productivity deal made their labour more valuable. Nevertheless, pay deals were negotiated which were supposed, rather half-heartedly, to raise output per man hour, and these were widely used to circumvent Chancellor Callaghan's pay freeze in 1966. Two years later the TUC, led by Jack Jones and Hugh Scanlon, the transport and engineering union leaders, rejected any incomes policy by 88 per cent of the block votes cast.

Harold Wilson and Barbara Castle's proposal in January 1969 for a conciliation pause in unofficial disputes had become a major political issue, creating a gulf between unions and government and within the Cabinet. The real point was whether the General Council of the TUC could dictate to the Labour government. Wilson and Castle found themselves alone in Cabinet with their policy, 'In Place of Strife'. The TUC, scenting victory, offered a 'solemn and binding' undertaking about

* The Rt Hon. Len Murray OBE, General Secretary of the TUC 1973–84

unofficial strikes. As no guarantees involving sanctions were offered, this was valueless, and another attempt to reform industrial relations had failed, but 'Solomon Binding' had entered the joke vocabulary.

Despite this setback Wilson tried again in 1969 to get some degree of wage restraint, and set out a norm for wage increases between 2½ and 4½ per cent; but in the event the increases were around 10 per cent. As Wilson is supposed to have said when his discussions with the TUC ended and his government fell, 'I don't envy Ted having to deal with this crew.'

Edward Heath's government in 1970 was determined to reform industrial relations by legislation, which would regulate trade-union power. It was also determined to avoid a statutory incomes policy. In both of these efforts it failed. There was no possibility that the TUC would be moderate or limit trouble. Jones and Scanlon were determined to defeat Heath's Industrial Relations Bill, which he described as 'reconciling full employment and free collective bargaining with the menace of rising prices and the inflationary scramble that ensues'. There was no discussion between government and the TUC about this – in fact there was a complete break in effective communication.

The Industrial Relations Act became law in August 1971. It made collective agreements legally enforceable, it made trade unions responsible for the actions of their officers in connection with collective bargaining, it prohibited the closed shop, it limited the right to strike and it gave additional rights to employees in the event of unfair dismissal. The TUC boycotted the Act and ruled that unions would be penalized by the TUC if they registered under it.

At the same moment, government and unions came into confrontation over wages. Government dismantled the conciliation procedures, deciding to stand firm and to apply shock treatment by non-inflationary wage increases. The result was, inevitably, a great deal of industrial trouble. The public, however, showed every sign of preferring industrial peace, even at the cost of inflation, which was a less obvious and immediate threat. So Heath and his Chancellor, Anthony Barber, determined to 'get the economy going again', and there began what was called the 'Barber boom'. By November 1972 the resulting inflation had got out of control and Heath started discussions with the CBI and the TUC. The TUC knew what it wanted – the repeal of the Industrial Relations Act and a return to free unfettered bargaining over wages. In the face of that attitude Heath felt he had no option but to introduce a statutory incomes policy, which he had sworn not to do. This started with a ninety-day wage freeze, announced in November 1972. That was the famous U-turn. Fear of being accused of this has introduced a great rigidity into all subsequent government policies.

The freeze lasted till March 1973. Heath then needed a stage two to 'bring wage increases well below price levels'. The TUC agreed reluctantly and resentfully. Stage three, due to begin in April, ran into instant trouble. Heath proposed a wage increase of 7 per cent or equivalent alternative. This was greeted by the TUC as 'unacceptable and probably unworkable'. The miners' executive was determined to break Heath's incomes policy, just as they had extinguished Wilson's guiding light. They claimed an increase of 40 per cent. They were offered 13 per cent plus 3½ per cent as an efficiency bonus, which they refused, and started an overtime ban.

At this precise moment the dark angel struck Heath's government. The Middle East oil prices were sharply raised, increasing all fuel prices in the Western world. This destroyed all the expectations on which the wage offer to the miners had been based. It was inevitable that the miners would strike for their claim, and equally inevitable that the government would refuse it. Heath declared a State of Emergency. A three-day week was announced from 1 January 1974. Murray's offer at NEDC to regard the miners' settlement as another special case was rejected by Barber, who did not believe the TUC could deliver any such bargain. The TUC interpreted this as a decision by government to confront the miners, and declared that the trade-union movement would be behind the miners. The miners voted heavily in favour of a strike, to start on 10 February. Heath declared his intention to stick to stage three and announced that there would be a general election on 28 February. Heath just failed to win the election and had to make way for Wilson's third administration.

Wilson presented, in the March and October elections of 1974, a 'new social contract'. This gave the unions the priorities they wanted and allowed them to continue their normal business of free collective bargaining. Heath's Industrial Relations Act would be replaced with legislation to increase trade-union power and workers' rights. The Labour government would 'control prices', attack speculation and set a climate fair enough to work together with the unions.

In 1974, however, wages rose by 29 per cent, prices by 16 per cent and unemployment by 200,000. Consumer spending fell. The balance of payments went into a deficit of £3.75 billion. The unions blamed this on Heath's incomes policy and Barber's boom. By the spring of 1975 earnings were rising at an annual rate of 37 per cent and the government feared they might be about to face an uncontrollable inflation and their own departure.

At that moment Jack Jones came forward with a plan for a flat-rate wage increase, tied to the cost of living index and based on average earnings. This would cut differentials and benefit the lower-paid. Jones admitted that the wage sacrifices would save jobs. In exchange for this offer, prices of essential goods would be frozen for twelve months. Jones was flying in the face of trade-union history but he wanted to save the social contract, which was very much his creation.

By July 1975, in a rapidly deteriorating situation, a government team led by Denis Healey, the Chancellor, and a TUC team led by Jack Jones agreed 'the development of the social contract', which was approved by the General Council of the TUC by nineteen votes to thirteen. In September the TUC voted two to one in favour, and Scanlon said: 'I looked over the precipice and didn't like what I saw.' The agreement was due to the conversion of Jones to wage restraint. He followed in the steps of Bevin and Deakin, also leaders of the transport union, who had taken the same line in 1948. The influence of trade unions on government had never been higher.

For the next three years there was a close working partnership between government and unions over pay policies, wage restraint and the control of inflation, which came down rapidly. The partnership survived the strain of an exceptionally bad £ crisis in September 1976. James Callaghan became Prime Minister in April of that year and inherited the prospect of deep economic trouble and rising unemployment. Inflation was back at 17 per cent. The TUC leaders felt it was impossible to find a new pay policy which their members would accept, so demands for a return to free collective bargaining became more insistent. Jones and Scanlon retired and their successors, Moss Evans and Terry Duffy, in those early years carried less weight. It was clear by 1978 that the unions were diverging from each other and from government. The flash-point came when the transport union, led by Evans, determined to return to free collective bargaining.

The government tried to hold the partnership together by advocating (as Wilson and Heath had done) that collective bargaining should be based each year on a broad agreement between government, unions and employers upon the maximum level of earnings compatible with keeping inflation under control. In September 1978 the TUC rejected this policy by a large majority. The Labour Party conference called for the organization of 'a campaign ... against control of wages' and this was described by the railwaymen's leader, at that time Sid Weighell, a supporter of the Prime Minister, as a policy of 'snouts in the trough'. Callaghan remained determined to win the battle against inflation 'even if it means a long, hard winter of strikes'.

The transport union took the lead in breaking up the government's pay policy: Ford Motors had to pay 15 per cent more and the road hauliers 20 per cent. The death of the social contract and the facts of trade-union power were set out in the government/trade union joint statement of February 1979. The unions, having made their point about the dominance of free collective bargaining, were willing to help the government, but not if it meant any infringement of the right of any single union to use its power in its own interests, and not if it meant a departure from free collective bargaining.

Although it was agreed that strike action should be taken only in the last resort, industrial trouble was brewing and the civil service unions called a strike in the middle of their wage negotiations. As the government came up to the general election they found they could no longer justifiably claim that only a Labour government could work with the unions. Wilson and Jones had managed to suspend free collective bargaining for three years. Callaghan, however, had been no more successful than Heath, although he was a fully-paid-up long-time trade-union man. By October 1978 the union militants could accept restraint no longer and their leaders did not have the will or the power to refuse them. The government could no longer accommodate the unions without imperilling the social fabric of the country. They went into the general election in May 1979 in a defeatist mood. The unions had openly used their industrial power to wreck the policy of a Labour government and had exposed the weakness of a government which opposed them. The question Callaghan was asking in the election was, 'Can any government govern the country without provoking a destructive reaction from the trade unions?' Margaret Thatcher succeeded him as Prime Minister in May 1979.

Thatcher's position on the unions shifted from time to time, but it was fundamentally hawkish. Her first meeting as Prime Minister with the TUC leaders was a disaster. But at the Tory Party conference she said, 'However often we may be rebuffed, my colleagues and I will continue to talk to the unions, to listen to their views and to give those views due weight in shaping national policy, so long as it is understood that in the last resort national policy is the sole responsibility of government and Parliament.'

Prior, meanwhile, as Employment Secretary, in consultation with the TUC was preparing his Bill, designed to achieve the minimum change in union status consistent with the Tory manifesto. Those who lost their jobs because of closed shops were to get compensation. Union ballots could be financed by government. Those claiming unfair exclusion from a trade union could appeal to the High Court. Employers not directly involved in a dispute could apply for an injunction against secondary picketing. Prior planned, but did not announce, further legislation dealing progressively with sympathy strikes then with trade-union immunities, and finally legislation to make unions responsible for the actions of their members, with recourse to union funds to pay for damages. By September 1981 Prior had moved to the graveyard of Northern Ireland and Norman Tebbit had become Employment Secretary.

Tebbit's Employment Act became law in October 1982. Its main provision was the reduction of trade-union immunity from legal proceedings in respect of actions which otherwise would have been unlawful. Tebbit's Act made unions liable for damages arising from inter-union disputes, secondary strikes and political or unrelated disputes. In addition substantial compensation would be paid to people sacked under the closed-shop arrangements and unions would have to contribute to this if the sacking resulted from union pressure. 'Union only' employment clauses in a contract were made illegal and, following a strike, individuals selected by management could be sacked. Ballots to approve an existing closed shop would not come into force till November 1983 to allow time for voting procedures to be prepared. This was much stronger stuff than Prior's Act and it attracted fierce opposition from union leaders.

In 1981 there were fewer strikes than for forty years, but during that year unemployment rose to two-and-a-half million people. In 1982 the transport union's call for an all-out strike at Heathrow in support of the baggage handlers collapsed ignominiously. Scargill's call, as president elect of the miners' union, for a strike on the 1982 pay offer was turned down by a majority of miners. Industrial action faded away at British Shipbuilders, British Steel, British Rail and among tanker drivers, along with countless local disputes. Even at BL, the old hotbed of strikes, the 'washing up' dispute lasted only four weeks.

Early in 1982 Robert Taylor, a journalist specializing in industrial and union matters, examined the trade-union scene. He found that the general trend in the unions was towards moderation, despite the sensational election of the militant communist Arthur Scargill as miners' president and the arrival of his deputy, the communist Mick McGahey, on the General Council of the TUC. Moderate trade-union leaders carried the real burdens of union responsibility, with militants snapping at their heels.

Most trade-union members, Taylor noted, fail to turn up at meetings and usually ignore opportunities to vote. In a sworn affidavit in a court case in March 1982, Chapple of the electricians stated, 'The union calculated from branch and lodge returns that 6,981 out of a total of 438,000 members, that is only 1.6 per cent attended the meetings at which their delegates [to conference] were elected.' The builders' union, with 300,000 members, recorded that only 0.5 per cent of the members attended branch meetings where key resolutions were passed: 1,322 members voted on 111 motions which approved withdrawal from NATO, affiliation to campaign for nuclear disarmament, support for Tony Benn and condemnation of attempts to drive 'Trots' out of the Labour Party (*Daily Express*, March 1982). Voting of this sort lies behind the block vote, used so heavily at trade-union and Labour Party conferences. The ten million workers which the block votes are supposed to represent usually boil down to a few hundred thousand.

Taylor judged that the Communist Party still exercised an enormous influence in the trade-union movement, despite its puny resources: BL and Ford remain prime targets for communists. In most unions full-time officers have to devote much of their attention to the militant activists, who try to control conferences, the union executive and wage negotiations. The Workers' Revolutionary Party and the Socialist Workers' Party have, however, not made much headway on the shop floor; they have made a tactical alliance with the communists and the Labour Left for election purposes. But Taylor found that most of the time these different elements remain divided. The communists defend 'as is', which suits them well; the Trots want more democratic accountability. Taylor thought that 10 per cent of shop stewards sympathized with the Communist Party, but that trade-union members would give considerable support to the Tories and to the Social Democratic Party. Members of unions show little enthusiasm for more nationalization, which is seen to have been tried and to have failed in Britain. Free collective bargaining does, however, remain a simple slogan to gladden the hearts of all those who believe in *laissez-faire*, or, for that matter, those who wish to debauch the currency.

Taylor judged that militants would continue to take advantage of the inertia of members and the decaying structure of the unions themselves, but would fail to arouse a radical left-wing political mood among workers. Members were increasingly anxious about keeping their jobs and had tried to combine with members of other unions to discuss with management how to survive and keep their place of work open.

In March 1983 Scargill and the miners' executive recommended strike action to prevent the closure of a worked-out mine in South Wales. Scargill tried to extend the issue to cover other possible closures and the appointment of Ian MacGregor as next chairman of the Coal Board. This attempt was a fiasco for

Daily Mail, 8 April 1983

Scargill and the miners voted in secret ballot 61 per cent to 39 per cent against strike action. The miners were, as the labour editor of the *Financial Times* commented, committed to a lifestyle which their fathers would have associated with management – 'They are no longer impoverished proletarians ready to be mobilized.'

As the demand for cars improved in 1983, stoppages began at BL's Cowley plant, Ford's Halewood factory and at Vauxhall works in Luton and Dunstable. Old habits are hard to shed. New tactics by management were treated with suspicion. 'Them and us' has been part of life for unions, management and workforce alike. Long years of bloody-mindedness and old-style management will not suddenly be forgotten.

The unions were on the defensive. In 1983 total union membership fell to under 10 million from its peak in 1979 of 12.2 million. Even the National and Local Government Officers' Association (NALGO) experienced a fall in membership, for the first time since 1923. Membership of the biggest union, transport, fell from two million to 1.5 million. The militants were in retreat. Roy Halverson, Chairman of the British Communist Party, was ousted from the national committee of the engineers' union, where he had sat for the last eight years.

The hard core of the problem lies in the public sector, which now employs a third of the total workforce. Militants there are sapping and stirring away on the unions' executives or national committees. In a few cases they have a majority on important trade-union committees. Their interest is the overthrow of democracy, in favour of some sort of communism. They do not like to accept the view of a majority of their members. They are unlikely to succeed in their purposes, but they will always be against democrats and Britain cannot avoid a constant battle with them. What is important for Britain is that, in contrast to the 'militants', the 'ordinary' union membership is moderate, law-abiding, bourgeois, and anxious to preserve jobs, increase pay and work with management for those purposes.

The performance of the monopoly public sector is not good. With few exceptions it is over-manned, inefficient and arrogant in its dealings with the public or its customers. There are some recent cases of great improvement, but there is not yet a critical mass swinging the whole sector towards lower cost and better service. The sector has created a huge unnecessary overhead cost which adds to the non-competitiveness of the rest of British industry.

Graham Turner, an industrial journalist of wide experience, reported in 1983* some interviews with public sector leaders: a manager at an important railway station said, 'If it weren't for the unions I could run this place for half the cost.' A senior railways staff man said, 'It depends on whether management wakes up on Monday morning saying, "Now for the fight". In reality they are much more likely to say to themselves, "How many more days have I got in this ghastly job? Why should I bother!" '

Sir Norman Siddall, then Chairman of the Coal Board, was asked how many of his 200 pits could stand on their own feet in private enterprise terms. 'Fifty,' he said. Sidall had been asked by government what he calls 'daft questions', like, 'How many pits

* *Sunday Telegraph*, 20 February 1983

can you close without causing a strike?'

Sir George Jefferson, Chairman of British Telecom, admitted that in New York engineers made an average of seven visits a day and that in Britain the average was four. In the Post Office a union district organizer said that his men have steadfastly turned down a productivity deal. In the past the union had sat down with management and they had run the place together, but now management were putting his men under 'constant pressure' – something is happening in BT.

Lord King, Chairman of British Airways, has cut the workforce from 58,000 to 39,000 on the way to 35,000 or lower. The unions privately admitted they had been getting away with murder for years. In the past at BA, 'if someone bought the wrong fleet of aeroplanes, people just said, "don't worry, we'll get over it" '. Making money was mentioned, but not often! Life is changing at BA too.

Take the case of Mark Young, formerly of the electricians' union, now general secretary of the British Air Line Pilots' Association (BALPA). Since 1974 he has been trying to get a combine of unions to work together in BATUC, the British Airlines Trade Union Committee, to which all business matters would be referred. At first he got one shop steward for every 1,500 workers in the twelve unions involved to meet in a national joint council, with a shop steward as chairman. This was the 'front' to meet the employers. It was too large an organization; the officials of the unions who came to the meetings had a good dinner, and to all intents and purposes things stopped there. So Young started again in 1979 with fifty shop stewards at the National Westminster Bank training college to learn about balance sheets and profit and loss accounts and how things looked from the company angle. After two such courses he asked British Airways to talk 'commercial sense' with BATUC – 'how to get the airline right!'

In 1979 BA proposed to cut out twenty-seven domestic routes costing £28m, but producing only £22m of revenue. BATUC, then led by Colin Varndell, said 'If you close these routes you will simply transfer the loss to other routes, because you have not eliminated the overheads.' BA listened, but went ahead with the closures anyway.

In 1981, however, BA proposed to close down the Highlands

and Islands service, which was losing £4m per annum, unless the shop stewards could turn the loss to a profit of £1m. A joint union/management committee was set up to consider what sort of organization would be created if the service was starting from scratch. The joint committee reported in December 1981. More than half the employees would be made redundant; everyone would be available to do everything – pilots would handle baggage! Everyone made a contribution by giving up something and becoming more flexible at work.

The BA board accepted the plan. A year later, despite a 17 per cent fall in traffic, the service was breaking even. The same treatment has since been given to routes based on Birmingham. BATUC think this outlook can be applied to catering, motor transport, and building and plant maintenance. The benchmark used by BATUC is the organization and cost which would be acceptable to an outside contractor. This is the key to public service cost and efficiency. It is a master key which would unlock most doors.

BATUC's philosophy is that change is inevitable and it is better to plan change together than to slug it out in confrontation and strikes. What's best for members must take precedence over what's best for the union. This infuriates old-time union officials, just as BATUC scares old-time managers who fear that their inadequacies will be exposed. BATUC is mapping out a new role for trade unionism. Union members see the short-comings of the old tradition, but they need help to understand the business situation. They need training and a perspective towards a positive, not a defensive solution of problems.

BATUC believes that Britain is unique in the degree of disinterest generally felt by its workers in their jobs under traditional management. BATUC's experience is that once the workforce has got involved in a major decision, like a closure, the small problems vanish. If the workforce stays bogged down with details the wrangle goes on; meanwhile the activity or the service bleeds to death.

The personnnel manager of BA in Britain, Cranford MacDonald, said of the Highlands and Islands experiment, 'it even expanded the airline's activity and profitability and produced a unique degree of staff enthusiasm and flexibility'. He recognized that this work trod on a number of organizational toes and that it was 'irreverent, businesslike, unconcerned about status and, above all, committed to the objective'. A practicable plan was devised, he says, 'to move from the "now" to the "proposed situation"'. The new chief executive of BA, Colin Marshall, coming in during 1983, said of BATUC, 'This has worked extremely well . . . we are finding ways of taking a few more £million off our operating costs'.* The success of this project probably lay in the terms of reference; simply 'to establish whether and how those routes could be operated profitably'. Inevitably the threat of closure was a stimulus and a starting mechanism, but the union side were 'treated as people who were interested, involved, knowledgeable and worth listening to'. The comparison of cost and efficiency with the private section was the essential yardstick. This is the ideal at which the development state should aim.

As I write, in the late summer of 1984, the miners' strike is in full swing and we are offered the prospect of a 'big bang' following the TUC and Labour Party conferences in the autumn. The strike will be a landmark in British history and the source of a huge literature. I cannot tell when it will end. Despite a growing dislike of Thatcherism, most British trade-union members have an even greater distaste for Marxism, undemocratic leadership, violence and intimidation; besides, they want to keep their jobs and their pay packets. Many unions, such as steel, power, electricians and engineers, deeply resent this strike and its methods. Most trade-union leaders protest their undying loyalty to the strike, its cause and purpose, but the support generally of union membership will, I suspect, continue to be half-hearted.

This will have immense repercussions throughout the trade-union movement and upon the political parties. It will also provide a once in a lifetime opportunity for a rebuild on the devastated site. A development state could, indeed, be founded on the rubble left behind by the miners' strike. The one thing Britain must not do is to fall into the temptation of carrying on after the strike, in the old traditional un-progressive way, as though nothing had happened.

Just listen to George Wright, General Secretary of the TUC in

* *Director*, January 1984

'Miners trying to break through police ranks in an attempt to disrupt
supplies of coal and iron ore being delivered by road to Llanwern
steelworks yesterday.' *Daily Telegraph*, 5 July 1984

Wales, talking to Michael Davie of the *Observer* (8 May 1983)
about the eight Japanese companies established in Wales.

> The whole Japanese approach is different. The Japanese know
> that it is better to carry people with you than to bully; they
> never adopt the 'we're the bosses' attitude. Every morning the
> foreman talks to the lads about what they need to do and how
> they're going to do it. There's nothing sudden about the
> Japanese. They're slow and very thorough. It's like dealing
> with a sponge when you start, but when they move they move
> very quickly. They're not daft or soft. They insist on tough
> terms and they get it by carrying people along. The British try
> to run things by instruction.

> What the British have to acknowledge is the genuineness of
> the heartfelt groan of our fellow countrymen when faced with
> plant or office closure or redundancy. 'We had to do something;
> what else could we do except strike.' This betrays a total
> breakdown in relationships between workforce, unions,

management, government, the political parties, education and human beings in a fast changing world. If ever there was a need for a new start it is in this complex of relationships. We must not be starry-eyed; the *cri de coeur* of the striker has been used by union leaders to bolster their declining membership and diminishing bank balances; also to further their political ambitions. But when all this, and a long, bitter industrial history, has been allowed for, nevertheless the hard fact is that there remains a real problem and need which, until it is solved and satisfied will keep Britain in a permanently under-achieving state, getting poorer, unhappier and more divided than ever.

The initiative for rebuilding has to come from management. Following twelve steel works closures, 140,000 redundancies and a long strike in 1980 the management of British Steel has rebuilt all the vital relationships on a plant and customer basis and has created a model steel industry, which refused to kowtow to the bullying of the miners' leadership. The steelmen had learned the folly of strike action – lost money, lost markets, lost jobs.

There is no computer program or magic pack which can tell managers precisely what to do in every possible strike-prone situation or how to build good relationships where there has been conflict. From my own experience, however, certain strands stand out, from which a pattern can be woven to fit many industrial situations.

● 'Where the rubber meets the road', is the vital spot ... Where the workforce and shop steward meet the foreman and the first-line supervisor. Conflict is never far away from the shop floor. All managers should spend time in this function, then they would understand the shop-floor culture and language (and the workforce would know that they understood) and the beginnings of an 'all one family' workforce would have been established.
● Quality Circles operate at the vital spot and there can be no argument against them; but 'handle with care'.
● The next level up is the departmental head, who should spend most of his working life on or very near the shop floor – not in his office. He must clearly be an executive part of the management team which is responsible for an easily understood

operating unit or profit centre, with which the workforce can identify. The workforce credit a good departmental boss with authority and knowledge. He should settle as many working problems as possible, quickly and firmly. A bonus scheme based on productivity or profit can best be operated at department level. Its workings should be seen by all and announced by the boss, who should regularly tell his department what has happened and what is likely to happen.

• The works manager appears very senior to the workforce. He has great responsibilities, one of which is to see that the workforce is working well. He it is who should form and lead a works council so that communication with the workforce, through their shop stewards, is unambiguous and up-to-date. Redundancy and closure may at times be unavoidable and it is vital that this is handled in a 'consultative' way, with counselling, good compensation and, if possible, using any unwanted premises by entrepreneurs who want to start their own business. The works manager should see that his plant is plugged into the local community, especially the schools, and arrange for 'open days' when local people can come and look round and have simple entertainment. He should be looked upon as a father figure.

• Director level and in the board-room is where all these activities should be watched and insisted upon. Unless the top is keen on them little will happen. Directors should join in plant activities clearly identifying themselves with the 'one family' progressive spirit. This should include 'in house' education and training. If management leaves it all to the state, their own need of a skilled workforce will not be met. In the middle-middle, white-collar, technical world, where Britain belongs, continuing education and training are of the essence and this is part of a director's responsibility.

What Britain has to leave behind is the image of t'works or t'mill as a local dragon which gobbles up the local population and spews them out exhausted at the end of the day, unthinking, uncaring, grinding away inexorably. That is the image which brought the trade unions to the peak of their power, as the only defence of a powerless workforce. That is what management has to replace with the 'all one family' reality, which is what the workforce wants, but does not believe it can get, in at least one half of British companies.

At department and works level trade-union officials have an important contribution to make. They can feel the needs of their members and the capacity of the employer to meet them. They can be assimilated easily into the development state. At national level many trade-union leaders seem to find irresistible the temptation to go 'politicking'. The membership does not like that. The great tide which carried the movement on up from the Trades Dispute Act of 1906 to the late seventies has ebbed away in the eighties and is likely to recede further. Some union leaders, however, have spoken of a 'new realism'. This has been shadowed by the miners' strike, but it is still desired, though latent, on the shop floors.

Positive moves in this direction have been made by the electricians' union which has signed four one-union, no-strike, binding-arbitration deals with Japanese companies coming into Britain. The electricians are touting hard for more such deals, getting membership via the management rather than via the workforce. If the electricians merged with the engineers a new reality would be forced upon other unions, which are like cats out of the bag – they could jump right or left, or not jump.

Most trade unionists regard their union in much the same way as they feel about their religion. They may not attend many union or church meetings, they may not even believe in all the doctrines which are there canvassed and they may not be much interested in the officials of either. *But* they expect help from both when in trouble, they are prepared to put up a few pence to keep them both going and they regard their right to belong to church and union as a precious part of British liberty.

We live in a post-traditional-Christian age and we are moving into a post-traditional-union age. The union leadership and the union membership are no longer necessarily one and the same thing – the miners' strike gave plentiful evidence of that. Whatever the unions do, management in Britain does now have its best-ever opportunity to make a positive, deliberate move into the progressive 'all one family' workplace. This would be an essential part of the development state and would open up the possibility of a gradual and fundamental move away from traditional trade-unionism to industrial unions decentralized into largely independent company or regional units. These would collaborate in the search for new markets, or the recapture of old ones, new revenues, new investment and new jobs. This movement should be fostered by the membership, management, government, media, the general public and even the unions themselves, as a new role and purpose for trade unionism in 'start again' Britain.

As Glen Watts, President of the Communications Workers of America, recently said, 'a new era is on the horizon of collective bargaining – traditional adversarial relations may be gradually modified by co-operative union/management endeavours'.*

* *Financial Times*, 17 February 1983

8 Half a Million New Businesses

Big business in Britain will continue to reduce its workforce. It has to because of the manufacturing disaster, the need to improve productivity, the effect of the microprocessor and the competition from Japan and elsewhere in East Asia. British manufacturers lost the competitive edge and market share, so until they improve that market share, they have to operate on a smaller base with a smaller workforce. Unless British business goes on adjusting to the new competitive pressures it will lose more markets and have to shrink further. To resist this downward spiral will be hard and it will be done only by much greater investment and improved shop-floor relations, of which there are so far only the first signs.

Of course, big business must go on reforming itself, but alongside has to come a surge of new businesses. As they start up they will inevitably be small businesses. Some will stick, many will fail and a few will grow into the medium and big businesses of tomorrow. They will manufacture goods, be sub-contractors, provide services, be distributors and traders; some will be in the professions, some will be craft businesses. They will cover every imaginable human activity, and so long as they provide a living for those who work in them, they will create wealth and jobs and, maybe, innovate. They should be greatly encouraged.

There is, indeed a new principle here – new, real jobs will come only from new investment programmes. Whether your activity is in business or in the public service, whether you make, sell or serve, whether you are big or small, you will take on more people only to operate a new or expanded function. Otherwise you will go back to over-manning, which was Britain's weak spot in competing worldwide. Investment is therefore crucial to new jobs, more national wealth and to innovation.

In the work I do now,* we have helped nearly 2,000 new businesses to start up or expand in the places where previously we had to close steel works. When asked what they do, I reply, 'Anything and everything better than sex shops!' We support anyone who is determined to make a success of running his or her own business. Of them, only 400 have failed so far. The others are likely to create well over 36,000 new jobs – many are in the new high technology. Over 20,000 of these jobs are on the ground already, after the worst recession anyone can remember. New businesses are starting up or expanding at a rate of one each working day on or near the former steel works, taken together, thus renewing the life of the previously steel-dependent communities. All over the country other local 'enterprise trusts' are springing up to do the same sort of thing – this is a great spontaneous movement.

With the Small Business Research Trust, Stan Mendham† and I have started an organization to find out the facts of life of small businesses in Britain. What we now know compares badly with the facts in competitor countries. The United Kingdom Organizing Committee for the European Year of the Small and Medium-Sized Enterprise (EYSME) commissioned the EIU‡ to carry out a study of the environment for small businesses in the ten member states of the European Community in 1983.

The overall rankings by the Assessment Group in order of their favourability to profit maximization was as follows:

1.	West Germany	6.	Belgium
2.	Greece	7.	Luxemburg
3.	France	8.	Irish Republic
4.	Netherlands	9.	UK
5.	Denmark	10.	Italy

* British Steel Corporation (Industry) Limited
† Stan Mendham is the founder of 'The Forum of Private Business'
‡ Economist Intelligence Unit

Britain comes very badly out of this comparison, despite recent improvements. No one should think that Britain is making the most of the opportunities for development which small business offers.

Small business could do much more for Britain than in the recent past. Our competitors in Europe, America and Japan have for years encouraged the small-business movement. They have seen how small business strengthens the economy by specialization and risk-taking, how it brings out local effort, how it reduces costs by cutting overheads to below big-company levels, how it can exploit innovation, how it makes for good shop-floor relations and satisfaction at work and, finally, how it creates jobs in a stable society where regular long-term improvement can take place. Professor Gallagher of Newcastle University has calculated that over half the new jobs in Britain are created by firms employing less than 100 people.* In the USA two-thirds of the new jobs are created by firms employing twenty people or less.

Britain was built up by small businessmen during the last four hundred years. They seized the opportunity to trade worldwide after the defeat of the Spanish Armada. They started the Industrial Revolution, which made Britain for a time the workshop of the world. They became discouraged in the face of the so-called economies of scale. Then they were crushed by big business, which itself was damaged by its management hierarchies and labour difficulties. The whole way of looking at things in Britain after the Second World War turned against small business, which was neglected and dwindled.

But now the tide has turned. During 1981 and 1982 the number of small-business new starts increased and, despite fearful losses, the known 'births' exceeded 'deaths' substantially. This is apt to happen in years of economic recession. Enterprisers would rather strike out on their own than go down in a big ship. The problem will be to keep this growth moving forward, when easier big-business conditions return.

Today no one knows for sure how many small businesses there are in Britain, how many they employ, what they do, how much they invest, or what percentage they contribute to the

---

* *British Business*, July 1984

whole economy. But Napoleon was right: we are a nation of shopkeepers and small businessmen. It is from this half-known world that much of Britain's recovery could spring, if it was encouraged to the same extent as in the competitor countries.

There must, of course, be good, strong, big businesses, with their capacity to produce in huge volume, to market products worldwide and to finance massive research and development. Without them Britain would be nowhere. But big companies would do better, and reduce their costs further, if they would sub-contract to small business more of their processes and more of the components they use. They would benefit if they were to sell off parts of their empires to those – maybe the managers – keen to buy and make them their life work. Small manufacturers can be very efficient, cheap and reliable.

The revival of small business in Britain is not an instant cure for unemployment and our other troubles. It will take care, time and effort. It will not happen unless government makes it an essential part of its policy, and discriminates in favour of small business. If too much is expected, there will be disappointment all round. If too little is expected, we shall miss a valuable trick. The development of small business in Britain is a valid long-term policy.

Government statistics indicate a total of 1.4 million small businesses in Britain, but private research, which also looked into the 'black' (no tax) economy, puts the total at around two million. In proportion to population there are probably 40 per cent more in Germany and America and nearly twice as many in France and Japan. In all these countries small firms are increasing in number. Another half million in Britain would be perfectly feasible by the end of this century, and the target should be 30,000 new births each year in excess of deaths.

The contribution of small firms to national wealth in Britain is estimated to be more than 20 per cent, but less than 35 per cent. Analysts in France and Germany, where the numbers are known more precisely, say that there the contribution of small and medium-sized enterprises to their national wealth is around 50 per cent. In America the contribution is 46 per cent. In Japan it is 68 per cent of manufacturing output. In Britain we cannot afford to forgo the addition of 10 per cent, possibly more, to national income. It would improve our whole economy in every way.

In terms of employment the best guess is that in Britain 40 per cent of the workforce are employed in small business. In France and Germany and America it is more than 50 per cent. In Japan the number is no less than 80 per cent. If Britain could move up to the level of competitor countries in this important sector, the unemployment problem would be as good as solved.

Small business is ahead of big business in 'them and us'. Most small firms revolve around one or two personalities; the owner of a small business usually works alongside his employees, who see him or her sharing their working conditions. Employees may or may not know that he is probably paying himself less and has everything at risk, including his house and home. Owners have found that communication, an incentive scheme and management time spent on the shop floor are essential for success. Consequently, small-business productivity tends to be higher, quality better and deliveries more reliable than in big firms, where relations with the shop floor are more distant.

Small firms have found that the workforce do not want to manage the business. The shop floor wants to be told what is happening, to share in the benefits, if any, and to be listened to carefully when making serious suggestions about improving the product or the process, usually concerning small details. The shop floor, given the least encouragement, gets involved in the detail, works better and feels happier.

Small businessmen know that they cannot take their workforce for a ride. The truth will soon out in a small works. So most small businesses have good communications, usually very informal. This does not leave much scope for the unions. Many who work in a small business are members of a trade union, but few want a branch to be set up where they work. Many small businessmen are rough, tough and gruff. They are allowed to be hard, provided they are fair, run a bonus scheme, communicate and clearly know what they are doing. Britain needs a great host of businesses run like that and the British like working in them. That will be so when government in a development state recognizes that rewards have to be in line with risks, as well as work.

Small businesses still operate under endless disabilities, even after the Thatcher government has made many improvements in their lot. No fewer than 230 different inspectors have right of entry into small business premises, to see that legal requirements have been carried out. Fortunately there are not enough inspectors to go round, but in consequence many businessmen have stayed in the 'black' economy, and have not grown as they could and should. The recent Keith Report* on the enforcement of taxation was exactly wrong. Instead of more machinery to catch small enterpreneurs who do not pay tax, we need less, by exempting the small man from tax. A new business should pay no tax in its first years of life, so that it can build up some capital. The collection of VAT by small firms is very expensive and a fearful chore. This tax should not be paid by firms whose turnover is less than £50,000 per annum: today the threshold is a miserable £18,000. The Keith Report says the Inland Revenue should prosecute 'moonlighters' to deter the growth of the black economy, now estimated to be worth at least 7 per cent of national income. Where would we be without the 'black'? Poorer and with many more unemployed! What we should do is encourage the 'black' to become 'white' and then to get bigger.

James Callaghan, when Prime Minister, appointed Harold Lever to his Cabinet to advocate the small-business interest. Early in 1982 Margaret Thatcher was saying on BBC 'Panorama', 'Prospects will be at their best . . . if we take steps to try to stimulate small businesses and new businesses.' She said† in May 1982:

> If you can find a way of making a living as your own master and start something new and creative, then that is the best way of all to live . . . I do not think my father could have worked for anyone else . . . It is a way of life that is full of worry . . . My mother always worked in the business . . . I have the clearest memories of helping in the shop . . . I look back on all that with great affection . . . There is a fantastic area of new jobs in the service industries.

At the same time the then Industry Secretary, Patrick Jenkin, was saying:

---

* Report of Committee on Tax Enforcement chaired by Lord Keith of Kinkel, 1983
† *Small Business*, May 1982

We believe strongly that . . . small businesses vitalize our economy and hold the key to our industrial future... we want to increase as far as we can the esteem in which small businessmen are held... in terms of social recognition. When we came to office it could fairly be said that the tax climate worked against small businessmen. Today it works most definitely in their favour... small businesses are overburdened by bureaucracy.

There are now encouraging signals. Management 'buy-outs' of parts of big business are running at a rate of over 200 a year. Local Enterprise Trusts and local colleges are standing ready to help. The banks are devising new schemes to help small business with loans and capital. Pension funds and life assurance companies are getting in on the act. Venture capital companies are hunting round for good opportunities. Local councils have set up business development offices. Government itself is active through many agencies. The media have 'discovered' small business.

Are there too many cooks, and are they spoiling the broth? Not so! Small businessmen like to shop around for the best deal going, if they have the time to spare. But it is true that a recent survey by Shell found that only one small businessman in twenty was 'spontaneously aware' of the information service, the consulting service and the government-guaranteed loan scheme available to him. We need 'yellow pages' in which entrepreneurs may easily and quickly find details of all the help available.

Understanding small business is an effort for big business, government, academics and, indeed, for bankers and investors. Small may be beautiful but it is also difficult, hard and risky. The small businessman is in it up to his neck all day and every day. He is very vulnerable, until he has built up some reserves out of retained profits, and he is usually short of 'ordinary' capital. The build-up of capital is a slow business. On a turnover of £50,000 the likely profit is around £2,500, which is not enough to pay for even one extra person.

In bad times people are slow to pay their bills and big companies are notorious for keeping small ones waiting. Employment regulations seem unending to the small businessman; he neither knows them, understands them, or keeps them. Taxation laws present another jungle in which small businessmen get lost. That is why so many small businesses are in the 'black' economy – no accounts and no tax!

There are compensations, of course. When you are doing well you walk tall, you are known and respected in your community, you can choose your suppliers and customers, you have the power of decision. The workforce appreciate the businessman who knows his trade and shows good judgement.

In America, Germany, France, Japan, Belgium, Holland, Scandinavia and Italy, to name only a few countries, the small-business way of life is recognized as having qualities which hold the country together, make people responsible, support law and order, encourage public service, increase the national wealth and provide most of the jobs. It seems that Britain has at last decided to go down that road and to encourage people to stride out on their own and become go-getters. Britain should now do no less than competitor countries to encourage, help, accelerate and discriminate in favour of the small-business community.

The small-business stories from my case book which follow tell their own tales of the difficulties, joys and agonies of starting up. As in big business, it is individuals and personality which count. Experience and skills are needed, but determination is the essential factor.

In America, where start-ups are easier, the estimate of the Small Business Administration is that two start-ups out of three fail. In Britain the Industrial and Commercial Finance Corporation (ICFC) – owned by the banks – reckons to lose one out of three. We have to get used to the idea of failures and liquidations and be ready to support those who are willing to 'have another go'.

North of Watford

Roger is a Watford man and knows the City crack about 'no investment north of Watford'. But he got City money and then swung on to the Enterprise Zone in the Midlands. He had to get there to avoid the rates (no rates for twenty years in an Enterprise Zone), to get the capital allowances on new machinery and to find room to expand and double his workforce. Without that he could not survive, because of the international competition. Ninety per cent of what he makes is for export to airlines – model aircraft, plastic tumblers, cups, meal trays, dishes, plates, cutlery packs. There are 650 airlines in the world and the market for these items is £150m a year. Roger now has 0.75 per cent of it. In five years he aims to have 4 per cent and a turnover of £6m. You never met a more determined man, but he has a long hard haul in front of him.

Roger was part of the post-war baby boom. His people were working-class. He got to Bushy Grammar School. Three 'O' levels, no 'A's, but lots of football, hockey and chess. His first job at sixteen was in a local plastics company as a machine-minder at £4 a week. He worked Saturdays and Sundays to learn engineering from the maintenance men. He got to know the engineering of plastics machines in every detail; soon he was a fitter, then he studied designing and making tools.

In 1962 he met Phil – same sort of guy. Today Roger's firm is really a two-man band: Roger and Phil, looking after different parts of their business, but interchangeable on any job – 'essential', says Roger.

In 1973 Roger spotted a business he wanted. It was then in Aylesbury. It was bust and was bought for £21,000 by a friend, who gave Roger half the shares if he would run it. Three years later Roger bought his friend out with the money from a venture capital firm in the City. That firm has done well out of it, making 30 per cent a year on their investment, but Roger is paying them off fast.

Roger caught a terrible cold from a salesman, who said he could sell all Roger's products abroad. Was it a 'con' or a muddle, who knows? But the deal cost Roger £70,000. Roger got over his cold, wrote off his losses and decided to move where rates were lower, space was cheaper, and labour was easier than in Aylesbury. The 'Highlands and Islands' was best for cash, but impossible for Heathrow and Gatwick. Wales was somehow not for him. Corby had everything. An Enterprise Zone avoided the rates problem: a special Development Area meant the highest capital allowances: the New Towns Commission meant a new factory waiting. It was all done within two months – out and in.

Some of his managers and workforce came up from Aylesbury.

He was grateful, so he gave Phil and two other managers 10 per cent each of the share capital and another 10 per cent was divided amongst fourteen others, who all voted as to who should get what. There has been no dividend yet, and at times salaries have to be cut back, but the enterprise is still bursting with energy.

In 1983 Roger got an order from BA to make 500,000 model plastic aircraft for sale in flight. Fine, but how to finance the working capital needed? Banks don't like lending on the security of the order-book alone. Roger is not yet in the clear and his 'days to broke' situation is serious. He might go down, but his business is good, he has huge determination, he has learned a lot; whatever happens he is a real start-again man.

What motivates Roger? Fear of failure, determination to see off the competition, just sheer animal spirits – all these play a part, and it is infectious. Given half a million people like Roger – 2 per cent of the total workforce – Britain's problems would be solved.

Father and Son

Another man called Roger was prepared to lose everything, and it came to that. His father, Ted, had been all his life an engineer in steel until 1979, when he took his redundancy and started a new small business, making cranes and hoists and gantries, giving a spares and repair service on a twenty-four-hour basis.

Ted is a mechanical engineer and Roger went to work as soon as he could with Demag in South Wales, as a sales engineer specializing in cranes and materials handling service. He soon saw how this work could be done without the heavy overhead costs which weigh down most businesses.

When Ted went into business, Roger left Demag and joined him. They started in Cardiff, with a van looking for orders to service cranes and as agents selling other companies' products. In the first month they took £337, but could not see a future unless they went into manufacturing. Ted had been on a management course; he drew up a business plan and they set off round the banks. They had no luck to start with; they had to live on Ted's redundancy money, and they wanted to save that for the business.

Then they struck gold, with a bank which offered £1 for every £1 Ted and Roger put in. No bank would do better than that, but it was not enough to start manufacturing cranes. So Ted, who had been in the British Steel Corporation, went to its job-creating subsidiary BSC Industry, which sensed the determination in Ted and Roger. They took Ted and Roger to the Welsh Development Agency, which provided a factory with a rent-free period of one year, then to the accountants Coopers and Lybrand, who produced a professional business plan and cash-flow charts. At that point they were introduced to the government's Welsh Office, for grants. British Steel also bought them £12,000 worth of plant and leased it to them on 'friendly terms'. By February 1980 they were into their new premises in Cardiff, ready to manufacture.

Ted gave Roger £5,000 so that he could be a genuine partner. They both pledged their houses to the bank and Roger's wife worked in the business too, on the accounts. They took very little out, less than £100 a week, although they had been earning two or three times that amount before. So they scrimped, but Roger's two children were well looked after and they drew a little extra for very special needs. They learned the curse of the marginal rate of tax, where if you draw a bonus of £100 so little remains to spend after tax. Roger felt the more secure because he was in charge of his own destiny but Ted, after all those safe years in British Steel, felt the insecurity of his new way of life.

At times Ted yearned for their grotty first premises on the Cardiff dock, where there had been no light or water but it was cheap and they scoured the neighbourhood for orders. The profit in the first six months was £5,000 and they felt encouraged; there were no complaints and they were giving a good service. But they moved into their smart new factory just at the time of the long steel strike. There was no business. The loss in the second half of their first year was £10,000, leaving them £5,000 poorer on the year.

They just made it. In June 1980 business started to pick up and their good neighbour, Capital Steel, gave them an order which would keep them busy for the next three months. They took on four steel-workers made redundant at Llanwern, nearby. This was an error, because in September 1980 business went flat again and they had saddled themselves with the wages of four men. By early 1981 they had lost another £10,000 and had called up the last reserves from the bank. They were depressed and frightened.

The bank manager asked if he could come over, and they felt sure he would put the shutters up. But he didn't; he suggested they should have a 'start-up loan' of £20,000 for five years with a year's repayment holiday. The interest was high, but it offered a chance of carrying on. The bank felt that Ted and Roger were professional and was prepared to invest in them. Ted and Roger realized that they were borrowing to replace their original investment, but they had learned a lot and their deep determination again came into play. So the bank became their new partner and they ploughed on.

Then the climate of business began to change. In May 1981 deferred work became active again, the big Ford engine works at Bridgend gave them an order, and then another, and by June they were all fully employed, working seven days a week. In that month they made a profit of £12,000; they felt much stronger after making mistakes and then recovering from them.

At one time they felt confident of keeping up their progress and they expected to move to a factory twice as big and to employ thirty people. Then they could make eight cranes a month, but they would need more money and they had no security left; everything was mortgaged and second-mortgaged. But Britain's economy took another turn and orders fell away; by the end of 1982 they were desperate. They failed, but not for want of trying. Ted has a bit of a pension and Roger has his professional skills. He has already started again.

New small businesses don't all succeed; many go down, and good people with them. Small may be beautiful, but it is also hard.

High Technology

Peter's family lived in Jarrow. In the next house lived the leader of the great Jarrow March, symbolic of the unemployment and distress of the thirties. Peter's family were working-class and poor but determined, particularly that the boy and two girls should do well. Peter was born just after the Second World War and was sent at the age of seven, on the family savings, to school in the south. Later his father also came south with the rest of the family to Swindon, where Peter attended the technical college. Peter then went into the merchant bank of Lazard in the City of London as a management trainee in the computer department – a long way from Jarrow in just eighteen years.

After three years Peter went to British Olivetti, who sent him on a long series of courses covering all aspects of computers. There he came to know all there was to know on the subject, and became a total professional. His life gelled round the computer very early, and he has not thought of much else ever since.

When the courses were over he went on the road, starting in London's E2 postal district, knocking on every business door selling basic accounting machines. His tenacity was rewarded and he exceeded all his selling quota. But Peter was ambitious; he left, and took a chance with an American computer company which was in difficulties. He organized the local management to make a bid to buy the European division from the American parent company. This was a very early management 'buy-back'; they are now quite common. The Americans agreed to sell, the customers agreed to stay loyal, the staff agreed to stay on with Peter's new company.

Peter went on a long weekend with his newly married wife. That was just the moment when the American parent company decided to renege on their agreement. Peter dashed back to save the situation but he was young, the assets were old and the banks were coy. Peter was made redundant.

He was lucky to get employment with DATA Recording (DR), but this company, too, had problems. Peter put a radical scheme together, but it was not accepted. After his flying start, Peter had conceived two ideas which he had been unable to sell. He was convinced his scheme for DR was right and he determined to put it into operation as his own company. He had a wife, a house, a mortgage, but no job and no savings. He had friends, however, and two of these became his partners in turning his scheme for DR into the successful Future Technology Systems.

The crunch came in the coffee bar of one of those London hotels which cater for seminars on business. The time was mid-morning on a November day in 1978. The audience of some

200 earnest seekers after the truth about computers streamed out of the lecture hall and Peter grabbed Martin, whom he already knew well, and suggested they should go into business together. Martin, a steady, solid, unflappable type – a professor at Cardiff University – just nodded and went along.

Martin is a Nottingham man, brought up in a council house – father a TV maintenance engineer. He went to Nottingham Grammar School and got just enough 'O' and 'A' levels to be apprenticed to British Thompson-Houston, the electrical engineers, in Rugby, and for the next five years had, as he says, the best education and training in theoretical and practical engineering that the world could offer.

Martin got a degree at Rugby Technical College and a BSc in electrical engineering. After two years he started teaching at Leicester Technical College. He went on to Cranfield Institute of Technology, as research fellow working on control systems, and then to Cardiff University. A great opportunity came in his life in 1969 with a year's 'sabbatical' with Boeing in Seattle – what Martin calls 'a tremendous, wonderful experience'. Boeing wanted to keep him and sent him to learn FORTRAN, the computer language of control engineers; this brought him into the world of computers, which he adopted as part of his world of engineering and teaching.

Back in Cardiff he won a £4,000 grant for a mini-computer in 1971, to study its use for data processing, and this led him to microprocessors and his first book, which was also the first book on the subject. So by the time he was approached by Peter he was already known as a writer and lecturer on computers.

Martin was clearly a prize. Peter knew he would find in him a partner to whom the unfolding world of new computers would be an open book. He knew himself to be an entrepreneur, perhaps a future millionaire, but he knew that one man can't do everything and they both saw the need for David, also in DR, who had developed expertise in the storage of data, of information which has to be retrieved exactly when and how it is wanted.

David is a Brummie. His parents had a greengrocer's shop in Birmingham, where he was born forty years ago. It was an ordinary family, but David got lots of 'O' and 'A' levels at grammar school. At Leicester University he studied physics, but got fed up with the atmosphere and left without even trying to get a degree. He was always technical and went first to the BBC as a studio technician, but when he was twenty-five he answered an advertisement for an engineer to repair computers. The employer was Honeywell, and it did for him what Olivetti did for Peter and Boeing for Martin. Over the next seven years he became wholly professional in the engineering side of the computer business.

All three men knew that they must launch their own ideas. Peter and his partners had seen that existing computer makers tended to be limited by and to the investments they had already made. Peter was for a 'green-field' start with nothing on the ground, except aptitude and ideas. They had spotted a gap in the market, which could be filled with a system which would completely computerize all current office practice in small as well as large businesses. This system could be installed in almost any business at a cost ranging at that time from £7,000 to £100,000. They called it Series 88.

It was clear to Peter, Martin and David that the system they had invented could be assembled from components already on the market. It was a rearrangement of existing pieces on the computer chess-board, rather than the manufacture of new and untried pieces of microtechnology. Design, assemble, test and market – like Weinstock! Their calculation was that they needed to raise £1m to launch this system with a good chance of success. But Peter and David were jobless and only Martin was established. Peter had the priceless gift of refusal to stay down. He had been knocked down twice already, but he was absolutely convinced that Series 88 could be made to work.

A super-professional presentation of Series 88 was prepared by a first-class firm of City accountants, who did it at way below cost to help a new small business. Peter went back on the road with this presentation and had no luck with the banks; the venture capital people, he found, wanted too much of the action. The pension funds and investment trusts were more helpful, and he got £250,000 from an out-of-town life assurance company and the same from an out-of-town investment trust. That got him halfway.

The Scottish Development Agency people turned up trumps, not only with the money but also by giving Peter and his partners the option to buy back their equity share at any time. Since the factory was to be in a Scottish steel closure area the job creation subsidiary of British Steel also came in, but a gap remained to be plugged by the partners. They second-mortgaged their homes and then sold their designs to the new company, Future Technology Systems, for £50,000, which they immediately used to subscribe for ordinary shares. These shares, plus shares from exercising the Scottish option, would give them 60 per cent of the equity. The capital of the company was therefore £550,000 by way of loans, £200,000 in preference shares and £250,000 in ordinary shares – a very clever solution. The date was 8 July 1980.

Building began near the old steel works at Glengarnock. Production quickly got going, and in May 1981 the first sales were made to a large British-based multinational which has come back for more. Five months later, 150 systems had been sold for £1.5m. Sales of £2.5m in year two meant profit. The organization was ambitious and had to live within the cash available. Turnover in 1983 was £6m. The business was worth around £12m. Peter was a millionaire – on paper, anyway. The business went on growing, but faster than Peter and David could cope with, on the business side. In 1984 new capital was frittered away and the backers called a halt. Peter went and David moved sideways, Martin remained as design engineer. The non-executive chairman performed perfectly and a new management team was formed. It is not enough in business to be a technician, you must have business skills as well.

The problems of starting and growing a small business are many and varied. The state of the market probably comes first, and it is amazing what enterprising small firms can do to extend their own market by means of good service and quality, achieved with personal care and efficiency. A small firm which sits back and waits for the market to come to it will fall behind and down. The survivors go and get it.

The second main problem is the cost, availability and management of finance; then there is lack of experience, trying to comply with the law and form-filling, taxation and rates, the pressure of big business and the difficulty of getting orders out of government. It can be a long list.

It is in the availability and cost of finance that British small and medium-sized enterprises are at greatest disadvantage in the face of their counterparts in Europe, America and Japan. British banks have so far defended their conservative position with great skill against all inquisitors. They hold that no viable proposition fails to get financial support from them. The other financial institutions – life assurance funds, pension funds, venture capital and investment trusts – join in this chorus. No doubt bank directors have greatly changed their policies towards small-business finance (they claim to be carrying out a banking revolution), but it is in the implementation of these policies by bank managers that the blockage comes. It is inevitable that managers brought up to lend short-term on security should find it difficult to enter what is in effect the risk business. There are endless stories of entrepreneurs who failed to get finance for start-up or expansion when there was not sufficient security available to cover the loan.

The government Loan Guarantee Scheme has done something to improve this situation, but the scheme has lent only £440 million in four years to some 9,000 firms. It is almost impossible, in the small-business world today, to earn margins which cover the cost of this money and leave enough over to develop the enterprise. The crying need is for financial packages available to small business at no greater cost than would be paid by big business.

The banks ask why their shareholders should subsidize small business. The answer is that the banks should not do so; in other countries the state has done so. The banks' reply to that is that they own an institution, Investors in Industry, which has a subsidiary, the Industrial and Commercial Finance Corporation (ICFC), which is supposed to do exactly what is required for small business and make money and pay dividends into the bargain, so why is any state intervention needed? The answer is that Britain, like other countries, needs more small business in the same way as we need more exports and agriculture, and these are state-aided. Small business needs money rates equalized with those of big business, which is what other more dynamic economies have provided to grow their small-business sector, and that means assistance of some sort.

Germany, whose population is only 10 per cent greater than Britain's, has financial institutions whose balance sheets together add up to £17 billion, lending only to small and medium businesses. In France, whose population is about the same as Britain's, the balance-sheet totals of such banks come to £8 billion. In Belgium, whose population is only ten million, the credit organizations for industry have balance-sheet totals of £6 billion. In Japan, whose population is double that of Britain, the small-business credit corporations have balance-sheet totals of £33 billion. It is a matter for regret that in Britain the balance sheet of Investors in Industry, which owns ICFC, amounts to only £1 billion.

No fair-minded person could suppose that ICFC could make finance available to small business on the same scale as the institutions in other countries listed above. Indeed, the ICFC congratulates itself on making £100 million of new loans a year. Compare this with Germany, whose state-owned KfW* lends £1,000 million a year – ten times as much to ten times as many small businesses. The facilities available to small business in Germany are much more extensive and helpful to entrepreneurs than anything we have in Britain. The German system works on the scale which the development state would require. In April 1981, to meet the slump, a special loan programme was initiated to increase the competitiveness of the German economy, to save energy and to stimulate innovation. The loans were for four years at $9\frac{1}{4}$ per cent interest. An amount of £300m was made available, and this was taken up in a few months. In Britain it took three years to lend this amount under the government Loan Guarantee Scheme and the cost to the borrower was not far short of double the German rate. The KfW has continued to lend at around £1 billion annually during the recession of the eighties, and the commercial banks carry the whole of the risk.

The French Crédit National has introduced a new *'prêt participatif'*, which we would call a 'subordinated loan', to increase borrowing powers and 'comfort' creditors by making these loans subordinate to all other creditors. Over-borrowed companies can in this way be rebalanced. The loans are for

* Kreditanstalt für Wiederaufbau (Credit Institution for Reconstruction)

between fifteen and twenty years and the repayment and interest conditions are 'easy' in the early years or if the borrower gets into difficulties. No security is required and the rate of interest is way below the commercial rate.

The American government in the thirties introduced the Reconstruction Finance Corporation, to save the banks from failure. This was followed by the Small Business Administration, which is very active today, reporting direct to the President, who delivers an annual statement to Congress on the state of small business in America. In Belgium excellent facilities exist for the development of small business – PME, *Petites et Moyennes Entreprises*. In Japan three big banks stimulate, correct and finance small business at a rate of interest around 8 per cent.

If ever there was a highly industrialized country which needed reconstruction in peacetime, it is Britain. We have been devastated by inflation, high interest rates, a high rate of exchange, high unemployment, low productivity, loss of market share and reduction in manufacturing capacity. Investment is needed for us to get into the new technology, to become competitive and to start new programmes and thus re-employ the workforce.

What Britain now needs is a new fund with a large state capital base, borrowing on government guarantee in the world's markets, lending to small business – starting up or expanding – on far better terms than are now available. The fund should pay no tax or dividend and carry no risk, but pay the commercial bank a commission for doing so. Banks would include the fund's money in the financial packages they offered to the small-business customers. The fund should be run by businessmen, not civil servants, and be very lightly manned. It should take over many of the other services now handled by government, such as the Loan Guarantee Scheme, the Business Expansion Scheme, the Small Firms Advisory Service, and the multitude of smaller programmes initiated by successive governments. It would operate nationwide and regional support schemes would become less necessary. The Small Firms Division of the DTI could be greatly reduced. The large disadvantage small businesses in Britain now suffer would begin to be eliminated. Growth in this sector would be increased rapidly and another half million businesses by the end of the century would become a possibility. The new fund might be called the Business Development Board, BDB. I return to this later.

Government is the big spender in every country. Of British government purchases, 'procurement', perhaps 5 per cent now goes to small business; no one knows. In America the percentage is 23 per cent and President Reagan has said that in 1984 $60 billion of federal procurement actions should go to small business. Small business in Britain will be lucky to get orders to a value of more than $2 billion.

Government purchasing in America is regulated by Public Law 95-507 of 1978. Each 'solicitation for contract bids' over $500,000 must contain a plan to sub-contract a part of the work to small business. Failure to do so should result in failure to get the contract. Unfortunately 'contracting officers have not been diligent in enforcing it', according to the President's report to Congress in March 1982, and 'a major effort to encourage the procurement agencies to enforce these sub-contracting provisions is necessary'. There is great activity on this front by the small-business lobby in the USA.

In Britain we are still far from the business outlook or political will which could bring about legislation on the American model. Nevertheless, there could be no more direct way of increasing the contribution of small business to the economy than by increasing the flow of government orders in its direction. Central and local government servants would dislike it, because it is much more troublesome to deal with a myriad of small firms than with a few big businesses. Should this be the decisive argument? We obviously could not rush up to the American level of 23 per cent at once, the capacity would simply not be there; but an increase would give an impetus to the whole movement.

Another major limitation upon small business is lack of business skills. Receivers in bankruptcy in Britain estimate that 70 per cent of business failures are due to bad management. The entrepreneurs usually know how to make a product or provide a service, within their own personal experience. They worry about the 'bottom line' but they often have only hazy ideas of how to get there. What is needed are the business skills of accounting, estimating, costing, financing, marketing and organizing a business in an efficient and profitable way. The entrepreneur must know where he is all the time and why the numbers, which he sees, are going up or down. There are undoubtedly 'naturals' at this but most people have to learn; if they do not the inevitable result is failure. The growth of the small-business sector will not come fast enough if Britain goes on losing 12,000 companies and 16,000 partnerships a year through bankruptcy, which is the present rate.

There are in Britain today a large number of business tutors, advisers and helpers in great variety. Some have been organized by government and its agencies; others have been set up by colleges and universities, sometimes by teachers as a spare-time activity. Some 2,000 places a month are available on courses for small-business start-ups. Local Enterprise Trusts, consisting of local councils, businessmen and others, have sprung up all over the country and there are over 160 of these in being and more in negotiation: they all contain useful elements for encouraging, teaching or helping new businessmen. There are excellent organizations in the private sector to assist businesses in trouble. Both BBC and ITV run highly professional programmes for budding businessmen. The problem is to get these facilities used by the entrepreneurs, and a recent report* by Barry Baldwin of Price Waterhouse and Sue Palmer of ICFC recommended a training division at the DTI, presided over by a Minister of State. I would prefer BDB to take responsibility for this and fund it out of its own resources.

Many more people would become go-getters and their training would be greatly improved if there was a more suitable legal form for small business. Limited liability does give protection, but it is cumbersome, bureaucratic and paper-heavy. It is absurd that a new tiny business should have to comply with the same complicated regulations as great historic companies like Shell or GEC.

The solution must be simple. For very small firms there should be a new legal form – 'The enterprise'. The would-be small businessman would complete a form, establishing that he or she was, in good faith, going to run a business under limited liability and this should be signed by a banker, solicitor or

* *Management Training for Smaller Enterprises*, EYSME, 1983

accountant – as when applying for a passport. A small fee would be payable and this would entitle enterprisers to receive a manual of current practice from the DTI, or from the BDB, updated and free of charge. The manual would spell out the minimum required of very small firms under the law and provide a simple credit-worthiness form and a space for the accountants' report. Is this idea so radical? You cannot get a driving licence without knowing the Highway Code, and government should be forced to rewrite the rules required to regulate very small businesses.

In every industrial country policies for small and medium-sized enterprises include financial assistance, management training and advice, technological help and guidance, tax breaks, encouragement in sub-contracting, priority in government procurement, regional aid and promotion of exports. What should be the framework for all this in Britain?

Margaret Thatcher was asked by *Small Business* in May 1982, 'Would a senior full-time Minister for Small Business be a sound idea?' 'No earthly good at all,' said Thatcher, 'it is a ridiculous idea that you can tackle any problem by setting up a new department. We have too much bureaucracy already ... the idea of a separate department is quite useless.' That was vintage Thatcher! But all the same, small businesses are too important to be left to sort themselves out as best they can. A Business Development Board modelled on the German KfW, not a new government department, would be a good institution which could also act as the professional advocate for other reforms.

More and better businesses would be a foundation stone of the development state. Only more businesses with new long-term investment programmes will produce more real continuing jobs, wealth and innovation. There can be no valid argument against this proposition. An increase in the number of small businesses in Britain – after failures – at the rate of 30,000 a year would need a huge and organized effort. But does Britain have the people to start them up and drive them along?

9 Ready for Work

If Britain really is going to make a great new effort to start again, to improve and to create a host of new businesses, we are going to need the men and women to make it happen. Plans, intentions, manifestos, promises, conferences, and indeed books are all pie in the sky without the people determined to get results, educated and trained to do so. A new start has been made in training. The time for a new start in education is ripe.

I must declare my interest. Upon the initiative of my friend and successor at British Steel, Ian MacGregor, we, that is to say BSC Industry, have sponsored a syllabus called 'Education for Entrepreneurship' for inclusion as an option in the curriculum of secondary schools – thirty-six periods in the final year, or a crash course of twenty-six hours in one term. We shall support that syllabus in schools in the steel communities which want to adopt it, but it will be available to all schools. Work done in preparing this scheme has convinced me that, as things stand, Britain is not ready to create new businesses and new jobs on a sufficient scale to ensure prosperous survival.

The facts are stark. In 1982 some 650,000 young people left school at the age of sixteen.* Nearly 100,000 of this total left with no formal qualifications whatever. Another 300,000 did not pass enough exams to qualify them for any further education. About 200,000 went on to study, and only 50,000 went to universities. British 'A' levels are equivalent to the French baccalauréat; in Britain 13 per cent of students achieve the same

* N.B. 250,000 of them then became unemployed

standard as 35 per cent of French pupils. In France and Germany between 80 per cent and 90 per cent of pupils get systematic vocational preparation, in Britain only 40 per cent.

The public money voted for education and science in 1984 was nearly £13 billion, one of the highest allocations in the budget. There are 26,000 primary schools, 6,000 secondary schools and 839 colleges, polytechnics and university institutions. There are 400,000 teachers; in 1982 Her Majesty's Inspectors (HMI) reported that 25 per cent of new teachers were noticeably lacking in the skills they needed and that some of them should not have been allowed to have become teachers at all. There are ninety-seven Local Education Authorities (LEAs) in England; HMI reported in 1981 that no fewer than ninety-one were not fulfilling all their legal obligations, and fifteen were making provision well below the required standard. There is a long and lengthening list of complaints by HMI of serious inadequacies. HMI's report on 1983 said that education standards are up to scratch in only fourteen of the LEAs and that one in three schoolchildren in England receive poor or unsatisfactory lessons, where lack of resources and poor teaching environment made 'worthwhile teaching well-nigh impossible'. Small wonder that, as Michael Young, Chairman of the Manpower Services Commission said in June 1984, 'less than half leave with a piece of paper that an employer is prepared to consider significant'. Applications from comprehensive schools for places at Oxbridge have doubled in the past seven years, but success rates have slumped by nearly one half.

Two million adults in Britain are illiterate. One million cannot do simple arithmetic. Three out of ten do not understand percentages. Six out of ten do not understand 'rates' of inflation, exchange, growth, money and so on!* All this has got worse in recent years and is still deteriorating. This is a dreadful result from 'one of the greatest reforms of the century' – Butler's Education Act of 1944. Free education was assured for all children in Britain for as long as they were able to justify it. What was once the admiration of the world has become a drag on British progress and a forcing ground for failure. British secondary education is widely regarded as 'a failure system'.

* *Financial Times*, 24 October 1983

What went wrong? Nothing much in the primary schools, which are generally a success; nor at Oxford or Cambridge, which have kept up their traditional academic excellence. Nothing is terribly wrong with the polytechnics or redbrick universities except that they ape Oxbridge and are insufficiently 'technik'. The Colleges of Further Education, the so-called dustbins, provide an opportunity for a second shot at exams and a link with the business world. The trouble lies in the secondary schools.

There are endless excuses about stop-go in the spending on schools, an 'unexpected rise and then fall in the birth-rate, movements of population, and the arrival of Asians and West Indians'. These excuses come from the educational establishment, which is a deeply entrenched and self-absorbed enclave. The overriding causes of failure on such a massive scale are two:

• Academic approach to teaching of young people whose instincts and lives are not academic, but practical, earthy and active.
• Poor-quality teaching, lack of discipline, mismatch between teacher qualifications and the subjects being taught, poor accommodation, bad deployment of available resources – in a word, bad management.

For those who choose the academic route there are excellent facilities and they sail away on a high tide, which unfortunately carries them far away from industry. But for most of the remainder the examination is too difficult, the curriculum unsuitable, and the last years at school a boring waste of time.

In the great wave of enthusiasm for social progress, which swept Britain in the latter years of the Second World War, equality of opportunity was taken to mean that all must have the same education. Education should be so good that any child could become a Cabinet minister, a senior civil servant, a professor, a company boss or a trade-union leader. The attitude of those days was, and in many quarters still is, that to teach practical things in school was to consign children to a humble status and to deny them the chance of getting one of the top jobs. Thus all children should be given the chance of going to university, and should strive to pass 'O' and then 'A' level examinations, or at least get a Certificate of Secondary Education. But there was a structural flaw built into the system – it was always recognized that at least 40 per cent of pupils would not succeed in passing enough exams to qualify them for any further or higher education.

What makes it so difficult to correct this flaw is the existence of another, of a structural nature. To get the church schools into the system Butler agreed to share control with the local authorities, who shared it with the school governors, who left it with headmasters, who are today's supremos. Heads are subject to pressures mainly from teachers, who are usually non-technical; from parents, who above all want their children to pass exams; and from employers, who find exam results a fatally easy method of selection.

Under Butler's Act, the Education Secretary would seem to have all the powers required. Part I says, 'The Minister's duty shall be to promote the education of the people and the progressive development of institutions devoted to that purpose and to secure effective execution by local authorities under his control and direction of the national policy for providing a varied and comprehensive educational service.' The power is not enough. A more specific power is needed.

The professional controllers of the system are the civil servants in the Department of Education and Science (DES), the school inspectors (HMI), the Chief Education Officers (CEOs) of the Local Education Authorities (LEAs) and the twenty Examination Boards. The latter are widely felt to be dominating the secondary-school curriculum and maintaining the academic tradition. In addition there are twenty-five national voluntary organizations, including the teachers' trade unions, all with a finger in the educational pie. The result is a mess.

It is now proposed by the Departments of Education in England, Scotland and Wales that there should be a new single exam, with seven grades at 16+ for all school-leavers and a new curriculum and syllabus to go with it. Such a move came in October 1983 in Scotland, which has a relatively small comprehensive secondary school system. By the summer of 1986 all Scottish pupils will be able to take a new Scottish Certificate of Education (SCE) in Maths, English, General Science and Social/Vocational Studies – the normal range of subjects will follow in succeeding years. SCE is divided into Foundation, General and Credit levels. Two Credit levels at sixteen will be more stretching for pupils than 'O' levels now. The Foundation level will be specially designed for the 40 per cent who are expected to fail under present arrangements. Awards will be made on a single seven-point scale. The lowest grade will merely indicate that a Foundation-level course has been completed. Great effort is going into a new curriculum and syllabus at Foundation level, which is breaking new ground, but in-service training across the curriculum at all three levels will be needed.

The teachers in Scotland are still dubious. They are worried about 'streaming' from the age of fourteen into the three levels. Their 'internal assessments' will be confined to Foundation-level courses and to practical tests at other levels. Nevertheless, they have been persuaded to go along with this reform as a means of avoiding staff loss, and by a promise of genuine consultation as the scheme works out.

A 'bold and ambitious plan' for state schools was proposed by Sir Keith Joseph, the Education Secretary at a conference in Sheffield on 6 January 1984. He cannot impose it because of the susceptibility of Local Educational Authorities, but without it the education service will get no real increase in money from government. Its success, he said, depends on active support by teachers and employers.

The purpose of this plan is to bring the education of at least 80 per cent of all sixteen-year-olds up to the same level as is now achieved by the top 50 per cent – a huge leap! Exams would be based on individual standards of attainment, not upon statistical rules, as now – high time too! All children would have to attain minimum levels in English, Maths, Science, History, Craft and Technology. All pupils would be expected to learn about design and manufacture. A new curriculum would be broad enough to develop personal qualities such as discipline, and skills across the full range of basic studies. It must also be relevant to pupils' experience of the real world (get rid of 'clutter') and balanced enough to develop pupils' real potential.

These principles, said Joseph, must be applied deliberately and by agreement, which will take time; he was ready to discuss them with others in the education lobby, including trade unions. He said, 'high expectations on defined objectives

Education Guardian, 25 October 1983

motivate pupils to give of their best and help teachers to develop pupils' potential more systematically'.

In May 1984 Joseph was proposing that parents should have a majority on schools' governing bodies. In the next month he proposed that 'O' levels and the CSE should be replaced with a single system of exams at 16+, to be known as the General Certificate of Secondary Education (GCSE) to start in 1986. Examining boards will be reduced from twenty to five, who will draw up national criteria for all syllabuses.

This series of initiatives has been widely welcomed, but will they get to the heart of the matter, academic as opposed to practical teaching, and . . . bad management?

The Secondary Heads Association, in its evidence to the Parliamentary Select Committee on Education in 1981, commented:

The British are obsessed with examinations in schools . . . which are deeply embedded in our traditions: as many as fourteen different families of examinations can be found. A pupil can be entered in as many as six of them in the same year . . . for too many children exams are a measure of what they cannot, or do not want to do . . . already some encouraging experiments are being carried out in the teaching of French . . . where they can progress from one step to the next, like graded exams in piano playing . . . this could be applied to cover a wide range of skills. 'Profiles', which gave a clear and comprehensible picture of what a school-leaver has done, would be attractive to potential employers.

Headmasters are in a position to see that the present system is producing a new division in British society: those who have passed their 'O' levels or got a Certificate of Secondary Education (CSE) and those who have not. As things stand, the failures are condemned to remain uneducated, unskilled and unemployed in a world where their chances of any sort of job are diminishing.

Most pupils want to learn how things work, how to use their wits, how to co-operate with and lead others and how to solve problems. This is just as important for the academically inclined pupils, who get all the prizes, as for the others who get little or nothing.

Only 10 per cent of British pupils go on to higher education, compared with 26 per cent in France and Germany. Somehow our secondary schools do not release the same energies, ambitions and inquisitiveness as in Europe. Nevertheless, there are signs of a new start. In the last few years some secondary schools at least have cast off their inertia. Some headmasters feel that 'subjects' are secondary to real learning and that what is needed is balance between areas of experience. Creative skills, numerical skills, reading and listening and social skills should be superimposed on subjects so as to get this balance and so that each subject contributes to others. Thus pupils would get used to judging evidence, to being coherent and to making progress. Indeed, each school should echo the principle of the development state by becoming a development society.

John Tomlinson, Chief Education Officer for Cheshire, responsible to that LEA for thirty secondary schools, offered

some forward thinking. Until Butler, education was for the
brainy by the brainy, as it had been for two thousand years. The
abstract and the intellectual awakens the mind to beauty and
truth and sustains the human spirit. Right, but most of us learn
from the heart and the hand as well as the brain. The past has
given to theory a big lead over the practical. Nevertheless,
education has to help people to solve actual problems. This
should not be done by offering unwanted answers to unasked
questions. Youngsters naturally respect craftsmanship and
technology – long-standing English strengths – and a bond
between education and working life is both natural and
essential.*

Tomlinson's conclusions represent the views of many
enlightened headmasters:

• We need an agreement about a framework for a curriculum. It
is ridiculous to leave thousands of individual schools to make
their own lonely decisions about curriculum and defend
themselves against a hostile environment.
• This framework must be on a national scale and at the same
time leave room for LEAs and the schools to be creative.
Teachers could then spend more time and energy doing their job
– teaching.
• Assessment of pupils cannot be divorced from the curriculum
and it must be for professionals to do this.
• Learning by experience and by making and doing must have a
prime place in the curriculum.
• Much good development has been 'blunted on the classroom
door'. We need ways of motivating and developing teachers and
of involving parents and employers.

The National Union of Teachers also advocates that all
pupils should be assessed by a 'profile', in the form of a record of
personal achievement covering the whole of their secondary
education. They stress that this need is particularly crucial in
the case of pupils for whom the examination system is
inappropriate and who at present leave school with no tangible
evidence of their abilities and achievements. This proposal,

* Charles Gittens Memorial Lecture 1980

which is still at the experimental stage, is supported by most educationalists, including the Examination Boards. It is also approved by the CBI, the TUC and the select committees of both Houses of Parliament.

If profiles were introduced nationally, would the exam system be necessary? Britain is almost the only country in the world which has a quasi-compulsory nationwide examination for pupils as they leave school. The whole life of the secondary schools is focused upon it. The school curriculum is squeezed out of practical subjects into the exam mould. The exam itself has a strong academic flavour which for most pupils means regurgitating partly understood facts which will never be used again. Passing the exams is a feat of memory more than a test of all-round ability.

A conference of leading educationalists at Salford University in April 1983 had no doubt that the examination system must be changed to include the 'assessment of competence'. Those educationalists wanted a new framework with emphasis on serving social and economic needs, and the removal of existing institutional and academic barriers to personal development. That would mean the end of the old, narrow academic exams. It would also mean the end of the division between education and training and between academic and applied studies. That would be such a change, such an explosion in education that a new Education Act would be necessary. But should not the development state aim for that? Is that not exactly the move Britain needs, to get away from bored, disaffected pupils? Should we not aim towards interested, self-educating pupils keen to try out what they have been taught at school in a job, where they can continue to learn and start to develop their practical skills?

Why not abandon the idealistic pretence that all children are potential prime ministers and accept that most children want to become competent, self-supporting, respected people in their own community? Don't worry about future prime ministers and other bosses, they worry about themselves; either they have got it in them or not; if they have, they will see to it that they study and pass the exams and qualify for top jobs. Maintain equality of opportunity in education, but for heaven's sake don't try to squash all children through the same wringer; the best are then shrunken and the less good dried out for life – the worst of both worlds. The 1983 Leverhulme Report on further education endorsed diversity. Young people are diverse, and to pretend otherwise is unrealistic.

Equal opportunity in secondary schools should be based upon a curriculum of core subjects with different options leading either to the academic or to the practical route. Academic advance should be by exams; practical advance should be by moving through grades rather than exams. All should be assessed by 'profiles'. The Schools Council, now defunct, drew up the 'practical curriculum', reproduced on the following pages. Much of this curriculum is essential core education under any system, but there is also provision for short courses. These should include computer studies and work experience, of most interest to the new start in Britain, which has to move towards *technik* as in other advanced industrial countries.

In 1981 the Department of Industry (DoI) through its new Industry/Education Unit, came out with a scheme to help all secondary schools to buy a mini-computer. Introducing the scheme, Margaret Thatcher said: 'The microcomputer is the basic tool of Information Technology. The sooner children become familiar with its enormous potential the better ... I urge LEAs to take advantage of this scheme and I hope that schools who do so will be supported by their parent/teacher associations.' By the end of 1983 90 per cent of secondary schools had taken up the DoI offer to fund half the cost of the microcomputer package, matching pound for pound funds provided locally. All schools participating had to undertake that two teachers would be trained in the use of microcomputers in education.

In 1982 the DTI proposed a similar scheme for the primary schools, which should be taken up by all schools by 1984. This time Margaret Thatcher was able to say, 'We know how enthusiastically and skilfully young children can use technology in problem-solving and as an aid to learning across the curriculum. Our future prosperity as a nation depends upon encouraging this enthusiasm to flourish from the earliest day at school.'

A growing number of heads and teachers in Britain have been amazed at the enthusiasm for computer learning among children who previously attended school reluctantly. They find that computers can in some way or other be used for every lesson, from English literature to physical education. Peter Wilby, the *Sunday Times* education correspondent, found that there was a lack of computer expertise among teachers and a dearth of suitable software. He commented that 'a single micro is a pretty slender resource.'* The test will come when the DoI funding of school computers runs out. As the London regional director of this programme says, 'It's difficult to convince heads and education committees and parents that money should go into computers when maths teachers and books are being cut.'

The last of the Schools Council's reports recommended short courses in 'work experience'. The relationship of schools with industry has promoted much public anxiety, because the attitudes of schools to industry have been generally negative. The CBI, TUC, the DES, the DoI, the Schools Council and many others have played a constructive part here, but progress has been dispiritingly slow. Schools are not gearing themselves to relate to industry. Careers education does not get on to the timetable till the third year of secondary school. Only some 10 per cent of pupils have work experience lasting a week or more and only 15 per cent of schools offer economics as a subject before the age of sixteen. There is very little teaching material available, and it is mainly historical.

Following research commissioned by the Donovan Commission on Trade Unions, pupils and teachers were asked, 'Do you agree that a business is like a football team in which managers and workers are on the same side?' Sixty per cent of pupils and teachers agreed with this, 'but only because they have to, to get things done'. Thirty per cent of pupils, but only 15 per cent of teachers, disagreed 'because managers and workers are basically on opposite sides'.

The hostility of schools to industry must have its roots in the first Industrial Revolution, and it is summed up in the story of a visit by pupils to an engineering works. As the class was leaving the teacher was heard to say, 'That's what will happen to you, if you don't pass your "O" levels.' Attempts to bridge this gap can be made only by detailed work at local level. One of the pioneers is the Schools Council's Industry Project (SCIP). The purpose is to link education and employment. The project includes careers

* *Sunday Times*, October 1982

About twenty subject titles would be enough to describe most of the curriculum in most schools. They would include:

       1 English
       2 Mathematics
  3, 4, 5 Science (including Nature Study, Biology, Chemistry and Physics)
6, 7, 8, 9 Social Studies (including Environmental Studies, Geography, History, Politics and Economics)
  10, 11 Foreign Languages
      12 Religious Education
      13 Music
      14 Art
      15 Craft
      16 Design
      17 Technology
      18 Home Economics
19, 20, 21 Physical Education (including Athletics, Swimming, Gymnastics and Dance), Games and Outdoor Pursuits
      22 Careers Education
      23 Short courses

Particularly for older pupils some schools may also include a programme of short courses in subjects such as computer studies, consumer education, childcare, community service and work experience. A programme of short courses might also sometimes include some of the twenty-two subjects listed above.

Above and right: from *The Practical Curriculum*, Schools Council Working Paper 70, 1981

education and guidance, skills for later life and better methods of assessment, but it is not concerned with job placements. It works very closely with LEAs. It requires changes in the curriculum. It gets CBI and TUC support.

This is the story of Springfield School, mixed, eleven-to-sixteen-year-olds, on industrial Teesside. The head formed a task force of teachers, employers, trade unionists, an industrial chaplain, a careers officer, a psychologist, an LEA representative and parents; he took the chair. The curriculum for fourth-year pupils was completely cleared for the task force, whose members were involved in the classroom alongside the teachers. Outsiders stayed for lunch with the pupils and for programmes in the afternoon. The head regarded this as a calculated risk: if the

	1	2	SCIENCE			6	SOCIAL STUDIES			10	11	12	13	14	15	16	17	18	19	20	21	22	23
Subjects	E	M	Nature Study	General Science / Biology	Chemistry / Physics	Environmental Studies	Social Studies	History / Geography	Politics & Economics	La^1	La^2	RE	Mu	A	Cr	D	Tk	Hk	PE	Ga	Ou	Ca	Short courses
Age of pupils																							
5	E	M	NS			Ev						RE	Mu	A	Cr				PE	Ga			
6	E	M	NS			Ev						RE	Mu	A	Cr				PE	Ga			
7	E	M	NS			Ev						RE	Mu	A	Cr				PE	Ga			
8	E	M	S				from Ss/H/G					RE	Mu	A	Cr			Hk	PE	Ga			
9	E	M	S				from Ss/H/G					RE	Mu	A	from Cr	D	Tk	Hk	PE	Ga			
10	E	M	S				from Ss/H/G					RE	Mu	A	from Cr	D	Tk	Hk	PE	Ga			
11	E_5	M_5			S_8		SOCIAL STUDIES$_6$ or H or G			La_4		a programme including RE_1	Mu_1	A	Cr	D	Tk	Hk_6	PE_2	Ga_2			
12	E_5	M_5			S_8		SOCIAL STUDIES$_6$ or H or G			La_4		a programme including RE_1	Mu_1	A	Cr	D	Tk	Hk_6	PE_2	Ga_2			
13	E_5	M_5			S_8		SOCIAL STUDIES$_6$ or H or G			La_4		a programme including RE_1	Mu_1	A	Cr	D	Tk	Hk_6	PE_2	Ga_2			
14	E_4	M_4			S_8		Ss or H or G_4			La_4		*	*	2 from A, Cr, D, Tk, Hk_8 PE/Ga/Ou_4								*	*
15	E_4	M_4			S_8		Ss or H or G_4			La_4		*	*	2 from A, Cr, D, Tk, Hk_8 PE/Ga/Ou_4								*	*

outsiders were late or did not turn up, or failed to deliver, the teachers had to pick up the bits and this lost the confidence of the pupils. The method was group work on industrial relationships, careers, community work, industrial appreciation, small businesses, change, new technology, leisure and trade unions. Pupils worked with unemployed local youths on local 'Youth Opportunity' courses. Pupils were frequently out of school. In school the emphasis was on participative learning.

After two years this has become a permanent feature of Springfield School and has been extended to the fifth year. A good rapport has grown up between pupils and visitors, extending to social life. Pupils take it for granted that strangers are constantly in and around the school; they reckon that any adult can be quizzed or asked for help about unemployment benefit or shop stewards or indeed any current industrial topic. The task force now has twelve staff. 'Personally, it has had a lot of effect on my teaching and the way I look on my job,' said one teacher. Pupils said, 'the teachers have got more confidence'. Parents said, 'the benefits are clear, more confidence and competence'. An industrialist on the task force said, 'I handle industrial relations differently now'; another said, 'I listen more'. A shop steward on the task force said, 'I find myself less hostile now to other groups'. The pupils said, 'they taught us things that teachers did not know'. A teacher said, 'the pupils have a new maturity'.

The secret at Springfield was the commitment of the head and the staff, combined with an influential group from the industrial community on Teesside. The actual trigger for success was the marking out of a whole year's curriculum for use by the task force on the Industry Project. The Springfield experience indicates that there is a persistent tendency to underrate the potential role of the school in the life of a local community.

There is nothing in this which constitutes a threat to teachers – indeed, teachers reported that they felt strengthened in their own profession. Local employers, particularly ICI and BSC, took a generous attitude, as did local trade unions. There is no real reason why the Springfield experiment should not be more widespread. How can the leadership be found to get this type of education going among 6,000 secondary schools? Schools/industry projects of this type are being tried out in fifty LEAs, and many others want to start. In many cases the curriculum is being rethought, with local industrialists acting as consultants. There is throughout the country increasing pressure bearing upon LEAs and headmasters to move in this direction.

Britain is not alone in starting to move down this road. It is already a feature of school and community life in America. In Sweden the compulsory school curriculum says, 'Schools must operate in partnership with enterprise and working life generally . . . This will mean some school activities take place outside school . . . other persons besides the school must be able to participate in lessons and free activities.' The development state would need this kind of education, first, because opening up schools like this will create work-minded communities; second, because pupils can learn the need for top quality in work at an early stage in life. Even those pupils who go on to further and higher education would greatly benefit from more exposure to industry. Pupils in the lower range (70% of all) may well find that their instinctive ways of thinking and performing lead them to one of the thousand ways of being useful and successful in life, instead of accepting failure at school and thereafter.

On 12 November 1982 Margaret Thatcher, herself a former Education Secretary, cut through the whole network of long-established consultative bodies and announced that trials of technical and other work-related courses are to start in state schools. These trials for fourteen-to-eighteen-year-olds are to be funded not by the DES but by the Manpower Services Commission (MSC), which will find £7m in the first year for ten experimental projects. Those that are successful will be funded for at least five years. Headmasters and industrialists, many of whom have been calling for a move away from academic instruction, will now have a chance to show what they can do.

For many years there has been a course in British secondary schools called 'Craft, Design and Technology' (CDT), aimed at filling the need for practical as opposed to academic teaching and learning. A team of schools inspectors reported in 1982 that they had visited ninety schools in England and Wales which ran these courses and that this was 'roughly 10 per cent of the secondary schools which were running technology courses at that time'. That means that only 15 per cent of the 6,000 secondary schools are using these courses. The inspectors found that 'technological activities are patchily represented over the country as a whole'; that there is a 'small cadre of teachers, largely self-trained, male, constituting an evangelical vanguard among craft, design and technology teachers as a whole'; and that 'periodic competitions can induce a spurt of activity, but cannot be a substitute for a sustained course to which all pupils are exposed'.

The inspectors concluded that a good technology course is a general preparation for any adult society, and they advised heads and teachers on how to make the best use of resources available to them. Their report conveyed the impression that they have been inspecting a 'way-out' subject to which they would not recommend any increase of resources, but which should make better use of such resources as existed. Surely we could do better than that!

The MSC is now striding to the front of the 'ready for work' column, as the provider of training from age 16+, with a new government funding of £1 billion from 1983. The MSC chairman, David Young, was explicit about it in the *Director* magazine in October 1982.

> Training should not be confused with education. Training is about work-related skills and is intimately concerned with employment, so training must ultimately be employer-directed. We can help prepare for economic recovery through providing efficient training and job placement services. We will concentrate on youngsters, disabled people and long-term unemployed. We must work with employers and unions to come to terms with new technologies. We will encourage initiative, enterprise and self-help. We shall demonstrate our faith in small businesses.

By June 1984 David Young was saying* that those pupils who have neither aptitude for, nor interest in the overwhelmingly academic curriculum should have the option of leaving school at fifteen for a combination of work experience and college studies. 'An early leaving option,' he said, 'might well motivate a lot of children to do better at school.'

* *Financial Times*, 14 June 1984

The MSC has been behind many schemes in the past – YOP, WEEP, UVP, TOPS – the initials, if not the objectives, are well-known. As from October 1983 there was one main scheme, the Youth Training Scheme (YTS), to cover 400,000 school-leavers who have finished their education at sixteen and some 17,000 unemployed seventeen-year-olds. They get planned work experience in factories, works, plants and offices and thirteen weeks of whole-time off-the-job training. At the end of a year they will qualify for a national certificate, recording the work experience and standards achieved. This will serve as a step towards further trade and industry qualifications. This scheme is intended to offer a fresh start to young people and to be financially attractive to employers.

There are many who feel that thirteen weeks' industrial training for school-leavers is much too short and that the period should be at least thirty-six weeks or even forty-eight weeks or cover three years, as in Germany. But we must not fall into the old trap of swinging from one extreme to another. What we should realize is that a new start in the vital area of industrial training, so long neglected in post-war Britain, is upon us. But the reform of British education cannot be left to the MSC, although it is proving a most useful stimulant. Britain does still not have an agreed core curriculum which is more practical than academic, so the first main cause of failure in education has not yet been dealt with.

If exams and the curriculum are hard to change, teaching and schools management will be even more difficult to improve. In March 1983 the Education Secretary announced government proposals for better teacher training – almost the only area where his department has control of the educational system. 'Newly trained teachers will be expected to have greater expertise in the subjects they teach as well as more practical experience and they will have to provide satisfactory evidence of classroom competence,' he said. He went on, 'The quality of teachers is the major single determinant of the quality of education.' There are now too many teachers, recruitment is low and the effects will be slow. LEAs themselves are proposing a new teacher structure, including an 'apprentice' scale at lower pay rates, which would last for three or five years. A teacher would then have to be competence-tested before he or she could move on to the 'professional' scale. Good teachers could jump up this scale two steps at a time.

In July 1984 the Permanent Secretary at the DES announced a programme for the assessment of teachers. The government is determined that good teachers should be rewarded and bad ones eliminated under radical changes in the profession, now being negotiated between the teacher unions and the employers. LEAs do not want teachers to sit for exams but to be marked by heads with help from HMI and outside consultants. Lists of essential attributes are being put forward. Teachers who are successful will be rewarded with promotion and extra cash; those who are not will have to mend their ways, or lose their job. (*Observer*, 15 July 1984.)

And not before time! The report of HMI on four schools in Haringey (North London) published in 1984 is calm and cool, but damning. The ratio of pupils to teachers in Haringey was better than the national average. The schools budget implied costs which were the second highest for English authorities. Nevertheless:

> the overall picture in the primary schools visited lacks sparkle and fails to make demands on pupils who consequently tend to under-achieve . . . the absence of such standards is regarded as the norm across the authority . . . All four secondary schools visited were affected by . . . higher than average non-attendance, disruptive or unacceptable behaviour and undemanding work . . . work in no more than half the subject areas was of broadly acceptable quality . . . the rest was unsatisfactory and poor . . . examination results were disappointing and below the levels that might be expected . . . There was a general absence of broad and coherent curricular planning . . . pupils' work had not always been marked . . . staff absences were at a serious level. There were social and behaviour problems that rightly caused concern to parents . . . poor attendance rates, unreasonable disturbances in lessons . . . open hostility and distraction by members of the fourth and fifth years . . . relationships appeared to be maintained by the staff not demanding high standards of work and behaviour and allowing matters to drift . . . under-performance does not appear to result from inadequate resources . . . the causes lie

with the quality of teaching, a shortage of effective leadership, inadequate checks on use of available resources and shortages in oversight.

Of course there were some redeeming features: some heads and teachers try desperately hard to swim against the non-achieving tide, but HMI concluded 'this is not a problem unique to Haringey, it is shared by other authorities with similar urban environments ... across the LEA there is a need to raise levels of educational thinking and practice and to establish a conviction that the mediocre or the second rate will not do.' *The Times* commented on 13 July 1984: 'the schools have been corrupted by a culture of non-achievement, the deliberate abandonment of objective tests . . . of competences and purpose and the substitution of a flabby regime, boxed in by trade-union selfishness, of academic under-performance.'

Meanwhile in the spring and early summer of 1984 the teachers' unions called for strikes in selected areas and refused to supervise lunch time or cover absent colleagues. This went on till the end of June when LEAs agreed to take the teachers' pay claim to arbitration, which government and Parliament is not bound to accept. Joseph said that if extra cash had to be found it would be at the expense of teachers' jobs or school books or maintenance and equipment.

In Britain teachers have for long been convinced that their efforts are undervalued and they constantly refer to 'the burdens' they have to carry. Teachers are infuriated by the popular belief that they have a cushy job and life with short hours and long holidays. In fact in secondary schools they work a nine-hour day. But teachers' pay has undoubtedly during the last ten years fallen behind professional groups, such as accountants and police inspectors, who now earn substantially more than they. Teachers need continual reassurance that they are doing a good and useful job. They face sullen or indifferent pupils, who question the value of education – they may be insulted or assaulted. Adults give them little comfort and Joseph refers to their inefficiencies and assessment tests and low pay, because the supply of teachers is greater than the demand. By taking strike action the teachers diminish their authority over their pupils and make their own jobs more difficult: they feel isolated, friendless and largely powerless. I am indebted to Peter Wilby for this penetrating analysis of a British problem of outstanding importance, which will not go away quickly or quietly.

In the declining welfare state I suppose that this problem might be allowed to continue: it is part of municipal socialism, which has plenty of money, but no vision of how schools can contribute to a full life. It undermines good, strong management and makes no demands on pupils. It is part of the decline and the development state could not allow it to continue.

Education in Britain is a management problem, even more than it is an educational problem. How to shift bad teachers and how to skirt round the negative influence of the majority of LEAs which, as HMI reports clearly show, are not managing the schools properly. No doubt Joseph has started more new initiatives in education than any of his predecessors, but is he grasping the management nettle firmly? Are his plans for parents as governors and for assessment of teachers enough? Behind the agonizing and the exhortation is there a cutting edge to do the major surgery needed? We do not yet know.

We now have to reckon with the fact that we have to start again in education as in other ways. No longer is Oxbridge the be-all and end-all. No longer do we believe that decentralization to local authorities, without overriding power at the centre, is the best way to handle education. No longer will we put up with a failure system. No longer are we happy that 6,000 headmasters – the senior managers of the education business – good as most are, should remain virtually unsackable. No longer are we content that the reports of Her Majesty's Inspectors should be thrown into the waste-paper basket. No longer will we put up with a slack, inefficient society, however cosy. It can clearly be seen that one of its stunted roots is in the schools.

We now need a new, not a modified Education Act. It would have an enormous agenda. Some of the preliminary work has been done and some of the headings are beginning to emerge.

• Exams should be for those pupils willing and able to try to move up to further and higher education.
• Profiles on a national scale should be made out by school teachers in respect of all pupils.

- A national curriculum of 'core' subjects should be recommended for all schools, leaving room for optional subjects, academic and practical.
- The 'core' curriculum should include information technology and work experience.
- Where possible pupils should advance in learning and proficiency by 'grades', as in music, which would be recorded in profiles.
- The improvement in teacher quality and training now planned should be taken further, and bad teachers should be pensioned off.
- The teaching profession should be put up in pay to rank level with the armed forces, the police and accountants; all part of the essential professional element in the development state: it should lose the right to strike.
- The system of teacher assessments should proceed as planned and cover headmasters as well as teachers.
- The Education Secretary should have power, on the recommendation of HMI and with the approval of Parliament, to override LEAs, school governors and heads in any way needed to promote the education of the people.

This would sound, as did Butler's Act, a great trumpet call to the whole education system in Britain. Most people would say, 'that's right'. Parents, employers – even the pupils – know we have got it wrong as it is. The silent majority, who want to change and improve, would follow a lead. They would support a radical move towards a highly educated and trained population, capable of improving the standards and performance of Britain. Populations which have come to terms with this are to be found in Japan and other countries in East Asia. Until we understand what is happening there we cannot grasp the immensity of the challenge we now face, not only in education, but in most other ways as well.

10 Japan

There has never been a more remarkable instance of starting again than in Japan on 14 August 1945, when Emperor Hirohito commanded all Japanese to surrender. This order was immediately and willingly obeyed and Japan began again a new life of peaceful and calm co-operation with the American occupying forces, to rebuild a democratic, capitalist, non-militaristic, industrial state.

Nearly three million Japanese had been killed in the Pacific War. Cities had been destroyed, an empire had gone, 40 per cent of the country's capital had been lost. Forty years later it is confidently expected that Japan, with half the population and few of the natural resources of America, will soon be creating more wealth each year and a higher income per head than the USA. Japan will be the greatest trading nation and exporter of capital the world has ever seen. Even in 1980 Japan made more cars and more steel than America. Japan will soon have two companies challenging IBM in computers and a capacity to compete with both America and Russia in the making and using of space satellites. Half the younger generation will have been to college; all will have had schooling to the age of eighteen; new engineers and scientists will be coming out of college at the rate of 80,000 a year. 'Copy and improve', as a Japanese motto, will have given way to 'leadership in technology by innovation'.

This amazing series of events can be compared to the Industrial Revolution in Britain, beginning in 1780, and to the development of America in the hundred years following the Civil War, which ended in 1865. In Japan, however, it was part-spontaneous and part-contrived under a unique combination of hope and ambition between government, business and workpeople. Professor Chalmers Johnson, in his work on Japan, pointed out that Japan made a conscious decision to abandon the militarist state and become a peaceful industrial and commercial state. All decisions and priorities have since then been graded in favour of high-speed economic growth. This situation is clearly a great threat to Britain's industrial position in the world. It is also a quarry where one can dig for new ideas, techniques and institutions. Just as, in the past, the Japanese have copied and then improved upon the West, so it is now possible for us to understand the Japanese experience and improve upon it.

Japan opened up its frontiers and discarded its old social and economic order in 1868. Unfortunately the Japanese military came to dominate the new order, but after the defeat of 1945 the Japanese, needing wide and distant horizons to inspire them, again shrugged off the past and at a signal given by the Emperor converted Japan into what became in effect a development state.

'Emperor Hirohito of Japan and Empress Nagako on a family outing yesterday at the palace of Crown Prince Akihito with (from left) Crown Princess Michiko, Princess Aya, Akihito, and Prince Nori. The Emperor will be eighty-three on 29 April.' *The Times*, 23 April 1984

Obviously some of the old feudal tendencies linger on, as, indeed, they do in Britain. There is still in Japan an awareness of the Emperor, who does not rule or govern. The Japanese have mixed but unexpressed feelings about the Emperor, who reigns in venerated seclusion, but to traditionalists he is the ultimate person among living men to whom tribute is owed. The Japanese have a great sense of debt to all that had gone before. 'Proper station' and 'harmony' are still respected in Japanese life – like 'fair play' in Britain, comments Sir John Pilcher.* They are part of feudal loyalty to one's leader, one's comrades and one's workplace; they override loyalty to family and self-seeking and produce a coherence between individual Japanese. The concept of obligation or indebtedness makes Japanese people very law-abiding, and they are taught not to commit 'faithless acts against honoured friends'. They wish to be 'loyal for life to a lord who will care for them in return and they will only leave his service if he casts a slur upon them'. Loyalty and harmony are still strong in Japan, but the idea of equality, copied from the West, is making headway against them.

Self-discipline is still greatly admired, as part of self-improvement, for which education is essential. The Japanese have to overcome the considerable difficulty of learning and using their own language, but having done so they are ready to absorb enormous amounts of other information. The competition to get into Tokyo or Kyoto University is fierce, because these are considered the places where one is trained as a top job-holder. But all down the line education is essential to Japanese self-respect, and this continues in the internal training, in most companies. Here again the Japanese comes to see his 'proper station' and understand his role within the organization, thus adding to its harmony and coherence. The Japanese education system is very deeply rooted – way before 1868. Sir Fred Warner† comments, 'it has carried the Japanese to the highest standards of technological education in the world'.

On the negative side a Japanese cannot easily admit to lack of knowledge or to being wrong, since that would be to lose respect in the opinion of other people. There is always the danger that a

* British Ambassador to Japan 1967–72
† British Ambassador to Japan 1972–5

Japanese insulted or beaten will turn against the system. Japanese do best when measuring their form against their own record, rather than against the performance of others. If you sneer at a Japanese he is likely to seek revenge.

To Americans and British, who see true democracy as the management and pursuit of one's own individual interests and happiness, the Japanese seem submissive. To the Japanese, on the other hand, Britons and Americans are lawless people who do not stay loyal to those above and below them and ignore the fundamental duty to 'keep one's honour'. *Noblesse oblige* continues in Japan, and hierarchy is still respected. Britons and Americans take pleasure in the fact that the dignity of aristocracy is passing away, because they believe that a greater dignity is to be found in equality, however elusive that may turn out to be. On a more practical level, 90 per cent of Japanese people consider themselves to be 'middle-class'.

Japanese are subject to depression and boredom and they fear any form of rejection, so they need a great vision. After 1945 they found life barren and suffered from lassitude. They decided to defend their good name by co-operating with the occupying Americans, as indeed they had to! Aggression had not paid off, and the Japanese took another direction. Japanese do not pursue lost causes; they are too pragmatic. They wanted to earn the respect of other nations and they had to rebuild Japan from the ashes of defeat. They sought a new vision and put their faith in Japan's 'Culture of Tomorrow', which they believed would provide Japan, their enterprises, their families and themselves with a 'proper station', which other countries would respect. It has!

And so the Japanese set off on their new tack with institutions and ideology for a peaceful, parliamentary democracy, within a competitive market economy. Land was given to tenants, unions were encouraged, the conglomerates were broken up (but later re-formed), as were the monopolies and cartels. Wealth and incomes were more evenly distributed. The Japanese, however, never accepted the Anglo-Saxon view that the greatest advance comes from firms pursuing individual interests, maximizing profits, and driving each other out of business. The Japanese were convinced that some ordering of economic growth would be necessary and many were worried about 'excessive competition'.

On 28 April 1952 the American occupation ended and Japan, poor and weak, was on its own again. Its annual average wealth per head was $188, which was below that of Chile or Malaysia. All Japan then had was an educated and skilled workforce, of which some were productive and well paid, others not, and a cadre of management good at organization, technology and engineering.

In the next twenty-five years the wealth of Japan increased ten times over, which is two-and-a-half times the world average. Japan put its faith in steel, electricity, chemicals, coal, electronics, cars, computers and optics, and its exports grew twice as fast as world trade. By the sixties, investment in plant and machinery was equal to a fifth of annual wealth creation and productivity was rising by 9 per cent a year, leaving other countries far behind. By 1970 the foreign trade surplus was $30 billion. The key to Japan's success has been the combination of 'harmony', investment and productivity by business and government. It is by no means certain that this formula will hold good as circumstances change; indeed, it did not hold good in agriculture or distribution, or in the modernization of small businesses.

This combination would not have been possible without great optimism about growth, a sharp perception of opportunities for profit and an aggressive chase after a larger market share. This created its own domestic demand and the conviction that long-term views of a company's results were essential, to get products developed and quality high. It was accompanied by high savings. Many town workers saved a fifth of their income and savings overall were three times the American rate. 'Copy and improve' was the industrial policy, and imported technology was encouraged and guided by the government. When world income rose by 1 per cent, Japanese exports rose by 3 per cent. The main thrust of industry, however, came not from government but from private firms and especially from big companies, soon to be multinationals. They relegated smaller firms to the position of sub-contractors and component makers, where they have made a unique contribution to industry, which we should note well.

Today after a world slump the Japanese are inclined to ask

themselves, was it all worthwhile? Can we regain the high-speed growth, based on high productivity and quality? Nevertheless, it is certain that this will return and continue to the limits of what is humanly possible for the Japanese.

For Britain, seeking a new industrial impetus, there are four main questions:

• How far did the Japanese government assist the country's spectacular economic success?
• How much was the Japanese system of industrial relations responsible?
• What will the Japanese motor industry do to Western car companies?
• How can the West compete with the Japanese in microelectronics?

It is widely thought that 'Japan Inc.' sums it all up. This misses the point. The Japanese have developed a system which combines administrative guidance and financial inducement by government with intense competition between Japanese firms for market share at home and abroad. The 'team' appointed by President Carter and Prime Minister Ohira in 1981 to examine the long-term economic relations between the USA and Japan reported: 'One of the most difficult aspects of the Japanese economic system for non-Japanese to understand is the government–business relation . . . the image of "Japan Inc." creates the false impression that Japan can manipulate exports and imports at will.' Business in Japan does not meekly respond to government fiat, nor is government the creature of business. Government relies on giving administrative guidance as the informal means by which it attempts to influence business, without resorting to legislation or regulation, as would be the case in America. This administrative guidance is usually exercised by the Ministry of International Trade and Industry (MITI). But MITI's wishes have often been thwarted and flouted by Japanese industry. MITI has been through many phases and changes of policy, but it has consistently pressed for high-speed growth in particular sectors of Japanese industry, to meet Japan's domestic needs and export opportunities.

Chalmers Johnson's study of *MITI and the Japanese Miracle**
is particularly enlightening. As he describes it, the Japanese
came late upon the industrial scene and flinched from the
American 'legal sprawl', the 'English disease' and communist
dictatorship. In Japan the state's role in the economy is shared
with the private sector: public and private sectors have together
perfected means to make the market work for development
purposes.

In this single sentence lies the secret of Japan's success and its
contribution to economic action. Capitalism is moving out of
the free-for-all stage; it is striving to defeat both socialism and
communism and to preserve liberty for the individual within an
ordered, harmonious wealth-creating society. Making the market
work for development purposes could not have been done in
Japan by any one institution such as MITI; the industrial
relations system, the high rate of savings, the early retirement of
top bureaucrats into industrial and banking companies, the big
companies, the nationalized corporations, the huge number of
sub-contracting and distributing small companies, the tax
system, the docility of shareholders and, in the past, the
Japanese Development Bank – all have been interdependent
parts of the system which produced high-speed growth.

What these institutions together have created is a mixture of
the market economy and the planned economy. It is in that
sense a mixed economy – mixed not on the basis of ownership,
some state, some privately owned, but on the footing that
government, giving top priority to industrial policy, works with
industry to increase the competitiveness of Japanese companies
in world markets. To understand, we must take a look back.

Before the Second World War the Emperor reigned, but as Sir
John Pilcher comments, 'whoever controlled the Emperor ruled'.
Today the Diet (Parliament) nominally rules and the majority
party governs, together with the economic bureaucrats, 'for the
sake of the citizens'. This is both elitism and meritocracy, with
administration in the hands of those able to pass the incredibly
competitive Higher Level Public Officials examination. There
is a great tradition in Japan of respect for such an elite and the
mandarins who compose it. Thus administrative guidance is

* Stanford University Press, 1982

said to rest on the *'samurai* sword', a cultural weapon of great beauty which in Japan is a great deal more effective than legislation and penalties. In 1945 the military were rooted out, but the bureaucracy continued unscathed, with their chief opponents out of the way. Bureaucracy ballooned with the need for post-war recovery. The democratic political system, encouraged by the Americans, was not strong enough to control it and in 1949 the Japanese adopted the 'bureaucratic leadership structure', which is the Japanese mainstream to this day.

The bureaucrats extended their influence to the Diet, and a quarter of the House of Representatives and a third of the House of Councillors have usually been ex-bureaucrats and members of the Liberal Democratic Party, which has controlled the Diet since 1955. The real debate on legislation takes place between the ministries before the Diet is able to consider it. There are 'deliberation councils', but these are ministry-dominated and not comparable to the committees of Congress or to the British Parliament. So the Diet is a ratifying body and the ministries are the real rulers. It is widely accepted that the bureaucrats speak in the national interest while the political parties speak for special interests, mainly local.

Nevertheless, the Diet is strengthening its position against the bureaucracy. It is a mediator between state and society, forcing the state to pay attention, for example, to agriculture and small-business and other interests. The Diet has forced the state to change direction on a number of occasions to deal with new problems – pollution is a recent example. But power still revolves round the triangle of the bureaucracy, the major political party and business, held together by a common interest – the development state. It is operated by an 'old-boy network' composed of graduates from many universities, including the leaders, Tokyo and Kyoto, and of those who have retired early from government to go into big business.

What Japanese bureaucrats really like is a government minister who will leave them alone, while at the same time taking responsibility for his ministry and protecting it from other ministries and competing business interests. The minister must therefore be a powerful politician without too many ideas of his own. This attitude is very familiar to the British, and has been enshrined in the popular TV series 'Yes, Minister'.

Clearly there are dangers in this system. Scandals and corruption can easily occur and can as easily be covered up. Public corporations may be created or kept in being as soft landing grounds for bureaucrats, who retire early on inadequate pensions. There is certainly petty corruption, with gifts, subscriptions, dinners and suchlike, but all the evidence is that corruption among higher officials in Japan is uncommon; the public places greater trust in the bureaucrats than in the politicians.

The latter have been in trouble on many occasions, the latest and greatest of which was the Lockheed scandal of 1976. Companies do in fact believe that having senior retired bureaucrats on their board will help them in getting favours from government. But companies also resist government to get what they want. There has evidently been considerable adaptation by business to government attitudes, especially in the industries which are given high priority in the development state.

Japanese bureaucrats defend their own ministry against other ministries just as fiercely as commercial companies try to beat off their competitors. MITI tends to be protectionist; 'Foreign Affairs' is internationalist, 'Finance' is stingy, and policy emerges when a compromise is struck between them according to the strength of each, which varies with the leading personalities and with political and economic events. MITI itself is the smallest of the economic ministries, but its strength lies in its control of the Japan Development Bank, the Electric Power Development Company, the Export-Import Bank, the Smaller Business Finance Corporation, the Bank for Commerce and the Japan Petroleum Development Corporation. This formidable array of instruments in some of which the Ministry of Finance is also involved is co-ordinated by MITI's Industrial Policy Bureau, which manages Japan's industrial policy.

MITI was actually set up in 1949, but it was not until the sixties that there was a model or theory of industrial policy in Japan. Even to this day there is no doctrine comparable with that of Adam Smith, Keynes, Marx or Lenin. The Japanese make it up as they go along.

MITI sees its function as the protection of Japanese industries from any foreign competition for which it is not ready. MITI is self-assertive, nationalistic, loyal and workaholic and its 'spirit', as Professor Johnson says, has become legendary. MITI aims for Japan to be highly competitive internationally, and gets irritated by the disorderly competitive scramble among domestic Japanese companies: it believes that success in competition is not measured by profit margins but by the development of new products, new technology, new sources of supply and new types of organization. MITI men are of enormous interest to a wide band of Japanese public.

The institutions and agencies which put MITI's system into effect were built between 1949 and 1955. Wartime controls had been continued in Japan after the occupation was ended. Further controls were needed to lessen the cut-throat competition of Japanese firms in their own home market. There was already a list of industries chosen by government for nurturing. MITI's main tool at that time was control over export and import licences. This was to safeguard the Japanese balance of payments, and it became a highly restrictive trade and exchange control system. The other tool was the Japan Development Bank (JDB), which provided 'positive finance' for industry, which was then capital-starved. Foreign exchange control projected Japanese industries as they recovered and grew after the war, and JDB enabled groups of chosen industries to borrow from their bank, guaranteed by the state, amounts far beyond their net worth or capacity to repay. Only 10 per cent of company financing in Japan in 1963 was by way of shares. Over-lending became a habit and was done on advice from MITI; the banks did not press their customers for repayment and the practice of taking long-term views of a company's performance became established.

The old *zaibatsu* companies, which had been broken up during the American occupation, again became very useful and MITI busily rebuilt them. The number of trading companies was reduced from 2,800 to only twenty big groups; through them scarce capital was concentrated at the point where MITI thought it would be most effective. The money thus lent came partly from the 'counterpart funds' resulting from post-war American aid. These funds were put on one side to avoid inflation and were used again later for capital investment. The second and much larger source came from accounts in the government-operated postal savings system. These funds grew fast because the accounts were not taxable and you could have as many of them as you liked. The monies were taken into the JDB, which under MITI's direction drew up an investment budget, distinct from the usual revenue budget.

In 1949 MITI drew up a 'policy concerning Industrial Rationalization'; this created an Industrial Rationalization Council and initiated a Foreign Capital Law, which said that only with the permission of the Council could foreign investors acquire assets in Japan. Then came the Enterprises Rationalization Promotion Law, which directly subsidized new machinery, permitted rapid depreciation and committed central and local government to a large expenditure on ports, roads, railways, electricity and gas supply . . . innocent enough, you might say, but none of these facilities was available to any company without the approval of MITI.

In 1952 Japan joined the International Monetary Fund (IMF) and in 1955 the General Agreement on Tariffs and Trade (GATT), but in the special category reserved for poor countries. In 1953 Japan concluded a commercial treaty with the USA. At the same time MITI introduced into the Diet the 'Stabilization of Smaller Businesses' law and the 'Export Transactions' law, which gave MITI the power to create cartels and subjugate its rival, the Fair Trade Commission set up by the Americans during the occupation. MITI has always held that a country gets better results without anti-trust legislation. In 1954 came the 'Comprehensive Policy for Economic Expansion', and then the 'Outline of the New International Trade and Industry Policy'. The Minister of MITI had become one of the most powerful men in Japan.

MITI's technique was drastic. It started with an investigation and a basic policy statement about the needs of an industry considered suitable for support. Then the foreign exchange authorizations required were given by MITI and the funds were lent by the Development Bank. Licences to import foreign technology were granted by MITI. Then the industry was described as 'nascent', which automatically gave it the right to accelerated depreciation of its investments. It was provided with improved land at nominal cost, and given tax concessions. Lastly, MITI created an 'administrative guidance cartel' to regulate competition and co-ordinate investment among firms in the industry. At first MITI concentrated on steel, electric power, shipbuilding and chemical fertilizers; later on synthetic fibres, plastics, petrochemicals, cars and electronics. These measures were the core of MITI's successful industrial policies.

The results were rewarding, as the table of growth rates shows:

Growth Rates 1955–65: Percentage Change over Previous Year

Year	Real Gross National Product	Civilian plant and equipment investment
1955	8.8	–3.2
1956	7.3	39.0
1957	7.4	25.1
1958	5.6	–4.7
1959	8.9	16.9
1960	13.4	40.9
1961	14.4	36.8
1962	7.0	3.4
1963	10.4	5.3
1964	13.2	20.0
1965	5.1	–6.4

Source: Arisawa Hiromi (ed.), *Showa keizai shi* (Economic history of the Showa era), Tokyo, 1976, p.371

In 1959 the IMF and GATT demanded that Japan should at once make its currency freely convertible and open its doors to foreign products and foreign investment. MITI resisted these demands on the grounds that high-speed growth would not work in an open economy and that an 'invasion of American capital', as had happened in Europe, would make its own role and work impossible.

In July 1960 Ikeda became Prime Minister and the day of 'liberation' had dawned. MITI's golden age had passed. It had supplied the impetus for a development state in the fifties, when conditions in Japan were uniquely favourable. The goal had changed from military to economic victory and the nation had remained mobilized for national survival under its economic staff. But MITI, in Johnson's words, 'now suffered from the greatest bureaucratic infirmity of all – fulfilment of mission and loss of function'.

For the next five years MITI's administrative guidance was foiled and there were charges of corruption and neglect. In 1964 Japan had joined OECD, where it came again under pressure to liberate capital investment. But MITI hated the thought of competition in technology, capital and management. Japanese firms, with their heavy debt capital, would be easy meat for foreigners. In 1968, however, the Yawata and Fuji steel companies decided to merge to make the world's biggest steel combine, and this started the merger boom to end 'excessive competition' and meet the demand for capital liberalization.

MITI's main objective then was to create a vast tangle of rules, which would deter the hardiest foreign investor. The industries completely liberalized were restricted to those where foreign interest would be small (Japanese wooden clogs is the most extreme example). Usually, 50 per cent of a company's share capital was all that was available to foreign buyers, and all joint ventures were made subject to MITI approval. Japanese industry knew that before long it would have to open up and liberalize to avoid isolation, and in 1969 Mitsubishi and Chrysler agreed to form a new joint company, but without MITI approval.

A new stream of thought was maturing in MITI and a new 'long-term vision' came out in November 1974. Energy conservation and knowledge-intensive industries were to have top priority, protectionism was seen as a serious threat and internationalization of Japan was considered essential. This required a plan for public/private co-operation. An Industrial Structure Council was made responsible for the co-ordination of budget priorities, investment decisions and research spending. The ISC did not find it easy to get consensus, which in Japan today is by no means automatic. Nevertheless, all industries were liberalized except the seventeen that MITI was nurturing. MITI gave up its powers over import and export licences and control of foreign capital. 'Freedom in principle' became the 'basic purpose'; but with huge trade surpluses accumulated, Japan could finally afford to lower its guard.

The aim of MITI after the occupation had been to combine export promotion and high-speed growth into a coherent policy. A supreme Export Council was created to set export targets and make their importance known. The Japanese External Trade Organization (JETRO) was to overcome 'blind trade' by providing international commercial intelligence, by finding agents to see what competitors were doing and to market new Japanese products. This organization has now largely completed its mission. The major Japanese industries had been built up behind high tariff walls on the basis of a large domestic market. Only when unit costs had been achieved which were highly competitive in the international field, and necessary trade information had been gathered, were the tariff barriers dismantled. They were then no longer necessary.

The Japanese refer to their 'torrential exports', but it is their sector-by-sector attack which has caused so much hostility in the West. The truth is that, whatever they say, the Japanese do not enter competition, they undertake conquest – conquest, not competition. It is like General Montgomery's North African campaign. He would not attack Rommel until he was certain not only of winning the battle of El Alamein, but also of removing the Germans from North Africa. This is not the way the British or Europeans – or even the Americans – understand international trade. This points up, in the sharpest possible way, why Britain and the West cannot carry on in the good old way. We have to rethink, revise and start again if we are not to be submerged by the Japanese.

Under MITI's 'new vision' programme of 1974 depressed industries – textiles, rubber, steel, shipbuilding and petro-chemicals – were given the protection of a cartel. This is now called a 'positive adjustment policy' and is widely applauded everywhere. Excess capacity was scrapped, under a large grant funded by the Development Bank. The method of electric power generation was to be changed from oil to natural gas or coal, and nuclear power was increased by 60 per cent. Blast furnaces were converted from oil to coke. Oil imports were reduced by 10 per cent and 100 days' use of oil was stockpiled.

Once again, by reacting to change and altering its strategy, MITI had led Japanese industry down the right road; by the end of the seventies Japan had caught up, in many respects, with Europe and America. The oil crises in 1974 and 1979 were surmounted, as was President Nixon's devaluation of the US dollar – very painful for Japan. In 1980 *The Times* declared that Japan had emerged as 'the world's leading industrialized nation'. Japan's wealth per head was drawing level with that of the USA, and this marked the end of another era.

MITI's published view, at the end of the 1981, was 'to aim at building a foundation for sustained economic growth'. MITI recognized that Japan had an important part to play in easing the strains on the world economy and must adopt an international trade policy which would help to revitalize the economy and assist developing countries to do what Japan had done. Within Japan the need to conserve fuel was a first priority, then came the problem of rising prices and falling employment. For this purpose technological development, the requirements of small business and regional activity have remained essential. The plan is set out in great detail in a MITI publication of May 1981 entitled *The Industrial Structure of Japan in the '80s.*

What Japan now has, and Britain lacks, is a continuous economic policy and staff. In Japan this grew from traditions: it tried self-control by industries, which flagged; it tried state control of industries, which flopped; and it came, in about 1955, to an industrial policy of high-speed growth, initiated by government but implemented by competitive business. This led to the genuine public–private collaboration and the high-growth era. MITI played a large and at times dominating role in that development.

Certainly mistakes were made and changes became necessary, but MITI, as the engine of government economic policy, was persistent and managed to roll with the punch. MITI as the economic staff – giving administrative guidance, using financial inducements, funded by people's savings through the Development Bank and supported by far-reaching and radical laws – was successful for the most part in guiding Japanese industry in the right direction, while keeping up full competitive, commercial pressure. The conditions in which MITI worked were favourable, because the need to be a development state was widely seen and approved of in Japan.

A detailed comparison between the development of MITI year by year since 1949 and the actions which British, other European and American governments took to improve their economic performance would, I believe, demonstrate that they were all moving in the same direction, towards more and deeper state concern in the economy, despite loud denials of any such intention. We would also find that the Japanese have been more self-absorbed, more persistent and more successful than we in this. The West has been distracted from consistent evolution from classical capitalism by its past success and accumulated wealth, by its inventiveness and its contempt for other systems. That is no longer a legitimate position. The Japanese are beating us at our own game; they will not play it our way, so we have to understand and improve upon theirs. It is impossible to escape the conclusion that Japan's spectacular economic success has been greatly assisted by the attitude, policies and actions of Japanese governments following the American evacuation of the country in 1952.

Japan's industrial relations, the subject of the second main question, are no less rewarding than the machinery of Japan's government. They are a gold-mine for the careful, progressive manager, and a mine-field for blundering, insensitive management. Not only do the Japanese have their three 'sacred treasures' – lifetime employment, an age/service wage system and company unions – they also have what I call the three 'necessities' – company bonuses, Quality Circles and in-house education and training.

The 'treasures' have for long been thought of as part of a tradition which is unique to Japan. But a recent study* by Harno Shimada, Professor of Economics at Keio University, shows that they are not just a simple cultural model but the result of the interaction of market forces and technology, and that they have to be 'maintained by careful and serious efforts by workers, unions, employers and governments'. The system works not because of ingrained habits but because of intentional efforts by the parties concerned.

It is widely believed that under the lifetime employment system in Japan the employer provides his workers with employment security throughout a complete working life, much as a father provides for his children, and that in return workers offer unlimited loyalty to the employer. Looking more closely, however, we find that a regular worker in a firm is not usually guaranteed employment after fifty-five years of age; between fifty-five and sixty he has to retire, at an age when he may well consider that he has a further ten years of work in him!

* Published by Japan's Institute of Labour, 1980

One might think that the employment of regular workers must remain stable, but in actual fact levels of employment fluctuate sharply with business conditions, not only in times of depression – as in the seventies and eighties – but also in times of rapid growth. Redundancies are likely to fall first on the second grade of labour – 'the contractors' – and in many Japanese industries this category accounts for as many heads as regular workers. The popular belief that labour turnover is nil also turns out to be untrue. Worker mobility in point of fact averages about 15 per cent, being highest in younger and older age groups. Lastly it is said that this system has been fostered by paternalism, inherited from a pre-industrial Japanese society; that may be, but it also arose from the rational desire of employers, after the war, to secure their labour when there was a shortage of skilled men, in the early days of high-speed growth. The system does not provide a comparable lifestyle for 'the contractors', many of whom live and work in disgraceful conditions.

The length-of-service wage system is designed to encourage loyalty to the company and discourage job mobility; it is not usually related to productivity. Japanese strongly believe that experience and knowledge, arising from length of service and education, are increasingly valuable in the highly technological and sophisticated industrial business world which they have created since the war. It can, of course, happen that a senior unskilled worker is paid more than a young skilled worker, but in Japan this is accepted, because in the end the skilled workers go ahead of all the unskilled. Japanese have so far accepted that wage differentials calculated in this way are rational and acceptable.

The third 'sacred treasure', the company or enterprise union, usually comprises all the workers in a company and complies with company policy. The typical union is, therefore, not strike-prone. Unions increased greatly in Japan after 1945, since when high-speed growth of work, wages and wealth has not given them much to complain about. They have nevertheless secured 'single status' for white- and blue-collar workers, they make dismissal difficult and they try to insist on lifetime employment. Unions have eliminated the arbitrary wage-fixing of the past and have insisted that bonuses go to all workers, not to managers only. As in other countries Japanese unions have pressed for greater equality in all aspects of working life, but they have so far been prepared to accept the same objectives as the employers and to range themselves alongside the workers and management in pursuit of common goals.

There is no doubt that the 'treasures' were secured by the phenomenal growth and investment which began when the American occupation of Japan ended. An economy which averages a 10 per cent annual growth rate for twenty years is surely above serious criticism. In some years investments rose to nearly 40 per cent of total expenditure and this created an almost desperate need for a stable, skilled, educated workforce. Both workers and managers saw that employment would be increasing year by year.

So far Japanese Luddites are unheard of. It was providential that employers were able to rely on a youthful labour force which did not demand high wages. Young people were in plentiful supply and this created the pressure to get and hold a job, while learning new technological disciplines. Lastly it must not be forgotten that Japan, coming late to industrialization, had to recruit and train raw peasantry. There was no pool of skilled labour such as Britain has been building up for two hundred years. Internal training and promotion became essential; recruits had to start at the bottom and climb up the ladder of experience and skill. In this way, the economics of the local market for labour have gone hand in hand with the cultural tradition of respect for 'proper station'.

The origins of the 'sacred treasures' may have been misunderstood, but they remain very important. Lifetime employment may be in difficulties in Japan, but it is starting up in Britain. A divide is opening up in this country between skilled or professional employees, who can be said to 'own' a job, and the unskilled or casual labourer whose employment is insecure and may be temporary. This will be the new class division. Payment by age and service is beginning to return, particularly in small businesses. Company or enterprise unions are the natural sequel to the breakdown of the national unions – bad for union officials at national level, but good for union officers at local level who in co-operation with local management can improve wages, bonuses and conditions and avoid closures.

Look now at the three 'necessities'. Japanese workers are no

longer poorly paid; indeed, their income has risen so fast that
they will soon be among the best-paid people in the world. They
are paid monthly according to age, skill, length of service and
responsibility on scales agreed after negotiation with the
company union. In addition there are substantial bonuses based
on results, which can in a good year average an extra four
months' pay. There are also retirement allowances, depending
again on age, skill and service, which can be equivalent to as
much as forty months' pay. Each of these elements in the pay-
packet varies with economic conditions, but they increasingly
conform to a general norm rather than to conditions in each
firm. The system is flexible and efficient.

The second 'necessity' arises from 'quality', a word so often
used about Japanese products. One can split this up into several
parts. One part consists of the education and training which
goes on within Japanese companies; another is the long, patient
search for agreement which is typical of the Japanese in all their
dealings. Yet another is the Japanese worker's desire to be
involved in his company's success and a further part is the
willingness of Japanese management to consult and adopt
suggestions from the shop floor. The long-standing industrial
motto, 'copy and improve', has led to endless advances. The
Japanese are never content with what appears to be the best;
they immediately start to redesign, re-engineer and reprocess
products, and they do this on the shop floor as much as in the
drawing office. Management, supervisors and workers really do
not approve of technical or engineering 'fixes' to correct design
faults. They think the covering up of flaws is wrong and that the
design itself must be changed, even if that costs money.

Professor Cole of the University of Michigan quotes* an
example of the obsession with quality in Japan. He reveals that
General Motors of the USA usually gets fewer than one
suggestion per employee per year and adopts fewer than one in
four of the suggestions received. Nissan Motors of Japan, on the
other hand, gets nine suggestions per employee and adopts three
out of four of them. In 1980 Toyota received eighteen suggestions
per employee and adopted nine out of ten. American car
assembly plants employ one inspector for twenty workers,

* *Technology Review,* July 1981

while at Nissan and Toyota the rate is one inspector for thirty workers!

Professor Sasaki of Sophia University in Tokyo quotes Japanese experience drawn from the C. Itoh Co.: 'These past two years our company has performed many active projects. None of them was initiated at the top. All started from the proposals of middle management.'

It is through the institution of Quality Circles that results are achieved. The first type of QC, as we have seen, is the foreman and his section meeting to improve their product and process. This achieves the essential involvement of the workforce with improvement and quality and builds up the authority of the first-line supervisor. It also restricts the shop steward to union business and keeps him away from operational problems. It is in this way that workable ideas come up from the shop floor and from middle management. The second type of QC has middle management in the dominant role, suggesting and modifying what should be done and how. It is in this sort of QC that 'line' managers plan and improve in conjunction with 'staff' managers, and the frustrations of line managers are thus eliminated. In Japan unions do not participate in this type of QC and this avoids the embarrassment of divided and conflicting interests, which unions inevitably feel when change is being considered. Behind it all is the Japanese desire to use to the fullest extent the creative capacity of the individual worker. 'The whole system is entrepreneurial and coherent, unlike some of the bureaucratic management in the West.'*

The typical career path for future managers starts on the shop floor or as a production scheduling clerk, well below what his brainpower would seem to justify. He must learn what is really happening in his own business, and its impact on the customer. His training will be focused on building up long-term excellence in product, process and service. A college boy is paid no more than a machinist and his opportunity for promotion has to be seized and justified. He has to learn to use both muscle and brain and talk like his co-workers. Japanese top managers have started 'where the rubber meets the road'. A Japanese manager knows that organization is people. Heroes and super-performers are

* Mr Ohmae; *McKinsey Quarterly Magazine*, Summer 1981

discouraged and no one can skip grades. Bright children are trained to help slower-moving classmates, and this makes them good managers in later life – 'The nail that sticks up will be hammered down' is the Japanese manager's terse comment.

The third 'necessity' is education and training. Japanese industrial relations differ greatly from Western practice in this, which has produced an unusually high motivation, proved by negligible absenteeism. It all starts at the primary schools, where each child is taught that Japan, without natural resources, can survive only by importing raw material, adding value to them and then exporting, thus earning the wealth to pay for food needed from outside. Children are taught, and adults still believe, that if they stop working the country would collapse and they would starve. They are also taught from the first day that they must learn to work with others. Britain please note!

Children go to school 240 days a year in Japan (190 in Britain). At the age of thirteen Japanese children are reckoned to be three years ahead of British children in maths, a comparable subject. The rate of illiteracy is one fifth of the rate in Britain. Nearly 100 children a year commit suicide for fear of exam results. Nearly all Japanese children go to school until the age of eighteen (22 per cent in Britain). Nearly 40 per cent of Japanese children go on to higher education (10 per cent in Britain).

There are a thousand universities and colleges in Japan, of which about half specialize in science and technology. Each year 380,000 students get degrees, of which 82,000 are in science or engineering (18,000 in Britain), 13,500 in agriculture (671 in Britain) and 11,600 in medicine (4,000 in Britain). The majority study law, economics and the humanities.

No less than 10 per cent of Japanese national wealth is spent on education (Britain spends 5 per cent). Japan's educational expansion has been achieved since 1960, when only half the fifteen to eighteen age group was in school and universities concentrated on an elite minority.

After school, college or university most go straight into employment, where they are expected to take 'on-the-job' opportunities, to continue to study and to absorb required skills. Comprehensive internal education and training are built into the whole life of Japanese companies. All larger companies implement them. Hitachi, for example, puts all its science and engineering graduates through a two-year basic training programme, with an additional fifteen-month course for technical school graduates. Fujitsu runs an elaborate series of training programmes that start six months before recruits join the company and continue up to the mid-forties when the entire staff has a three-month development programme. Kawasaki gives new recruits a one-year on-the-job training, then a year doing the rounds of all shop-floor activities. In the third year many recruits become junior managers or join research teams. All these companies also offer courses on music, Western literature and poetry as well as on all manner of technical subjects.*

Most medium-sized companies and many smaller companies are now following suit. The Japanese passion for the education and training offered to them has been harnessed by employers to their own needs for skilled and loyal workers, and this is now part of normal business life in Japan. Education and training in the great majority of British companies are either non-existent or lamentable. Even the great old British system of apprentice-ships is diminishing as companies see no reason to train people who will leave them and go to work elsewhere. The new Youth Training Scheme will go a short way to correct this, but one year in elementary training at the age of sixteen will not get us very far.

If you put the Japanese 'treasures' and what I have called the 'necessities' together, you get a system of industrial relations very different from those in the West, and they have certainly greatly contributed to Japan's astonishing economic success. Britain and the West cannot precisely copy the Japanese system but we must take the steps necessary to get the same results. We shall not be able to compete with Japan until we have done so.

The third of the original questions was what will the Japanese motor industry do to American and European companies? The Japanese now make as many cars and commercial vehicles as the Americans. Japanese motor companies have been consis-tently profitable while the Americans have been through an unprofitable period. Japanese motor companies receive no special taxation assistance from their government.

* *Financial Times* (Charles Smith) 6 July 1981

Harbridge House, Europe, made a detailed assessment for BL of the consequences of the Japanese motor explosion. Harbridge consider that the formative period of the Japanese motor industry was from 1952 to 1968. It was then protected so heavily that the Japanese financial institutions, which own over half the industry, were tempted into putting up the capital to increase annual production for the home market by a factor of no less than seventy times! The drive which generated this growth was the intense competition between Toyota and Nissan. By 1970 these two had settled for an 80 per cent share of the home market between them (leaving the remaining 20 per cent to the six smaller companies) and had decided to indulge their competitive spirit in the export markets. The basis of their competition was in design, reliability and price.

In the early years the industry got protection from imports together with permits to import foreign technology, tax reliefs and protection from foreign capital investment. MITI's efforts to structure the industry into fewer larger units did, however, fail, due to violent opposition from the industry itself. Japanese government policy about stringent pollution emission control was nevertheless successfully imposed in the home market. It assisted the industry in capturing the American market as well!

Harbridge has collected labour costs in 1980 for Toyota and BL which show that straight wages, overtime and bonuses are higher in Japan. Statutory social costs are the same; voluntary social costs are, however, higher in Britain. Japanese labour costs are very nearly the same as in France and Germany. If Japan has a weakness it is that educated, skilled workpeople are getting restive under the system of promotion by seniority and retirement at fifty-five. Labour costs – especially in the social elements – are likely to rise sharply, but productivity is likely to rise to meet the increased costs.

The cost of finance has been held artificially much lower in Japan than in the West. Not only are interest rates substantially lower, but investors have been prepared to accept a much smaller yield on their dividend-paying ordinary shares. Honda's convertible loans, for instance, carry interest at 2 per cent per annum. Toyota pays out 12 per cent of its earnings in dividends and Nissan 16 per cent, but so confident are the Japanese investors in their motor industry that dividend yields are down to 1 per cent or 2 per cent. This no doubt reflects investors' belief that earnings are understated by as much as half. Most of the motor companies' debt has now been repaid. Toyota has no debt. Nevertheless, the companies spent £7½ billion on raising capacity by 750,000 vehicles in 1979–81. Toyota and Nissan can now borrow, if they so wish, for long or short periods on the best terms available anywhere in the world, but as Japanese financial markets become more sophisticated borrowers will have to pay more for their money at home.

Japanese cars are very consistently priced in the middle of the range but they fit, as standard, equipment that is optional elsewhere. They are remarkably good buys. In the export market they do not rely on the undervalued Yen; they price themselves against the market rather than the currency.

The Japanese motor companies have announced plans to raise annual production from 9,363,000 to 11,276,000 vehicles. The extra two million vehicles would all be exported, and this would secure for Japan 30 per cent of world markets by 1985. Only 500,000 units would be sold to developing countries and no more cars will go to America, unless the voluntary restraint agreement breaks. Where will the balance of 1.5 million vehicles go? The eleven widely divided countries of Europe are natural victims of Japan's motor offensive. The Japanese business community knows that this is likely to produce a wave of

'It took six Ford workers at Halewood to produce one vehicle in the time taken by three at Saarlouis and one at Toyota's Tsutsumi plant'

protectionism against Japan and many feel that the motor industry is endangering Japan's future.

World demand for vehicles is expected to rise to forty-three million by 1990. So confident are the Japanese in the value of their own cars that protection from imports has been entirely removed, as have regulations governing foreign investment in the Japanese motor industry; non-tariff barriers remain very effective. Financially the Japanese motor industry is the strongest in the world and lower unit costs, derived from higher levels of investment and productivity, are leading steadily to rising profits. It is probable that 85 per cent of Japanese car components are supplied by captive suppliers. The Japanese motor companies are likely to modify their growth target, but there remains the fear that despite voluntary export restraint the Japanese motor industry will damage the disunited motor industry of Western Europe. The Japanese share of the European car market was 9.5 per cent in 1982. It was over 10 per cent in 1983. In America the Japanese have 20 per cent of the car market, but lost some share in 1983 as General Motors, Ford and Chrysler fought back hard.

Britain has four main options in meeting the Japanese challenge, and they are much the same for the other car makers in Europe. The first option is to protect the motor industry against the invasion of Japanese cars with tariffs or quotas. There is, however, very little inclination to do this among the member states of the European Community; indeed the Germans and the present British government are hostile to the very idea of protection. The European motor industry would like to get an agreed limitation of Japanese car imports, but European governments have so far defeated this. Limitation by administrative guidance, as in France, requires a much tighter control over the banks than exists elsewhere in Europe. The reality of the situation is that Europe is very divided, likes Japanese cars too much and does not believe that protection is really the right solution anyway. What would be much more sensible would be for the European motor manufacturers to agree and practise common standards for parts and components and common regulations for safety, emission and roadworthiness. Then Europe would have the chance of real mass marketing.

The second option is to accept inward investment; for example the setting up of Nissan in the North East of Britain, as has happened in Tennessee. This will establish a tight, self-contained unit which will not spread the influence of Japanese technology and business methods. It will create temporary employment, but not additional long-term jobs, because the British-made Japanese cars will simply replace the same number of British cars. This option will in the long run be good for the Japanese and bad for Europe, but it looks good politically in the short run.

The third option would be to copy Japan, as Ford is trying to do with its 'After Japan' policy. Ford started off with a six-point programme giving much more responsiblity to production workers and introducing full flexibility between jobs and workers on the shop floor . . . Ford is not finding this easy.

This might seem a possible course for Britain, but there are difficulties: for example, a serious shortage of engineers in Britain. More serious is the fact that although small European cars, including BL's Metro, now have comparable unit costs and compete on more or less equal terms among themselves, the cost of similar vehicles made in Japan is 30 per cent lower. Is there a realistic chance in this labour-intensive, mature industry that the Europeans could catch up on a lead of that order? The extending use of robots by Japan indicates that the margin is more likely to widen than to narrow.

The fourth option is to collaborate, as General Motors has done with Toyota in California. The Japanese would like to manufacture in Europe. Obviously there is the avoidance of potential tariffs, but more significant is the wish to get near the European markets, to study them closely. For this privilege the Japanese should pay, and collaborative deals should insist on gaining widespread manufacturing benefits in return. Nissan already has collaboration agreements with Volkswagen and Alfa Romeo and BL has developed a relationship with Honda. Collaboration is not free of problems and it has to be between partners of similar management styles who are ready to compromise and get economies of scale by swapping components. There are six smaller Japanese companies, now moving out of their home market, so there is plenty of scope for those willing to go down the collaboration road. Copy and improve is still the name of the game and one should add – 'if you can't beat 'em, join 'em!'

Fourth is the question of how the West can compete with the Japanese in electronics. It is in this domain that the Japanese are preparing to take the world technological leadership. They trail far behind the Americans in space, defence and biotechnology. It is the 'knowledge intensive' industries which the Japanese have decided to master, and microelectronics is the key to these. Investment is now accelerating, and there is every indication that they will try to repeat what they did in the motor industry. MITI's largest research projects are Fifth-Generation Computers (FGC) and Opto-electronics. In the field of electronics America and Japan are way ahead of the rest of world. In Japan the government is leading the team, as well as planning and funding generously. In due course the banks are expected to come in and invest long-term.

The Japanese long ago realized that the silicon microchip is the essential element in current electronics, and in 1981 ten Japanese companies heavily increased their existing investment in making 'chips with everything'. These chips will be applied to a pocket TV, home movies on the Box Brownie model, microcomputers for small business, a typewriter that accepts dictation and a voice-input language translator, to name but a few domestic developments. Production of chips in Japan is rising sharply. In 1987 Hitachi will offer a silicon chip storing a million units of information – a so-called dynamic read and write memory chip.*

It is, however, in electronics for offices and factories that the greatest strides are planned. In 1979 IBM sold as much 'computery' as all its competitors worldwide put together, but two years later Hitachi and Fujitsu sold more computers in Japan than IBM. IBM has reacted strongly, almost violently, and has now gone ahead again, but it remains heavily dependent on Japanese components. The struggle between these giants is for the ultra-fast FGC.

MITI has voted up to £200 million to support the FGC plan. In

* *Financial Times,* 7 January 1984

hardware silicon chip technology will be pressed to its limit and post-silicon techniques will be reached. In software the idea is to get to 'man-level' intelligence and to have a machine which is 'user-friendly' and can converse in natural languages and reason and cope with totally unforeseen problems.

MITI has made it clear that the future prosperity of almost all industries in Japan will depend on how quickly advanced information technology can be made available to them. In typical Japanese way MITI is establishing agreement about desirable progress. It will then publish precise objectives and make the money available to reach them.

Japanese manufacturers have kept their feet on the ground, but they do expect that MITI backing will give them opportunities to manufacture novel customer items. They recognize that a National Plan for information technology is sure, as in the past, greatly to accelerate technical advance, but they complain that government funding of R & D in Japan has been quite inadequate! The Japanese are looking not only for translation systems and voice typewriters, but more especially for robots that can see, hear, have a sense of touch and respond to the unexpected. They are also quickly developing enormous data storage systems from which all the world's knowledge would be made available to everyone, through equipment no greater in size than a paperback book.

Computer-Aided Design (CAD) of limitless application, followed by Computer-Aided Manufacture (CAM) to create products without human intervention, are also Japanese objectives. Indeed, the Very Large Silicon Integrated circuits (VLSI), now too complex for design by hand, are themselves now designed by computers, thus massively extending the power of the microchip.

Out beyond FGC is the concept of using pulses of light instead of electricity for computery. This creates the optical computer, and yet another technology takes off! In Britain these ideas are well known, but will we get down to their commercial application?

These plans were presented by MITI at an international conference on FGC in October 1981. It is possible that MITI does not, in fact, know which route to take in FGC and is anxious to continue its 'copy and improve' policy at the same time as it tries to take the technological lead. There may even be a sense of duty in MITI that an advanced nation, as Japan certainly now is, should play a leading part in promoting world technology. Perhaps MITI was just trying to flush out the West's last few good ideas before committing itself; certainly some Japanese computer companies planned to pay large sums to obtain IBM's latest secrets, a plan which misfired badly.

In the sober words of a British Department of Industry report in 1982:

> High long-term growth rather than short-term profitablity is the driving force behind the Japanese electronics industry. Emphasis on growth and competitiveness has encouraged diversification and technological achievement and this is now yielding benefits. The main areas are computers, telecommunications and large-scale integrated circuits. Research and development is regarded by the Japanese as a major weapon and both private companies and government are investing heavily in it. Through MITI the programmes are brought together and the results are achieving product leadership in markets at home and abroad. To keep parity with IBM, MITI is sponsoring research into a new generation of super-computers and the fifth-generation computer project is Japan's first bid to gain world technological leadership in systems research. The Japanese Telecom is sponsoring a redevelopment of the public network and information service network for commercial and domestic subscribers. Japanese are strong in components and hardware products, but weak in software.

The DoI recommends that we collaborate with the Japanese because fourteen Japanese electronic companies, employing over 5,000 people, are already established in Britain, and English has become the second language in Japan. Japanese make all classes of computer and also new products to offer a joint relationship with British companies. Choice of partners is from a number of Japanese companies, willing to enter licence agreements. Collaboration on software, and in some hardware, offers possibilities to British firms, where Japan is weak and the British could push 'niche' products.

Collaboration with the Japanese will be much more even-Steven if we in Britain go strongly ahead with our own fifth-generation computer, as proposed by the Alvey Committee.* The report of that committee clearly owed much to the Japanese example both in technology and in co-operation between firms and with government. The Report said, 'We have taken account of recent developments in Japan, USA and Europe. These pose a serious potential threat to the UK. They also provide a yardstick of the scale and type of effort required, but it is a trap to assume that we should automatically follow what others are doing.' This is a prime case where British government saw the need to start again and did so, as we shall see in the next chapter.

In the great new wide world of electronics Britain has the brains, the inventiveness, the need and the opportunity to catch up with the competition. America and Japan are far ahead, but we could lead the rest of the field. We are still in the early days of this, the third and most fundamental industrial revolution of them all. It is not too late to play a leading part. To succeed we must invest heavily, collaborate to the full in research and compete like crazy in the market place. The Japanese are showing the way.

Drawing the threads of this chapter together we see that the essence of Japan, a new industrialized country which has retained its old habits of respect, loyalty and 'harmony', lies in wide agreement to go for high-speed growth. A public/private consensus has made the market work for development purposes. Japan is not a socialist or communist or religious or welfare state, it is a development state. Japan used organized capitalism, at first to save itself from breakdown, due to lack of resources, then to grow fast by 'copy and improve', and now to lead the world in technology.

What is the West, and in particular Britain, to do? It seems impossible that the West should adopt the system as practised in Japan. Rodney Clark, a lecturer on Japan at the University of London, has compared the Japanese and Western company systems.† The Japanese are unlikely to abandon their system,

* Report of the Alvey Committee, DoI, HMSO, 1982
† *The Japanese Company*, Yale University Press, 1979

first because it has been so staggeringly successful, second because it has a logic which is hard to upset, and third and most importantly, because it is approved of by those who work in and benefit from it. The system is vulnerable to slower growth, to rises in the price of imported materials, to ageing populations, to pressure and desire for bigger company dividends, to stronger unions, to Western influences, to a diminishing role for industry in society and so on. Nevertheless, the Japanese are moving away from the Western system and any convergence is, as Rodney Clark points out, 'discontinuous and desultory'. As you look down the contrasting characteristics in Clark's list (slightly edited by me) you see that each system is logical within itself, and that one could not be put on top of the other. Each could borrow items from the other, but there is no likelihood of merging the two.

JAPAN	THE WEST
Industry	*Industry*
Company usually part of one industry.	Company covers many industries.
Company does much sub-contracting.	Company likely to be self-sufficient.
Shareholders not primarily interested in profit or dividends.	Shareholders primarily interested in financial results.
Success measured by market share.	Success measured by profit.
Company financed mainly by debt.	Company financed largely by shares.
Relations with other companies depend on age and size.	Relations with other companies depend more on prospects.
Labour	*Labour*
'Lifetime employment' an ideal for half the workforce.	No ideal of lifetime employment.
Recruiting by age and education for general job vacancies.	Recruitng of particular skills and experience for specified jobs.
Employment practices related to size of company.	No close relationship between employment practice and size of company.
Bigger the company the better the quality of the workforce.	No such relationship.

JAPAN	THE WEST
Internal Organization	*Internal Organization*
Company a community.	Less so.
Managers and workers not differentiated.	Sharp distinction between managers and workers
Strong hierarchy and defined ranks.	Manager's position more related to his function.
Promotion by age and services.	Promotion by supposed ability.
Age and service increases attachment to company.	Attachment weaker, depends more on skill than on age.
Company (enterprise) unions.	National trade unions.
Labour mobility limits managers' powers.	Trade unions challenge managers' powers.

High-speed growth in Japan has now slowed down, partly because of the great size of the Japanese economy, and partly because of the long-term, cyclical world recession. Growth in 1982 was the lowest since 1975. In future there will be ever greater demand that individuals in Japan should share more in the benefits of success, most of which are now being enjoyed by the business companies. One can expect that promotion by seniority and early retirement will weaken, as will industrial disciplines. The unions may come to play a greater part in forcing change in employment conditions, especially in the smaller companies, where wages are relatively low. But when all the downside possibilities have been counted, Japan remains a most formidable, perhaps *the* most dangerous peacetime competitor Britain has ever had to face.

But Japan is not alone. This is made very clear in *The Eastasia Edge* by Hofheinz and Calder.* Hofheinz was a Professor of Government at Harvard, where Calder teaches the Political Economy of Eastasia. Japan since the Second World War has, indeed, been the leading edge in Eastasia's development, and has accounted for most of the region's advance, but other countries there are rising fast and now contribute a third of Eastasia's growth. A chart showing the narrowing gap between America and Eastasian countries during the years 1950 to 1980 shows how Singapore, Hong Kong, Taiwan, North and South Korea and

* Basic Books, 1982

The Narrowing Gap: Gross National Product per Capita, 1950–80

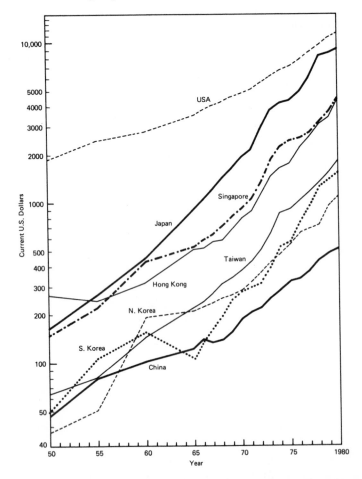

NOTE: Data represents annual Gross National Product in native currencies divided by year-end population and by the year-end exchange rate for the U.S. dollar. The basic data sources are as follows:
1950–1977 (except China, Taiwan, and North Korea) from World Bank, *World Tables* (Baltimore: Johns Hopkins, 1977, 1980).
1978–1980 (Except China, Hong Kong, Taiwan, and North Korea) from International Monetary Fund, *International Financial Statistics* (Washington: International Monetary Fund, June, 1981). China from National Foreign Assessment Center, *China: A Statistical Compendium* (Washington, D.C.: Central Intelligence Agency, July, 1979) and *China Business Review*, July–August 1981. Taiwan from Council for Economic Planning and Development, *Taiwan Statistical Data Book* (Taipei: Executive Yuan, 1979).
North Korea from Joseph Sang-hoon Chung, *The North Korean Economy: Structure and Development* (Stanford: Hoover Institution, 1974); and National Foreign Assessment Center, *Korea: The Economic Race Between North and South* (Washington D.C.: Central Intelligence Agency, January, 1978). 1980 figures for Taiwan, Hong Kong and North Korea were derived from data given in Far Eastern Economic Review *Asia Yearbook,* 1981.

From *The Eastasia Edge* by Hofheinz and Calder, Basic Books, 1982 even China are catching up America in terms of national wealth per head. Just think what would happen if China's population (the biggest on earth) and natural resources were effectively allied with Japanese industrial, commercial and financial skills! They are already converging. North and South Korea's population is nearly as big as Britain's. Taiwan has as big a population as Belgium and Holland together. Hong Kong and Singapore, powerful city states, have between them seven million inhabitants. All these countries are dynamic in the same way as Japan, and they are setting an example for the whole Pacific basin.

Eastasians have established government agencies designed not to dole out welfare, but to create wealth. They have encouraged production, protected their home industries and 'rallied the population around economic causes with national significance'.

They see that economics is the key to the future and they are not afraid to concentrate power, whether public or private. A partnership has been forged between public and private power. A major role of government is in providing information and ensuring a stable business climate (rather than twisting company arms), and business pursues its own interests with what Hofheinz and Calder call 'a fanaticism and determination which the robber barons of the American West would have envied'. It is the aggressive private sector, combined with progressive technical bureaucracy despite a strong conservative and protectionist element, that drives Eastasia along and makes it such a formidable competitor for the West.

We in the West have to face a rival capitalist system not only in Japan, but in other countries of Eastasia. We could not adopt that system but there are ideas at the back of it, not always obvious, which are of the greatest interest to us. Japan puts these ideas into practice when manufacturing in the West, employing Westerners successfully. If we are to compete with the Japanese system, we must make our own system work better. We must do this by learning from each other and by using the intelligence, innovation and flexibility which centuries of enterprise have given us.

These Western qualities have now to be focused upon the industrial problem, which at one time we thought had been solved. The problem has returned in acute form for many reasons – the rise of Japan and Eastasia is one of them. The editor of the *Financial Times* wrote 20 August 1982:

> Perhaps Japan's greatest achievement is to create an environment which encourages a flexible response to new economic challenges and market opportunities . . . Industrial policy is important not least in facilitating the contraction of old industries and the phasing out of new ones. MITI has perfected an array of market conforming methods of intervention, which act as a stimulus to the private sector and avoid the inefficiencies usually associated with a powerful bureaucracy. In Japan government intervention serves to accelerate change, not, as in most Western countries, to slow it down.

One might perhaps add that unless that intervention is obviously economically justifiable, it will not succeed. In Japan government intentions do not work out in practice unless the companies can see a profitable future in them.

Of course Japan has its problems. MITI's predictions of economic growth proved over-optimistic and had to be revised downward. Premier Nakasone stopped the publication of MITI's five-year plan in 1982. MITI is now in the doghouse. Nakasone tried to carry Japan rapidly on to the world stage, which was not popular in Japan. The Liberal Democratic Party lost control of the Diet and now rules with a coalition. The wretched story of bribes said to have been taken by former Prime Minister Tanaka lingers on. But Japan's growth has now resumed and is expected to exceed 4 per cent in 1984. The record balance of payments deficit in America has given Japanese companies the opportunity to make a killing. The threat to the West from Japan, leading Eastasia, will grow rather than diminish.

This new challenge has caught short the whole of the Western world, which is only now beginning to react to it. One of its most striking features is that Western men and women workers clearly respond well and happily to being employed in Japanese factories, set up in the West and managed by Japanese, or by Westerners trained in Japan, or by Japanese. This must cause us to ask if our cultural differences from Japan are so great after all.

Enthusiastic working in groups is thought to be a Japanese eccentricity, but do not the British have the same reaction, if they are well led and managed? A good firm or factory, ship or regiment, school or college, town or community, football or cricket team produces just the same interested, positive, stimulated atmosphere in Britain as in Japan. Like the Japanese, the British want to identify themselves with the unit in which they live and work, especially if it is small enough, well managed, and offers opportunities for making a contribution through work, being a fan, or even just being a voter. I do not think of myself as having been in the British Army, but as a Grenadier, not as having been in industry, but in British Steel, not as living in the South of Britain, but near Windsor, where I am chairman of the local theatre. I sing regimental songs, wear BSC ties and am proud of the theatre – just like a Japanese.

When it comes to actual work it is clearly observable that the British like to work steadily with care and attention; they resent their mates arriving late or being absent; they get furious when materials do not arrive on time, so that they cannot get on with the job. These natural reactions get clouded by the trade-union group culture in big units, where it is fashionable or advisable to go along with the unenthusiastic, 'why bother' attitude to work. But in smaller firms and plants the natural interest in work is evident, especially if it is encouraged by and gets a response from management.

The Japanese wear an armband when they are on strike, but they go on working. The British wish strongly to register their disapproval of treatment they consider unjust without losing their pay, and when they strike they say 'we simply *had* to do something and what could we do except strike?' Surely good industrial relations could find a way round that, by developing company unions. 'Them and us' bites deeper in Britain than in Japan, but it was not always so. It is only post-World War II that the Japanese, through education, have moved up to 90 per cent middle-class. In Britain we are on our way – just go to any one of the ITECs (Information Technology Centres) set up in 100 British towns and see the advance of those who were once thought of as working-class youngsters.

No doubt the Japanese are subtler than the British, more tense and self-absorbed, keener on education and improvement, less

given to political and economic theorizing and more loyal to
their own more successful society. Nevertheless, we are closer
to the Japanese than we think. Although neither the British,
other Europeans, or the Americans are likely to imitate Japan
precisely, there are features of their system which must cause us
to pause for thought.

- Should we not adopt an attitude to life and work focused more
on creating wealth than on how we distribute it?
- Should we not focus more on harmony and co-operation rather
than getting the better of each other?
- How could we combine the dynamic of private enterprise with
the force of government?
- Do the Japanese have methods, practices or institutions
which we should understand and improve upon?
- If Western people work well and happily in Japanese-owned
and -managed businesses should we not adopt their methods?
- What are the weaknesses in our own Western systems which
have been exposed by the better performance of the Japanese?
- How could we repair those weaknesses and still move 'with
the grain'?
- How could we make the market work for development
purposes?
- Are we too preoccupied with the short term?
- How much time do we have?

The experience of the Japanese is subtle – they are very clever
people. It show that success does not come from simple
alternatives – plan or don't plan, confront or negotiate, invest or
neglect, spend or save – it comes from the correct choice of one
of a myriad in-between positions. It shows also that there is no
one policy, action or institution which alone can bring success –
it is the correct combination which opens the door of the
strongroom. It shows, lastly, that it is the relationship between
management and all those interests and parties with which
management has to deal which decides whether success is
achieved, or obtained in only a small way, or missed altogether.

   In Britain we are on our own. If we do not or cannot make and
sell our products and services in price and quality competitive
with the Japanese, we shall go down. By the end of this century,

very soon now, it will be desperately late. Before then we have to take ourselves in hand and start again in a conscious and determined way.

The last chapters in this book are about how to eliminate the weaknesses which have appeared in British economic life. Britain does have to move – the system is imperfect. Japan has exposed this, brutally, by setting much higher standards of performance. Britain and the West have to meet these standards or suffer inevitable further decline.

But there is neither East nor West, Border, nor Breed, nor Birth
When two strong men stand face to face, though they
Come from the ends of the Earth!
(Rudyard Kipling, 'The Ballad of East and West')

11 Micros

'The face of manufacturing industry has been changed, irrevocably, in less than a decade by new techniques . . . based on relatively cheap computer power . . . the unmanned factory could be a reality within five years.' Thus the *Financial Times* on 16 July 1982. What on earth has happened: how, why and what does it mean? Is this just academic sci-fi? Why has there been no resistance . . . or has there? Why is IBM overtaking General Motors as America's most important company? Is information technology something we ought to know about? Kenneth Baker, Minister for Information Technology (IT) in Thatcher One and Two, quoted the results of a wide poll taken in Britain in 1982: 83 per cent of people asked had no idea at all about information technology, but 53 per cent said it was the most important thing for Britain and that if we did not get our act together the country would be totally washed up! Since then awareness of IT has steadily increased, but to understand we must go back a bit.

What has happened is that forty years ago two streams of thought, whose springs were in the last century, flowed into each other. Twenty years ago, a powerful pump turned the streams into a new, irresistible flow, and this is the source of the third, latest and most fundamental industrial revolution.*

The first stream started with the search for a mechanical calculator by Charles Babbage, an English mathematician who died in 1871, at the age of eighty; he is the father of the computer. The second stream began in 1879 when two English

* See *The Mighty Micro* by Christopher Evans, Gollancz, 1979

218

scientists, Thompson and Rutherford, discovered the electron. The streams joined in the Second World War. By the fifties electron valves had been overtaken by transistors invented by an American, William Shockley, who went on to invent the silicon chip, which reduced the cost of transistors, tenfold. The pump, primed by billions of US dollars, was the space race to get a man on the moon. This required the miniaturization of the electronic calculator and other devices to save weight and room in the spacecraft. From this came microelectronics and micro-processors, which are in fact mini-computers.

These devices were taken up by the commercial companies in competition, and they are now incredibly cheap. They lie at the heart of the new machines which are today taking over in our factories, offices, homes and defences. The microprocessor or mini-computer is as important an invention as the steam boiler, or the electric light bulb, or the internal combustion (motor-car) engine, and it is still at the beginning of its career. It will come to develop more power and wider application; it will become even smaller and cheaper. It has caused the development of the new technique known as IT.

That is the skeleton: it deserves some flesh on the bones. Babbage made two machines: the first, 'the Difference Engine', he showed to the Royal Astronomical Society in 1822; the second, 'the Analytical Engine' (actually a model of it by Babbage's son), can still be seen in London's Science Museum. What Babbage was trying to do was to eliminate the long routine of making logarithm calculations. Could this be done by a machine? Babbage was determined that his analytical machine would be able to tackle each particular task with unique internal 'patterns of action', in fact a programmable computer. It had a processor which Babbage called 'the mill'; it had a control unit for the programme; it had a memory, where numbers were stored till wanted. It had methods of feeding in numbers and an output mechanism. It was hand-powered, and bells rang when the sums were done. But Babbage could get no support for his engine and died a disappointed man. His ideas lay dormant until the 1930s, when they were reactivated by the needs of the coming war and the possibility of applying electricity to drive the analytical engine.

If Babbage was the father, Herman Hollerith, an American,

was the godfather of the computer. Hollerith invented a tabulating machine to cope with the USA census of 1890. It used punched cards which were sorted and counted by electricity. The idea was very widely used and Hollerith merged his company with many others. By the time he died in 1929, it was known as the International Business Machine Corporation, today IBM.

IBM was then run by Thomas J. Watson, a cranky autocrat who, as the Second World War was breaking out, allocated $1m to Howard H. Aiken, a young mathematician at Harvard, to develop a general purpose computer using Babbage's ideas and electromagnetic relays. This was quickly related to defence purposes and was first switched on in 1943. It was enormous, noisy and slow and was called 'Colossus'.

In Britain, electric calculating machines were being used in great secrecy to crack the German codes; this was Churchill's secret weapon, described in the Enigma story, and it was steered by Alan Turing, who had written a treatise 'On Computable Numbers'. In Germany, Zuse and Schreyer produced a calculator using electronic valves which greatly increased the speed of calculating, but Hitler thought it would take too long to build and turned aside from it – another of his fatal errors.

Back in America, at the Moore School of Engineering, the first electronic calculator was installed on a weapon-proving ground in 1947. This was a prototype of the computer as we now know it. Its chief snag was that its programs could be changed only by rewiring the machine. The mathematician Von Neumann, working in America on nuclear weapons, had already spotted the fact that computers were more important to mankind than nuclear bombs and he introduced the missing link, the idea of the stored program. Von Neumann's idea was to store the programs within the computer itself. The Moore School's next model incorporated this idea and the stage was set for the commercial companies to design computers for general use. While all this was maturing the control of electricity, known as electronics, was making astonishing progress. Electrons can exist independently of atoms and they can travel in a vacuum or within crystals; they move at random, unless they come under the influence of an electric or magnetic field. Electronics is the technology of controlling the flow of electrons, and links input devices like gramophone pick-up heads, microphones and photocells to output devices like loudspeakers and alarm bells. The input devices are called transducers and they convert vibrations, sounds or light into electric signals, which when magnified and activated can be heard on loudspeakers and seen on TV screens.

Electronic apparatus consists of a few basic components. Resistors, capacitors, inductors and oscillators are passive components which simply control the flow of electric energy. Silver and copper are good conductors, porcelain and polythene pass no current and are insulators. In between lies germanium and silicon and some new materials which are semiconductors and it is of silicon that most transistors, which are active components, are now made.

Before transistors were invented, electronic valves were used: they were hand-made, variable in quality, short in life and expensive. The early Moore School computer used 19,000 valves and used enough electricity to keep a small power station busy.

The breakthrough came in 1947 when a team at Bell Telephone, led by William Shockley, invented the transistor, for which they won the Nobel Prize. Evans commented, 'The most important single invention within the whole complex of inventions which we today call the computer is undoubtedly the transistor.' The transistor is a switch. As such it can be 'on' or 'off', which can be 'one' or 'zero' or 'yes' or 'no', and these are its basic uses in a computer. As Ed Goldwyn said in his BBC TV series 'Horizon', 'the transistor murdered the valve industry with a speed that was brutal'.

The Japanese quickly saw its possibilities and became world leaders in the manufacture and use of transistors, especially in radio receivers. This was, indeed, Japan's first great technological achievement. But it was not long before the lead passed back to America. In 1955 Shockley left Bell for Stamford University, where he discovered that silicon was a much better semiconductor material for making transistors than germanium, which stopped working when warmed up. The US Army allocated $15m to Shockley to make a transistor capable of standing up to battle conditions. Silicon transistors were light, small and cheap; they could withstand vibration and shock, they required no heat and only a low electric current; they were the answer. But Shockley was a difficult man to work with; his eight assistant scientists left him in 1957 and set up a rival company with Fairchild under their manager, Robert Noyce. In this factory they developed a British idea of making several transistors at once. These were called integrated circuits, and they won the lead back from the Japanese.

It was at this point that the powerful pump of Space Race dollars came into action. By 1963, eight transistors could be formed on a single chip and the cost had been reduced by 90 per cent. Today, 64,000 transistors on a chip is standard and a million is within sight. The cost of a standard chip is measured in cents rather than dollars. But the stunning change came in the size of the transistors – what used to be a cubic centimetre in size was reduced to a small pinhead!

The demand for minute transistor circuits was enormous, for use in spacecraft and in guided missiles. San Francisco became the centre of production and a valley at the south end of the bay became known as 'Silicon Valley'. Scientists peeled off from Fairchild, and the 'fairchildren', as they were called, now populate Silicon Valley and the surrounding towns and countryside. Noyce is still king of the fairchildren and he has achieved the amazing feat of condensing a whole computer on to a $10 chip – this is the microprocessor.

It is the cheapness and the size of the microprocessor which are so staggering. Evans calculated that the human brain is made up of some ten thousand million neurones, each of which is a minute switching unit. In 1945, in the days of valves, it would have been impossible to make a computer of similar capacity because that computer would have been as big as Central London. Ten years later, the first transistors would have enabled the computer to be reduced to the size of the Albert Hall. Ten years later again, when the silicon chip was first available, the computer would have been as big as a London bus. Today the computer with the switching capacity of a human brain need be no bigger than a human brain. A modern computer can switch billions of times in each second.

But what is the purpose of all this frenetic switching? The computer switches between O and 1; by adding 1 to 1 many times over it multiplies, and by subtracting 1 from 1 many times over it divides. When the computer copes with 2 it uses 10, 5 is 101, 8 is 1000, 15 is 1111. This is binary arithmetic, and is the oldest method of calculation known to man. It is possible that the neurones in the human brain work in this way. The one and zero symbols can also be used for letters of the alphabet for words and for logic such as 'true' or 'false' or, indeed, for the simplest answer of all, 'Yes' or 'No'. For calculating machines there is no conceivable system so convenient as binary, provided the switching is fast enough, the machine (the hardware) cheap enough, and the instructions to the hardware (the software) comprehensive enough. The first calculator to use binary was made in Germany in 1936, but that technology got lost until after the Second World War. With the arrival of the transistor all computing, everywhere, became based upon binary arithmetic.

The computer or microprocessor has its own binary arithmetic into which numbers and letters must be coded and, after completion of the calculation, decoded. It must also have coded instructions such as whether to multiply or divide, work out percentages, relate inputs to facts stored in its memory, or a thousand other types of calculation, all done by 'switching.'

The software programs, which tell the computer what to do, are, as of now, a limiting factor, because the spectacular advances in hardware have so far not been matched by the software. It is very likely that program-writing techniques will sharply improve, using computers to write their own software. The number of program-writers is greatly increasing, as gifted amateurs start to make their own computers and experiment with new ideas.

There remains massive scope for innovation in both hard- and software and in the products and processes to which it is applied. Already domestic cookers, ovens and washing-machines are controlled by microcomputers. Machines need no longer communicate by needles on dials, but by displays combining charts, characters, even animation and three-dimensional pictures. You can buy a computer-controlled machine which will talk to you in your car and tell you why it won't start! Children can teach themselves by pressing buttons and getting the reply in clear English. Blind and handicapped people will be able to

A British company — Servis Domestic Appliances — claims the distinction of being the first firm ever to get a microcomputer-controlled washing machine on to the market.

The single-chip microcomputer which now controls the wash timings, sequence, temperatures and speeds is shown on the left. The electromechanical system which originally did the job is on the right.

Ease of operation (the user can select any of seven wash programmes by the touch of a button), versatility and great reliability are some of the advantages conferred by the microelectronic approach.

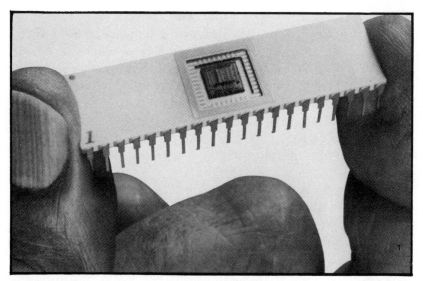

Europe's first microprocessor. The Ferranti F100 is the first (and so far the only) European-developed microprocessor. It is ¼-inch-square and 0.015-inch-thick.

use and read machines by touch, breathing patterns, eye movements and, it is believed, by brain impulses.

Sir Clive Sinclair, who pioneered the home computer and flat-screen TV, is a British businessman as well as an inventor. His pocket TV set, smaller than a paperback book, appeared in time for Christmas 1983 – cost: £80 (the Japanese equivalent cost: £250). Sinclair's new QL (Quantum Leap) personal computer for business use costs £400. The programs that come with it include word-processing and financial analysis. The American equivalent by Apple costs £1,400. Sinclair plans to sell 100,000 QLs in 1985. He said in 1983, 'Sinclair is much more than a TV and computer company. It is working on a whole new range of personal communication products.' A start-again man!

Word-processing, which is the automatic processing of letters and documents, can increase a typist's output by 300 per cent and make the job more satisfying. The move is towards a single office information system with all the data stored in an information bank, which can be drawn upon at a touch of a button by those who are authorized. Not only secretaries but all staff, including directors and chairmen, will need to be able to operate keyboards.

Each function in an office can now be worked by a single operator with a word-processor, a video display screen, a print-out and access to the central data bank; a telephone and telex can easily be built into this. Book-keeping, pay, management accounts, investment analysis, standard costing, employment records, sales analysis, order processing, stock control, quality control, production schedules, cash flow and bank accounting can all easily be brought into the integrated office information system.

But it is in the factories that the most extensive and revolution-ary changes can be made by using microprocessors. This is the heart of the start-again process for Britain. It gives us the chance to catch up with the industrial lead nations. Of course, if we fail to take the opportunity we shall be worse off than ever, because other industrializing countries will come up from behind and we shall slip ever further down the league tables of wealth and living standards. Our Department of Industry has seen this dilemma and helps firms willing to move into the 'Flexible Manufacturing System' (FMS), into 'Computer-Aided Design and Manufacture' (CADCAM) and into the world of robots.

Flexible manufacturing brings microelectronics and mech-anical engineering together on the shop floor, to get *economies of scale in small-batch production.* Just as a data bank in an office can be the central control point, so in a manufacturing process a central microprocessor can control the machine tools and the transfer of components and tooling. Software programs can now be easily and quickly changed over from one purpose to another, leaving the memory data in store. An operator can move from one batch of work to another without the need for 'long runs', which was the basis for the economies of scale and the great advantage of large companies. The computer and the microprocessor have brought these economies within the range of small businesses. This is of great significance for British industry, because it enables a whole new range of businesses to manufacture, as sub-contractors or on their own account, as cheaply and as well as a big manufacturer.

An outstanding example is the way Austin/Rover and Jaguar

became successful small motor manufacturers by intensive use of the flexible manufacturing system and robots. This was done in competition with the international giants, and all Britain should note.

We don't go for this in a big way as yet, although many of our competitors do. We are held back by our conservatism, our reluctance to change and take risks, our lack of technical education, our lack of industrial capital and, perhaps, also by our lack of commitment to the endless improvement essential to survival in modern industry.

CADCAM is nothing new, it has been applied by big business to complex problem-solving for more than a decade. What is new is the arrival of the microprocessor, which makes everything computer-aided, cheap, easy and quick. There is no manufacturing firm that cannot benefit from it in design, drafting, planning, estimating and manufacturing. The output of design staff, rare birds, can be increased threefold. The waiting time between design and production can be cut by a quarter. Errors are eliminated, the cost of improving design is greatly reduced, the repeat of orders is easy, the quality of the product is greatly improved.

Once CADCAM is into a plant it tends to spread. It permits a complete overhaul of design and production. It is lack of awareness and fear of the computer which are holding back the advance of CADCAM. Great efforts are being made to educate businessmen in the new opportunities before them. There is no logical, valid reason why we should not now full-heartedly plunge into this.

People are scared of computers and of 'robots' too – it is an intimidating word, like 'entrepreneur'. Once again the microprocessor is at the heart of these reliable, capable, sophisticated machines, of which the short description is a 'reprogrammable mechanical manipulator'! Robots can weld, spray paint, load pallets, feed machines, transfer components, assemble, press, mould and operate machine tools. They save waste and ensure consistent quality.

In Japan there are in 1984 about 30,000 robots in use – five times as many as in America. In Britain the number is only 1,500. The Japanese aim to be using over 50,000 robots by 1990.

Teaching by teaching arm, as demonstrated on the Hall
Automation CompArm

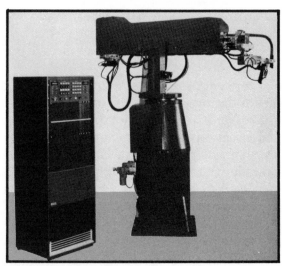

Microprocessor-based robot-control system

Their research may not be as good as ours or America's, but they are incredibly successful at the use of robots in manufacture. The British Department of Industry has offered £10m to support the making of robots, and by 1984 this scheme was overspent.

In 1981, nearly a third of the robots installed in Britain were British-made; in 1982 less than a quarter were British-made and the number imported from Japan had doubled. Once again we are losing market share. Robots are exactly what British engineering now wants as part of FMS and CADCAM. As with all microprocessor-controlled machines, robots can easily be switched from one operation to another, just by changing the program. They provide flexibility in manufacture and enormously increase the range, speed, quality and cost savings of the small and medium-sized enterprise. They do the long, repetitive, sometimes dangerous jobs on the factory floor, where turnover in manpower is usually high, and their use in a factory makes its employees more secure in their jobs. This, as the British Institute of Management said in 1980, 'is likely to change the whole nature of the industrial environment'. The TUC reported: 'the new technologies offer great opportunities not just for increasing the competitiveness of British industry, but for increasing the quality of working life'. The beauty of the robot controlled by a microprocessor is that, as our Department of Industry says, 'The worker who formerly did the job can program the computer and supervise the robot.' The experience is that robots are proving to be more cost-effective than expected. They are, above all, cheap.

The robot is part of the manufacturing system which is controlled by the microprocessor. Flexible manufacturing, automated small-batch production, computer-aided design and manufacture, together with robots, are the systems of the third industrial revolution, changing all our ideas about manufacturing industry. The 'dark satanic mills' are disappearing fast; the white coat takes the place of dungarees; intelligent, careful, machine-minded British workers take easily to the microprocessor system. The old working-class outlook is fast disappearing and the classless society is approaching. Nothing can hold up this powerful force for long. Managements, if they are reluctant, or timid, or ignorant, can slow it down and let the competition get further ahead, and that is damage enough, but an essential part of the development state package is the rapid extension of these new techniques to everything concerned with 'more and better'.

The microprocessor will go on being improved, and the systems in which it works will be extended. The range of our knowledge and of what we can do with it is now seen to be limited mainly by our capacity for communication. There is building up a flood of traffic for telephone lines – voices, pictures, texts, numbers, seeking new routes. Information technology has to cope with this and needs greatly improved transmission systems. We need a high-capacity 'star', as opposed to 'branch' network, and we don't have one. The trunk and local telephone exchanges are being improved by microelectronics. We have now to move from copper wire to fibre optics, hair-thin transparent glass or silica fibres that will transmit information in the form of pulses of light. This was pioneered in Britain in 1960, but it has been developed worldwide by others. By 1990 world sales of fibre optics are expected to reach £1,500 million, and at last Britain is on the verge of enough manufacturing capacity to make several thousand kilometres of this fibre a year.

Fibre optics is better than copper wire for telephone cables because it permits thousands of telephone conversations to be carried at the same time along a fibre as thick as a hair. Optical fibre cables are smaller and lighter than copper, and are easier to install. They need fewer amplifiers and there is less interference. They cannot be tapped and, above all once again, they are cheap.

Opto-electronics converts light to electric current and vice versa, generating optical signals for transmission and converting the signals for display at the receiving end. The market for these displays is already large and growing fast, and they are an essential part of our electronics industry. Britain invented the liquid crystal used in display equipment and we are still the largest suppliers of it, but other countries are hard on our heels.

Kenneth Baker summed up the position in 1982:

The world market for information technology equipment and materials is now over £50 billion a year, estimated to increase at a rate of 14 per cent a year. If we add together the information technology equipment sold by the six biggest

British companies in the business, we get to a total about equal to that of Siemens of Germany or Philips of Holland, but these companies themselves only rank five and six in the world league.

The report of the Chilver Committee* of November 1981 to the National Economic Development Council stated that the British electronics industry is in relative decline and that 'current trends would imply a further decline in Britain's share of the world market and an equivalent loss of trade, profit, and job opportunities'. Chilver pointed out that 'British manufacturers have not concentrated on leading edge business which . . . explains why annual growth in British output in the late seventies was only about 7 per cent compared with growth in world markets of 10 per cent. By 1990 Britain's electronics industry could be showing an annual trade deficit of £1 billion.' It will be £2 billion in 1984!

Chilver proposed that government, industry and users together should encourage rapid adoption of the latest electronic systems in banking, insurance, local and central government and the health service. Suppliers and users should work together and users should be allowed 'more than 100 per cent tax deduction for the purchase of such systems'. Chilver stressed that firms in the industry 'will respond positively to government leadership in making the final choice and in co-ordinating and implementing policies'. He emphasized that 'firms will need increasingly to work in collaboration with each other because of new development'. He concluded on a more hopeful note: 'We have begun to identify those sectors, within which Britain could build up competitive businesses', and 'work is now in hand . . . to develop appropriate strategies for the business in each of these sectors'.

Two prime factors came out of the Chilver Report:

● First, unless our leading firms do get together in some effective way, Britain could drop down to only a minute share of world trade in microelectronics and be on the receiving end of massive imports.

* Sir Henry Chilver is Vice-Chancellor of Cranfield Institute of Technology

● Second, there has taken root the beginnings of co-operation between government, suppliers and users in Britain, on much the same lines as in Japan.

In America and Japan the information technology revolution is moving very fast. In Britain some ten million people are in the information business, including teachers, scientists, journalists, managers, office staff, banks, telephonists, printers and administrators of all kinds. This total is increasing at the rate of around one million people a year. Are they being provided with the best and latest equipment, and are they learning how to use it?

A decisive breakthrough came on 28 April 1983, when the Industry Secretary, then Patrick Jenkin, announced that the government would support the report by the Alvey Committee, which the government had appointed as a sequel to Chilver. He said, 'this is the first time in our history that we shall be embarking on a collaborative research project on anything like this scale'. A Tory government has taken the lead in bringing industry and academic work together with government to plan the fifth-generation computer. Government agreed to contribute £200m and private-sector companies £150m. It was perhaps at this point that the development state in Britain was conceived.

John Alvey, British Telecom's technical director, admitted that the trigger was 'the unveiling in 1981 of Japan's fifth-generation computer programme and the invitation to other countries to come and discuss participation in it'. Alvey's argument continued (and it is the argument for the development state):

● The scale of this and other Japanese IT programmes has to be seen as a major competitive threat, to which America is bound to respond, leaving Britain miles behind, unless we respond too.
● Japanese are applying IT to 'those parts of society where increases in efficiency and productivity could be most beneficial' – making IT easy to use and applying IT to the processing of knowledge.
● In Britain, 'collaborative endeavours are essential if we are to preserve and strengthen our capability and competitiveness in IT' as part of an overall British IT strategy.
● Action plans are needed to develop the four 'enabling technologies':

1 software engineering: better ways of instructing computers;
2 Man/machine interfaces: making computers acceptable to their users;
3 Intelligent knowledge based systems: transferring knowledge to computers;
4 Very large-scale integration: chips which cram components together to get extremely fast working.

• There is solid agreement among industrialists and academics on programmes and priorities, which have been widely welcomed and supported.

• Without government support collaboration between firms and with academics is not possible. Government should fund 100 per cent of academic research and training. Government should fund 60 per cent (later reduced by Thatcher to 50 per cent) of the remainder.

• The programmes should cover 'pre-competitive activities' – basic research, design tools, communication between researchers, testing and assessment. Individual companies have the job of translating the results of the programming into totally competitive marketable products.

• People must be trained and educated to mount the technical programme; 'the number of skilled practitioners is very low'.

• The programme must be a British effort; foreign participation should be permitted only where security is guaranteed.

• A new director within the Department of Industry must drive the programmes firmly and have power to act quickly and flexibly.

• Government must continue to support product development with public-sector purchasing and promote IT, particularly in the service sector.

• Unless all this happens British prospects of competing successfully in the world IT markets will be sharply reduced. This would be extremely damaging to

    employment prospects;
    industrial efficiency;
    Britain's economic position.

• So Britain has three options:

    seek the leading edge of technology; or
    rely upon imported technology; or
    opt out.

● To opt out is invalid; imported technology is unreliable. Britain has major technical strengths in IT, but these are not always effectively focused and unless we build on them, they will wither.

● 'The only option is to have a domestic capability in the enabling technologies and this means a national effort based upon collaboration, because:

No single organization has the know-how to go it alone.

No one organization has enough resources.

Compared with competitors Britain is fragmented.

"Precompetitive" collaboration is consistent with fierce competition thereafter, as the Japanese have proved.'

● 'The greater the level of government support for the programme the more its results are public property, available for exploitation by British industry generally. Government support is the basis for collaboration and it provides more opportunity for effective commercial exploitation, particularly as far as the small-business sector is concerned.'

● The programme should 'go live' in April 1983.

Well, it just did!

Brian Oakley, Secretary of the Science and Engineering Research Council (SERC) was appointed director. He said:

> In some areas co-operation can come quite naturally. It is much more difficult when you have a bunch of firms competing in a particular area. You have to say to them, on the Japanese model, 'you can't do as much as you want to do on your own – get together with these other firms, share the research programme and then compete like hell in the market place'... Working individually British companies are just too small to compete. That's what it's all about.*

During the last week of April 1983 a professedly non-interventionist Tory government not only approved the Alvey Report but also gave the go-ahead for a £3.5 billion investment to 'cable' half the country. The Minister for IT said, 'We are the first country in Europe to go flat out on both cable and

* *The Times*, 17 May 1983

research collaboration between industry, the universities and government.'

Cable TV will add to entertainment and to the possibilities of home shopping, home banking, home security, to working at home and to being able to call up all the information in the world on to your home TV screens. Take together 'Alvey', 'cable', industrial robots, microprocessors, a mini-computer in every school, IT centres in every city and a huge increase of media coverage of IT and personal computers, and you have the new industrial revolution beginning to invade everywhere. Bio-technology and other new technologies are still in the hands of the researchers, but they could come up over the hill very quickly.

Nevertheless, Brian Benjamin, a computer man for twenty-five years and chairman of the government-promoted Information Technology year, IT 1982, had many reservations as 1982 closed. 'Half of all British industrial companies have no IT at all . . . There is a pitiful approach to training and retraining of managers in industry. Few companies are willing to try advanced technology and change their approach to take advantage of the opportunities for innovation.' 'Where,' he asked, 'are the risk-takers?' Benjamin sees Britain as a country 'drifting along without enough purpose, a declining economy, and a work ethic unsupported by opportunity'. He also sees in Britain 'a variety of cultures, interests, personal goals and political ideas. These create their own system of checks and balances and provide a civilized basis for living. The great advantage of technology is that it is a powerful ally to all of these interests and it will help us to maintain our heritage.'*

The development state in Britain can be said to have been conceived in 1983. We must hope that there will be no miscarriage and that it will grow to full estate in most British activities. The Japanese have had a policy of 'copy and improve'. The British policy should not be to copy, but to learn from the Japanese experience and to adapt our ways so as to be able to compete with it.

'Change is the only constant factor.'
(Lee Kwan Yu, Singapore, October 1983)

* *The Times*, 16 November 1982

12 The Development State – Heavy End

The stories and studies recounted in this book illustrate my belief that:

- British people are highly individualistic, tolerant of most things, except injustice, and remarkably easy-going. Indeed, they are slack – almost inefficient – but they become magnificent in a short-term crisis.
- As a society Britain has remained self-absorbed and largely unconscious of developments elsewhere, more given to analysis than action, somewhat inert and strangely anti-industrial.
- The institutions by which Britain is governed and managed continue to suffer from serious and chronic constipation, an absorption with the past and a recurrent urge to retreat into it.
- The exceptions to this include agriculture, the oil industry, distribution, pure research, television and international finance in the City. The outstanding successes are a handful of companies, the armed forces and the Royal Family.
- The laggards have started to change, and this could be accelerated.

I take the liberty of confronting this Britain with the development state, as a way of moving on from the welfare state. Britain has always kept its political economy moving – on from absolute monarchy and feudalism through Parliament to constitutional monarchy, then oligarchy, democracy, liberalism and *laissez-faire* to a 'methody' socialism and the welfare state. This last state is now showing unmistakable signs of wear and tear – a sacred cow, which looks sick. At the same time our industries lose market share and competitiveness and employ fewer people.

What do we do next? We can't just sit enjoying social security; that would be soul-destroying and anyway it has to be paid for, and who is going to do that? At the present time the taxpayer and the North Sea pay. Without the oil Britain would be in one hell of a mess, but the oil revenues, now at peak, will have greatly diminished in a few years' time. British people may be easy-going but they are not stupid, and they cannot want to potter along to the brink of disaster and then say, 'Why did we not deal with this danger years ago?'

The development state would be very different. It would protect Britain's three treasures – parliamentary democracy, freedom under the law, and social security for the needy. But it would be much more than that: it would foster creative, innovative, educated, trained, practical, technical people; learning, investing, collaborating, taking risks, making more and better goods and services and getting satisfaction from doing that well, better than the competition.

Those who lived in this state would be concerned with the improvement of all the things they did. It is not possible to make superb cars out of sub-standard steel or components. It is desperate trying to be efficient if the public services don't work properly. You cannot be competitive if the price of energy, water, transport, the rate of exchange, or the use of technology is out of line with the competition. It is impossible to make or service a good anything, if the management is inadequate or if the workforce couldn't care less. The development state would offer everyone a point, a purpose, which is to do one's job with more quality in it; that means more care, more *technik*, more thought, more economy of materials, energy and time. Instead of working ourselves out of a job, as now, we would work ourselves into jobs, because the results of our work would once again be the preferred choice at home and abroad. That is the long-term policy to be pursued every day.

If you reply that such an attitude is impossible, you have not been on the shop floor or in the offices of whizzing small businesses in Britain. You have not visited the plants of big companies, which for fear of death *did* start again in almost every way. You don't know what *is* happening in many of our progressive organizations and schools. The problem is how to get the performance of the best extended across the whole field. The need is for an idea which is largely self-explanatory. 'Development State' is clearly dynamic, hopeful and unifying.

The organized capitalist state lies between a planned economy and Adam Smith's free-market, *laissez-faire* economy of 200 years ago, which is now part of history. The development state would move with markets, but would not always accept distortion or damage by them. It would, as in Japan, use markets for development purposes. It would accept that Britain is not a completely self-adjusting economy and that corrections must be induced. It would deal head-on with the British disease.

The development state would point up the direction and encourage the methods needed to improve the 'tradeable' economy, and everything which bears upon it. An inefficient country inevitably makes poor-quality products, and people won't buy them. Sadly, we have allowed Britain to reach the borderline of inefficiency. The development state would promote movement towards success. Social security can catch the needy, but the competent, the enterprising, the successful have to lead and create and reap reward. The penalties of failure exist for them, as for those who get stuck at the bottom. Just as every organization has objectives, so the development state would work out and announce the general direction and progress which sectors of the economy could be expected to make. The decisions and the actions of government would be aimed at those targets, above all others.

Why is all this not happening now? Surely someone, some-where, is doing all these sensible things? If it pays people to invest and manufacture and provide services and develop old and new business, why are they not doing it? Why should they need help from the state? Would that make any difference?

The answer is that some organizations and businesses are doing all these things. But the majority are not. Most business-men are licking their wounds, trying to protect their markets, reducing their costs and their workforce, and hoping that they can go on surviving. In fact they are stuck in a situation in which strong confidence is still lacking; there is a need for leadership. British managers and businessmen do not believe that continuing prosperity is just around the corner. What they want to believe is that there is a government determined to assist, in a steady, imaginative way, the promotion of profitable business and efficient organization, to create the wealth and employment we all see that Britain needs.

Most managers appreciate that Britain faces horrendous difficulties; they do not see why they should not have the intelligent support of government. There are at least six major problems, and the solutions to them are neither simple nor comfortable. Overshadowing them all is North Sea oil, paying for imports, paying for the government spending deficit, and wasting away every year.

First, the public cost of carrying on as we do now, as a nation, goes on soaring. Despite determined attempts by the Thatcher Cabinet to cut government spending, the percentage of national income spent by government – 40 per cent when it came to power – was 44 per cent in 1983. Social security, including health and education, take over half the gross government spend. So! Either we cut the services, which nobody wants to do; or we increase taxes, which everybody wants to avoid; or we borrow more, which we cannot go on doing for ever; or we raise output and wealth – which would get top priority in the development state – in order to pay for the services we want.

Second, we have to deal with at least three million unemployed people – a number which will increase considerably, if we do nothing about it. What we do is crucial. The only way genuine jobs will be created is by doing more business, and that will come only by better management and more investment. The development state's purpose would be to stimulate new investment, to create new business and thus new jobs and, on the basis of competitive costs, improve management, quality and efficiency to regain lost market share at home and abroad.

Third, we are at the beginning of a technological revolution which is making most of our old ways of doing things hopelessly out of date, as did the use of steam, electricity and oil in their day. Britain has been slow in reacting to this – that is one of the reasons we are losing market share. Britain needs positive stimulus to move into the new technologies. It is not yet too late to catch up, but it soon will be. This would be part of the main purpose of the development state.

Fourth, most managements, unions and workforce representatives are still clinging to 'them and us', with all its frustrating loss-making non-satisfaction. The movement towards progressive companies has begun, but it needs steady continuous pressure to get results in good time. There are still elements which resist progress for all they are worth. It is not only a question of reducing over-manning, it is about improved performance everywhere. The welfare state neglected this. In the development state 'them and us' would be progressively eliminated.

Fifth, the competition from Japan and other newly industrialized countries in East Asia is increasing all the time. All the European countries are feeling this, but because Britain is at the bottom of the productivity league we are feeling it most. Unless we organize a strong industrial recovery we shall go on down further. The development state would exist to improve British competitiveness by every means available, and to regulate trade in the way proposed by Dave Roderick, Chairman of United States Steel:

> Free trade doesn't exist. Anyone who believes in free trade is just being theoretical. But conversely, protectionism is a disaster. So you have the tooth fairy on one end of the spectrum and a disaster scenario on the other. How do you avoid these extremes? You do it by taking those areas where you're having trade frictions, where you need time to solve a problem, and the nations involved work out a mutually agreeable solution.

This is the development state in action.

Sixth, the standards of much of British management, the traditions of many trade unions, the education and training of shop-floor and office workers are not yet linked to the huge task of turning Britain around. Each of these will be difficult to move. They all bear directly upon Britain's real economy and would be very much the concern of the development state. There will be managers, unions, workers, teachers, bureaucrats and others who are unable or unwilling to change. The development state would have to bypass them and find others to do their work. I have seen this at close range and I know how difficult, but how essential, these changeovers are.

You may say that this is not the sort of thing the British do, nor the way they go about their business. Look, then, at the National Governments of the thirties; at Churchill's wartime government; at Attlee's government, which brought in the welfare state. Look at the Tory Party in the late seventies in opposition, which positively promoted the defeat of inflation over full employment as a policy for their next government. In exactly the same way the promotion of the development state over the welfare state, after the defeat of inflation, would steadily, methodically, intelligently move Britain towards a solution of our long-standing, deep-seated problems. This will be possible only given three conditions:

- a gradual return of genuine wealth creation, worldwide;
- a willingness by British management on British shop and office floors to accept and encourage endless improvement, co-operation and *technik*, and to take longer-term views of markets and investment;
- a government in Britain which can lift its eyes from the traditional political issues and drive at 'more and better' as a first and continuing priority in all legitimate activities, by all legitimate means.

Of these three the first, as I write, has begun to happen and there are some signs of improvement on British shop floors. It is the third condition which will be the hardest to satisfy. When will the political parties realize that economic development, which they see to be necessary, is not compatible with the old easy way of life, which is enjoyable for some, but has caused Britain's decline, unemployment, poverty and poor prospects for the many? This has almost reached the point of no return. The post-war consensus about full employment, parley with the unions, demand management, fair shares, endless welfare, lame ducks and don't let's be beastly to anyone came to an end in 1979. Thatcher One accepted none of these things, although most of them did to some degree continue. The bulldozers went in, inflation was driven down, perhaps as much as a quarter of

British industry was driven to the wall, public expenditure was brought under greater control, the unions were pushed aside and dazed management was expected to pick up the pieces. Survival became the name of the game – batten down and hope to carry on as before, when the bulldozers have left.

Can Thatcher Two get round to the job of construction on the cleared site or will it be occupied by weeds such as loosestrife and London pride, as after the Blitz? The greatest opportunity for reconstruction since 1945 is now open to Britain. A move on out of the welfare state, taking our three historical treasures with us, would meet with a strong response from the five million managers and self-employed people – the 'driving ten'. There can be no leadership from passengers. Why does not a radical government get its mind round this most exciting, logical – indeed natural – programme? Call it the development state, or a 'go-getter' society! Britain is on the verge of it already. Sir Peter Carey, as he retired from being Permanent Secretary for Industry in 1983, said:

> The aim is to spur industry to perform better, to erect a framework which encourages and supports good managements and points directions. What we can do is to collect a lot of information about particular firms . . . and then make a judgement about what has to be done. We can look at the market place of the future and identify technologies which are going to be of great importance . . . and then give support. Market forces have primacy which government can nudge, but not indefinitely arrest. There is too little understanding in Britain of the importance of industry.*

This was the threshold of the development state.

The thrust for the onward move is unlikely to come from within government. It could come from back-benchers in Parliament, from the political parties, from the lobby groups or from the media, but most likely from the 'middle middle' sector of our society. These people have initiated most of the changes, reforms, improvements and advances throughout British history; they are the doers, critics, nonconformists, entrepreneurs and

---

* *Financial Times*, 5 May 1983

"Good morning, I'm from the
Treasury—I've come to read
the gas-meter"

Financial Times, 6 March 1984

radicals, and no resounding reform can be successful without
their active participation. It might just be that the development
state will creep up on us unawares under the Tory 'doing good by
stealth' policy but, as I write, I detect a contrary inclination in
government.

A major hang-up surrounds 'intervention' by government in
business. Tories say they do not intervene because they believe
in Adam Smith's free-market philosophy. But Tories do, in fact,
intervene all over the place. They do it, however, half-heartedly,
stealthily, as though they were ashamed. So they seldom make a
success of it and finish by giving themselves another reason for
saying that they should stick to a 'hands-off' policy, after all.
Labour governments have intervened greatly and openly.
Socialists profess to disbelieve in markets and private enterprise,
but in fact they have to go along with market-dominated free
enterprise, again in a rather half-hearted, unsuccessful,
unorganized way. The Alliance Party's industrial strategy sets

out a policy which moves towards the development state –
'meeting the needs of industry should be recognized as the top
priority in the formulation and implementation of all government policies'. But when will they have enough political
strength to give effect to it?

What Britain has not yet experienced in peacetime is a
government confidently collaborating with private enterprise
to get the sort of economy it believes in. America witnessed
some of this in the New Deal of the thirties; Germany under
Adenauer, France under de Gaulle and Japan since the Second
World War were steered in this way.

The key to successful collaboration lies in government
encouraging, steering, facilitating and accelerating 'more and
better', and the private sector responding, but remaining free
and competing fiercely between themselves and with the
competition from abroad. The development state would
recognize that government has a central responsibility for the
health and success of the economy, and that it has to provide the
social services. In Britain we acknowledge the second part, but
Tories, at any rate, have baulked at the first part. That is one of
the reasons why our society is out of balance – government
insists upon spending citizens' money, but takes precious little
trouble and care to see that the money so spent has been made. If
it is not made, government borrows, and that unbalances the
economy further.

The whole purpose of the development state would be to
ensure that the supply side covers the spend. If war is too
dangerous to leave to the generals, business is too important to
leave to the chairmen. Many of the stories in this book validate
this. The experience of Japan in particular proves that a
powerful central government influence on the supply side,
accompanied by intense competition between companies, does
in fact produce a strong, viable economy. The development
state would seek to deepen the relationship of government with
managers in order to create more business and thus more jobs,
more wealth and more satisfaction.

Government 'intervention' in the past has often been inept.
The projects government has sponsored have been too big, too
ambitious, too optimistic, too political, with too little
attention to management. Civil servants are not businessmen,

entrepreneurs or risk-takers: they turned their back on that life when they joined the civil service. But they are careful, cautious, objective collectors of facts and views over a wide field. They will, of course, nearly always swing with the minister, if he is in dispute with business; that is predictable. Civil service advice on a business problem is usually worth listening to. You don't have to take it. I do have to say that with nearly twenty years' experience of working with senior civil servants, I have found them always trying to help, often intelligently opening up the view, usually departmentalized, seldom innovative, but honourable, uncorrupt, and patriotic – a most valuable part of British life.

I agree with Sir Douglas Wass that reforming or tinkering with the civil service would be pointless and damaging to Britain's prospects.* The machinery of government which they operate is another matter.

The civil service can build and operate a development state to suit Britain's needs, in collaboration with private enterprise, if that was government policy. The civil service could not initiate such a move; it reacts rather than proposes. It is, however, certainly now in a position to carry out the four essential functions – encourage, steer, facilitate and accelerate – necessary to assist the turnaround of Britain after the demolitions of Thatcher One.

In the development state the government/business relationship would be crucial. It would be based upon consultation, initiated by either side. The consultation might well involve other companies and other government departments. When it is complete the company's decision must be its own, and it must carry the responsibility for the results. The company must always feel free to disagree with, or even disobey, government. I have done this and I know it to be essential in any relationship which business may have with government.

If the development plans of businessmen – investment, expansion, merger or closure – were prematurely exposed to debate in Parliament, managers would rapidly retreat into secrecy. It is unfortunately the case that many Members precipitate themselves upon rumours of any industrial change

* BBC Radio 4 interview, 25 January 1984

in their constituencies. They are generally believed to be drawing attention to their zeal for their constituents and their value as a Member. Many good pieces of business have been lost in this way.

It would be desirable to change the machinery of government as little as possible. The Departments of Trade and Industry have already been amalgamated by Thatcher Two. That would be helpful to the development state, but I do not believe that the new department should seek to become a British MITI. It would not be sufficiently broadly based. It now sees its role as 'to encourage, assist and ensure the proper *regulation* of British trade, industry and commerce'.* Regulation is the wrong word; it should be *development.*

The key to the development state in Britain would be the involvement of the Prime Minister, without whose constant public pressure the shift of emphasis from welfare to development would never be made. Fortunately, the Prime Minister of Britain today also takes the chair of the economic committee – the 'E' committee, with all its sub-committees – of the Cabinet. It is this committee which would have to lead, drive and steer the move from welfare to development. On it sit representatives of the economic departments of Treasury, Trade and Industry, Environment, Employment, Energy and Transport. It would be the requirements of this group of ministers which should prevail in Cabinet, in the administration and ultimately throughout the economy, overriding all else.

If economic objectives are constantly bypassed or thwarted by other heavy interests, they are weakened and will not be achieved. The difference between 'as is' and the development state is that wealth creation in the development state would take top and continuous priority over all other objectives except defence, liberty and the necessary needs of the people.

As things stand, each department within government prepares its own brief for its Minister and in the end compromises are struck between departments to reach consensus. Civil servants have developed a very sophisticated expertise in doing this, but the consensus they reach is to suit the departments, which is not necessarily the same as suiting the best interests of Britain.

* Norman Tebbit in DTI *Aims,* 1984

CABINET COMMITTEES
ECONOMIC AND INDUSTRIAL

Committee Initials	Chairman	Functions
EA	Margaret Thatcher (Prime Minister)	Economic strategy, energy policy, changes in labour law, the most important EEC matters
E(EX)	Margaret Thatcher	Exports policy
E(NI)	Margaret Thatcher	Policy sector strategy and oversight of the nationalized industries
E(NF)	Nigel Lawson (Chancellor of the Exchequer)	Nationalized industry finance
NIP	Nick Monck (Treasury official)	Official committee on nationalized industry policy
E(PSP)	Nigel Lawson	Public sector and public service pay policy
E(DL)	Nigel Lawson	Disposal and privatization of state assets
E(PU)	Norman Tebbit (Trade & Industry Secretary)	'Buy British' policy for public purchasing
E(CS)	Peter Rees (Chief Secretary)	Civil service pay and contingency plans for civil services strikes
E(OCS)	Peter le Cheminant (Cabinet Office official)	Official committee for preparing contingency plans
PESC	John Anson (Treasury official)	Committee of finance officers handling the annual public expenditure survey

The Cabinet committee list is an extended version of a chart contained in Sources Close to the Prime Minister *by Michael Cockerell, Peter Hennessy and David Walker, published by Macmillan*

Departments are like companies and trade unions; they have
their own separate lives and hopes and fears, over which they
fight and compete vigorously. The development state would
need at the centre a unified group whose constant and sole
attention was on the advance of the real economy, irrespective
of the separate and traditional position of departments or
ministers. Britain is being torn apart by interest groups; what we
need is a strong group which puts Britain's interests first.

The 'E' committee of the British Cabinet, in the development
state, should have working for it an economic staff. This should
not be cobbled together from the ranks of the deputy secretaries
in the civil service, who would always be looking over their
shoulders at their bosses, the permanent secretaries. One half of
the economic staff should be recruited from the best people in
the whole civil service, and they should normally spend much
of their life on that staff. The other half should be recruited from
the private sector – businessmen, scientists, academics, administrators, trade unionists who believed in the objectives of the
development state, and party political specialists to reflect the
political ambitions of the party (or parties) which formed the
government of the day.

A strong and influential economic staff, servicing 'E' committee
of the Cabinet, emerges as the first new piece of machinery
needed for the advance out of the welfare state into the
development state. It would have to resist the claims of short-
term crises, being 'blown off-course' and hostile actions of other
countries. It would have to hang on to the development state
through changes of government, when enthusiasm for it would
wax and wane. It would have to be ready to move, in the same
way as business does, with the changing economic cycles and
technologies and fashions. It would have to believe passionately
in itself and its long-term mission; to break through the colossal
and so far unresolved problems which have been allowed to
accumulate in Britain.

To quote Sir Douglas Wass again:

What the Think Tank [the now defunct CPRS] should have
concentrated on was the 'balance of policy', the way the
government's programmes fitted into its strategic objectives
. . . whether, for instance, more resources should be put into

industrial policy and fewer into social policy ... it should be continuously involved, as the Treasury has to be, in all the important parts of the government's programme.*

The economic staff would have to work out how to harmonize *for development purposes* the powerful rates of foreign exchange, interest, inflation, taxation and growth which to a great extent dominate economic life. There is another category, less obvious but equally powerful: the rates of money supply, savings, investment, profits and productivity. The levels of prices, output, unemployment and the balance of payments are of equal importance. Unless these rates and levels promote industrial development and the advance of the real economy at a steady pace, Britain will not be able to compete and catch up with the competition.

Here is the heavy end of economic management – macro-economics – where the financial totals are added up, to make a model of the whole economy. It is very much Treasury country, but the Treasury does not have much of a 'feel' for business or for industrial problems and trends and needs, and it is here that the economic staff should concentrate and specialize. Sir Peter Carey said, on retirement, 'The Treasury takes too short a view of industry. It is remote from the market place and loses sight of the impact of its macro policies.' Sir Frank Cooper, Permanent Secretary for Defence, said, 'Treasury officials live in a different world from the rest of humanity.' The present Permanent Secretary to the Treasury, Sir Peter Middleton, talking to the authors of 'Yes Chancellor' (BBC 1984) said: 'I don't think there is any way in which the Treasury as such can produce a successful economy. You can produce conditions in which a successful economy can take place, but a successful economy takes a good deal more than that and it takes a good deal of time.' Quite so; that is exactly the argument for the economic staff, the development state and the purpose of this book.

In the development state taxation, together with the other principal rates, should be the concern not only of the Chancellor but of 'E' committee and the economic staff. (It is, for example, inconceivable that in the development state the

* Second Reith Lecture BBC, 1983

rate of exchange would have risen to $2.46 = £1 in 1980. It fell to $1.30 = £1 in 1984. Nor would inflation have risen by 10 per cent in 1979 as a consequence of changing the rate of VAT.)

In the spring of each year the whole of the British economy comes under public scrutiny at the time of the Budget presented to Parliament by the Chancellor. Sometimes this is a damp squib, sometimes it arouses intense passion – as did Sir Geoffrey Howe's deflationary budget during the 1981 recession – and sometimes it stirs up some excitement, as did Nigel Lawson's budget in 1984.

The first positive move towards a development state Budget was made by Howe in 1980 when he introduced the Medium-Term Financial Strategy. Lawson, as junior Treasury Minister, was the architect. The first MTFS had a bumpy ride: its forecast for government borrowing in 1983/84 was £2.5 billion, equal to $1\frac{1}{2}$ per cent of national income, the out-turn was £10 billion, equal to 3.3 per cent of national income. Nevertheless, after a number of revisions and experience gained, MTFS won some credibility and became a useful tool. Government spending and borrowing came under control, inflation was reduced, and all without radically altering the shape of the welfare state.

Not much development was done in those years of deep economic recession, but a rational base was put together for construction when the climate changed. Expectations of wage increases came into line with reality. The industrial adjustment from 'smokestacks' to 'micros' began. The long slide in British competitiveness was at least checked, and the climb up that endless ladder became possible. The price paid was three million or more people unemployed, but few will deny that a price *had* to be paid or argue that it could have been much less, in view of the previous gross over-manning.

Thatcher Two faced a different situation. The site clearance had been done. Indeed, early in 1984 Thatcher admitted that government spending could not be much further reduced. That was a key signal, among many others in 1983 and 1984, that a new start was coming. If you cannot spend less and will not borrow more you are irresistibly forced to earn more money by developing your assets. That was where Lawson found himself when facing his first Budget. He had a fine inheritance, he was at an easy point in the economic cycle and he knew his job better than any of his predecessors. His Budget made a small move towards development, taking welfare along too. It was a start, but no more than that: it will be harder henceforth.

Lawson's 1984 Budget was clearly aimed at new and service industries, investment and small business, and trying to accelerate the production and service of more and better. The old inflation route was shunned and the development route was signposted for five years ahead, as this table shows:

	THE TREASURY PLAN		
	Inflation* annual % rise	Tax cut £bn	Money GDP annual % rise
1983–84	5.5	—	8.2
1984–85	4.8	—	7.8
1985–86	4.3	2.0	6.7
1986–87	4.0	4.5	6.0
1987–88	3.5	3.5	5.7
1988–89	3.0	3.5	5.1

Financial Times, 15 March 1984
* Annual % rise of GDP deflator
Source: Financial Statement and Budget Report
and *FT* calculations

That is what should be done in principle, but will it fare any better than the first MTFS? Many winds, from home and abroad, could blow it off-course, but what it needs more than anything else is a strong, steady business recovery in Britain. Under Lawson's first Budget unemployment and Britain's ageing roads, railways and sewers were not directly improved and the 'poverty trap' was not closed, but these very desirable objectives can come only from new wealth created by development of business. Lawson rightly, as in a development state, put the horse before the cart. What he did not acknowledge was the colossal size of the problem and the effort needed to turn Britain around, nor the much more extensive measures which will be needed to bring this about.

The heavy end of the British economy still has to create the conditions in which we can reverse the manufacturing disaster and replace the income from North Sea oil, as it declines from now on. This is what the turnaround is about. Now look at where Lawson has placed Britain in relation to our main competitors:

● Britain is shooting at a 3 per cent growth rate, which would be level with Germany, but America and Japan are going for 5 per cent.
● Britain is struggling to keep inflation below 5 per cent, but Germany and Japan are at half that rate.
● Britain has a rate of interest of 10 per cent, America's is higher, but in Germany and Japan it is 6 per cent.
● In Britain government spends over 40 per cent of national income. In America and Germany it spends 20 per cent and in Japan an incredible 9 per cent.
● Worst of all, the British government expects that in 1984 exports will grow 5 per cent but that imports will grow by 7 per cent.

On these numbers Britain is simply not going to be able to catch up, and without even starting to catch up how do we turn around? Without a turnaround how do we catch up? What can break the vicious circle?

The limitation on Britain is not only macro policy at the heavy end of the economy, it is also management at the sharp end. The turnaround cannot all be done by Chancellors' Budgets. Management has to take the action needed to give quick and long-term effect to macro policies on the shop and office floors, in board-rooms, in laboratories, in committees, in banks, in the administration of government, in schools and colleges and in our homes. Only management can get high-speed growth without inflation. So, we must see that British management is professional enough, innovative enough and bright enough. The fear remains that the British disease has lingered on and will abort the new start. It is at the sharp end that we have fallen down in the past; that is where neglect could be fatal.

'For now sits Expectation in the air.'

(*Henry V*, Act II)

13 The Development State –
Sharp End

Unemployment will be for many years a great smog looming over Britain . . . a curse, to which almost any alternative will seem preferable. The economic staff would have to keep its head and recognize that it is not just jobs we are short of, it is *business*. Jobs are a by-product of many other things. If you go for them direct, you usually fail to find them and you may well make things worse. Jobs come from profitable business and business comes from people willing to invest and take risks, in the hope of satisfaction, fame or fortune. It is by encouraging entrepreneurs to start or expand their businesses that jobs will be found. New real jobs will come only from new investment programmes, in high tech or low tech, designed to produce more and better . . . whether for war or peace.

Recovery from the recent worldwide slump is coming as businesses adapt and adjust to new technologies and different expectations. Britain must be part of that, but in addition there is a huge field here at home ready for planting with new enterprises. The scope for making things, providing services, sub-contracting, government contracts and exporting is very great – 'more and better'. For all these activities investment, innovation, good management and training schemes are essential. Palliatives such as job-sharing will help a few people, but won't get far. Phased retirement, compensation for short-time working, community programme schemes, voluntary early retirement and job release schemes will all make some contribution to the reduction of unemployment. But nothing will take the place of, or be as good as, new or expanding businesses led by determined entrepreneurs. This is where the new start in Britain is taking us, and this should be at the top of the economic staff agenda.

The need for drastic action is a direct consequence of the 'British disease'. Many on the management side in Britain and in competitor countries see this plague simply as over-mighty trade unions, usurping managers' functions, denying productivity and pricing Britain out of markets and men out of jobs. It is much more complicated, deep-seated and hard to cure than that. The root causes of the disease, as opposed to its symptoms, are:

- A system of public secondary education which is largely irrelevant and boring for most pupils.
- Lack of business skills and commitment in management and workforce – the reluctant industrialists.
- Too many old-style non-progressive managements.
- Too few entrepreneurs and insufficient cheap capital.
- Adversary attitudes on all sides.
- Lack of investment in innovation and technology.
- Inadequate planning, care and financial control.
- Wage payments unrelated to productivity.
- Emphasis on consumption rather than investment.
- Short-term rather than long-term views.
- Lack of any purpose in British life – 'I'm all right, Jack'.
- Lack of confidence that Britain can compete industrially.

It is these flaws which prevent Britain bouncing back after recession and developing our full potential; they have allowed other countries to take our market share and to put us in great danger.

There is no doubt that political, social, financial and trade-union attitudes in Britain have made the job of management harder. The best news in Britain in 1984 is that the ambitions and performance of management have strengthened, and are likely to get better still. A new start has in fact already begun, but it is still tentative and should be nurtured and accelerated, before it is killed off by the British disease. The roadblocks on the development route should be removed and government should stimulate a 'could be' mentality, away from acceptance of 'as is', to which British people are remarkably prone.

To cope with these problems a battery of tools should be grouped round the economic staff, which would be responsible to Parliament through the Prime Minister, as chairman of 'E' committee. One of the existing tools, which should be more used, is the Industrial Development Advisory Board (IDAB), set up to advise the Secretary of State for Industry on the use of government funds in British industry under the Industry Act of 1972. Some of the best people in British business have served on this Board and the advice they give is from deep experience, and entirely objective. The Board's function is limited to advising government on the merits of propositions and projects put to it by the Industrial Development Unit of the DTI. Unfortunately its writ does not run in Northern Ireland, or the de Lorean fiasco would have been avoided. In 1982 IDAB held fourteen meetings to consider thirty-nine applications for government money. All except one of these applications 'met the relevant criteria and were approved'.

IDAB should certainly continue its advisory work as at present, but it should be detached from the DTI and become a tool of the economic staff. The economic staff should use it for advice on investment, on research, on collaboration, on mergers before reference to the Monopolies Commission, and for advice on the adequacy of top management in any company which was seen to be failing. IDAB should also be the instrument used to bring about necessary changes in management in consultation with the big shareholders, non-executive directors and bankers. This can be done. The old Industrial Reorganization Corporation did it, as I know, and in most cases it was successful. Why should Britain suffer from and put up with continuing bad management?

Here are some extracts from the IRC report of June 1970:

Low productivity, late deliveries, slow switch of markets, mediocre products and a lack of management control characterize many companies ... IRC is using its influence to stimulate British industrial companies to effective and profitable reform, without recourse to merger or takeover by others. In all its dealings with managements IRC proceeds by advice and persuasion, which it has found effective in a rational society. In the year under review, IRC has reached agreement in every case ... IRC has been surprised to see how disinterested even professional shareholders are in the performance of managements to whom they entrust their money ... the statement by the Chairman of the Prudential Assurance promising their weight in 'revitalizing flagging industrial managements' is very welcome . . . Existing managements have no prescriptive rights and if they fail to deliver the goods they should make way for those who can ... IRC has seen many of the installations of our competitors overseas and is of the view that to keep our place we shall have to renew and extend our industrial apparatus selectively, but on a scale larger than is now taking place ... There is a need in Britain for a concerted effort by industry, finance and government to catch up by massive but selective investment. Many countries have done this successfully; we have a chance to do this now and we should take it.

Well, we did not take that chance! Heath was in a non-interventionist Tory mood and he abolished the IRC five months later. I sit writing at the same desk as when I wrote that IRC report *fourteen* years ago! A last quote from that report: 'The major influences upon objectives are market forces and government's overall economic and industrial policies. IRC works at the micro level with individual companies.' That job has still to be done and IDAB, working to the economic staff, could do it.

Pundits can say what they like about investment in Britain in the past, but it is now certain that if Britain is to catch up, massive new investment will be needed in new technology and innovation in industry and in the roads, sewers, communications, docks and railways, without which Britain cannot function effectively. As the Director General of the CBI said, 'Britain is falling to pieces'.* I believe that an economic staff would recommend any government in Britain to get on with that work urgently. Part will be for government account, but if government will not invest, why should private enterprise? It won't.

* Sir Terry Beckett, February 1984

In the private sector there is a lack of investment projects. Confidence is not yet strong, costs are still too high, money is still too expensive and there is anxiety that the unions may demand a share in the results of investment before those results have been produced. For big business there is plenty of money available, awaiting investment in projects which have good prospects. But that money is expensive, if it comes in the form of loans. What hauled Britain out of the slump in the thirties was plenty of *cheap* money. Cheap loans are needed today, together with real capital, equity, ordinary shares, which are entitled to what is left over after all other costs have been paid and provision made for renewals and expansion. If capitalism is to be effective and survive, it needs capital. That means that investors must be prepared to take longer views with some of their money, and 'wait for it'.

The heavy end of the development state would need to be greatly concerned with the rate of interest. It is far too high to permit the investment surge necessary to get lasting recovery, to say nothing of development. In Japan and Germany, countries with far stronger economies than Britain, the cost of money for investment is much lower. Savings in Britain fell in 1983 to half the volume of 1982. Britain is busy spending, not investing, and that is the wrong way round – fun for a government which can claim it has presided over recovery, but bad for the country, which needs above all investment not consumer spending . . . which goes largely on imports!

Investment in the new technology is vital for all parts of the economy. As we have seen, Britain lags far behind, in both the production and the use of microelectronics and IT. This lag is seriously damaging to Britain's recovery. The government has recognized this in appointing an excellent Minister of State and he has a small budget which he makes go a long way. The economic staff would get on to investment and innovation in technology at once, because of its effect upon almost everything Britain should be doing.

It is at this point that the second existing government tool should be brought into effective action – the British Technology Group. This has unfortunately been a political football, kicked around between Tories and Labour for many years. It is now an amalgamation of the National Research and Development

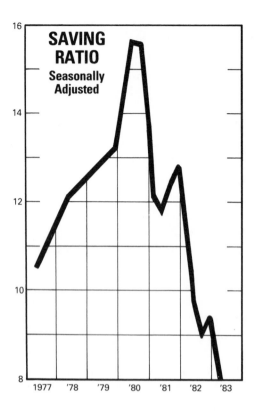

Council (NRDC) and the National Enterprise Board (NEB). BTG should make a positive contribution to the development state. Let the Research and Development role continue, but put the weight of BTG on to stimulating the production and above all the use of microprocessors throughout the British economy, in communications, machine tools, robots, drawing boards, schools, offices, homes – everywhere.

There is a huge task to be done in stimulating the transfer of the new technologies from universities, polytechnics and big business into new businesses, which will develop them commercially. The British passion for squirrelling ideas has to be overcome. The BTG, working with the Welsh and Scottish Development Agencies, decentralized to, say, fifteen local offices, could create a market-minded organization which, manned by businessmen, would talk to businessmen in their own language. It would cut red tape and above all escape from the deadly civil service dogma that if anyone is to have a benefit from government all must have it, and if all cannot have it, no one should.

The BTG Chairman, then Sir Frederick Wood, stated in April 1982 two 'overwhelming top priorities':

- to identify technology which has commercial value and will strengthen our industries;
- to be the pathfinder for private-sector investment by identifying investment opportunities.

BTG, rooted in advanced technology, should operate in the competitive sectors of the economy and form a bridge between state support and private enterprise. It should act as a small trigger for releasing a large charge of private-sector funds into targets which will advance the real economy. Britain's main competitors do this – without it Britain is disadvantaged.

The German government plans to spend £800 million to boost, by 1988, both development and application of micro-electronics, computing and communication technologies. The programme is the most ambitious of any so far put forward by a European government in response to American and Japanese competition. The German electronics industry intends to collaborate in the research programme. Schemes for increasing training in electronics, robots and computer-aided engineering are included. Venture capital in electronics will be encouraged. Public procurement of electronic goods and services will have a coherent strategy.* The German scheme is 'Alvey plus', put forward by a conservative government, dedicated to private enterprise, which has seen the need to link companies and university research with government as a top national priority.

The British response was announced by Trade and Industry Secretary Norman Tebbit in March 1984: another £180 million is to be made available to high-technology industries, including £120 million for the Microelectronics Industry Support Scheme, to be spent by 1989. Let us be generous and add in Alvey (£200m) and the £55 million already made available by the British government, and we only just reach one half of the new German

* *Financial Times*, 9 March 1984

scheme. This is it in a nutshell – Britain will be tail-end Charlie once again.

Is BTG another sacred cow? Kill it off if you must, but it would be better to give it a positive, precise job of getting that money spent on the microprocessor and other new technologies made and used in Britain. BTG reports to the Minister for IT, who should be a member of 'E' committee of the Cabinet in his own right. He should be one of the most important people in Britain.

The development state would have to tackle head on the British 'them and us' problem. This drags down our productivity, causes most people to be more miserable and poorer than they need be and makes us a laughing-stock to the outside world. Quality, delivery and service have become inferior and the world has turned away from our products, so that Britain's share of world trade has halved in the last twenty years. How can any government stand aside from this situation? Well, some have because they were afraid of offending managers, and others for fear of the trade unions. I offered the unions in steel a 'steel contract' which would have enabled management, unions and workforce to plan the evidently necessary restructuring of the steel industry in an agreed way, without 'aggro' and without strikes. The unions would have had new rights and new duties. They turned aside from it, because it would have infringed the imaginary absolute autonomy of each union to do whatever it likes, whenever it likes. I am convinced that only very rarely, as in the case of British Airways' Trade Union Committee, and in the electricians' union, will the solution of 'them and us' be made easier by a British trade union. I have to add that many, perhaps even most, managers in British industry hold traditional views which keep 'them and us' alive in their business. It is all very well for Norman Tebbit as Employment Minister to tell managers, 'take the workforce along with you', but will they do it?

Owen Glendower, in *Henry IV*, says,

> 'I can call spirits from the vasty deep;

To which Hotspur replies,

> Why, so can I, so can any man;
> But will they come when you do call for them?

This situation is much too serious to leave to exhortations. It calls for an agency to follow up the comments on consultation, involvement and participation which, by law, company annual reports must now provide. This could be called the Industrial Co-operation Agency (ICA). Its creation would draw screams of horror and rage from unions and employers alike, because their sacred territories would be invaded. They would give every assurance, solemn and binding and all, that they would attend to the matter themselves, but they would not do any such thing. It is here that the cancer of the British disease is to be found. If it could be easily treated it would have been cured years ago. It has not been treated because of fear. Inadequate old-style managers fear exposure and an extension of union power. Defensive union officials fear a loss of their bargaining power and questions about the purpose of all the functions they have assumed. In between, the workforce would like to be told, and to say, more about their jobs, to be more involved and to have some participation in the results of their work.

It would need a determined government to tackle this situation. The first step has been taken by requiring directors to report progress, but they report to shareholders, and what can *they* do? They have to trust their management, unless things are going very wrong; but the remedy for 'them and us' lies *with* management. In May 1984 Tom King, the Employment Minister, said that all company reports on industrial relations are to be carefully monitored. But what then? A positive remedy would be to create an agency with the following terms of reference:

The Agency may, for the purpose of promoting industrial efficiency and profitability and assisting the economy of the United Kingdom:

1   promote or assist industrial co-operation through communication with, involvement of, and participation by the workforce in any company or corporation in the private sector of the British economy;
2   if required to do so by the Secretary of State, promote the same purpose in local authorities, health, education or water authorities or in nationalized industries or any other public organization whose activities bear upon industrial efficiency in the United Kingdom.

The Agency should never employ more than one hundred people and its budget should be tailored accordingly. The directors should be mature businessmen aware of the damage done by 'them and us' and determined to improve shop-floor relations. There might be one or two trade-union leaders who would work for the same purposes, just as the late Les Cannon,* on the IRC board, worked to improve company and trade-union efficiency. It would be important to ensure that the unions were prevented from making themselves the channel for communication, involvement and participation. The initiative and drive must come from management and make direct impact upon the workforce. The relationship between managers and those they manage has to be direct, immediate and trustful, if 'them and us' is to fade away. A rerun of the Bullock Report, which proposed trade unions as the sole channel for management/shop-floor communication, is to be avoided at all costs. Britain is not yet ready for worker directors: the elimination of 'them and us' is much more important.

It is to the positive side of life that people respond positively. It is above all a positive attitude which Britain's shop floors should adopt. We need a way out of the endless bitching, which has become a habit. Taken by itself, an Industrial Co-operation Agency would not stand much of a chance. It belongs, however, to the group of measures which the development state would promote, in order to turn Britain around.

So much for existing business; given the right managers, new investment, innovation and determination to eliminate 'them and us', great strides could be made by British industry into the world of new technology, as it emerges from the years of recession. But that would not be enough to replace the business and jobs lost in recent years.

What Britain needs is a new swarm of small ventures and many more middle-sized companies. Many of them will certainly fall by the wayside, but many will succeed. Some will grow into the middle ranks and a few will become the giants of the future. Every big company was once a tiddler, as can be seen from the stories in this book. Britain needs a source of finance, run by businessmen to act as did the famous but mythical Aunt Agatha

* President of the Electrical Trade Union: died 1970

in the last century: 'Here's some money, my boy, to put in your business. Let me have it back sometime . . . No hurry. And if you have a problem, have a word with Uncle Bill – he's very sensible!'

The first Thatcher government had some experimental schemes, like the Guaranteed Loan Scheme, the Business Expansion Scheme, the Small Business Engineering Scheme and the Enterprise Allowance Scheme. But these are puny and timid in relation to the size of the problem and the need. Government is not a bank, with the civil service as clerks turning over short-term funds. Government should aim to make an overall advance through time, losing here, winning there, but working to declared progressive objectives – 'more and better'. Government needs a positive, confident, central economic staff who would never say, 'it can't be done'. They might say, 'the impossible takes a little longer'. That is the attitude required to get a turnaround. That is what Britain, in a small way, has already started to do.

In a previous chapter, I described an organization in democratic, capitalist Germany, whose title could be translated as 'the credit organization for reconstruction'. In 1982 Shell allotted me £10,000 to study this and other similar organizations, and I sought the help of the Economist Intelligence Unit (EIU). We sent our report to the Chancellor in December 1982. We greatly favoured the German organization* and proposed that the British government should set up a Small and Medium-Sized Business Organization, which I now prefer to call the Business Development Board (BDB).

The purpose of BDB would be to increase the size of the small and medium business sector in Britain up to the same level as in other industrialized countries. That would mean another half million businesses. That could be done by the end of the century but it would need a strong, concentrated effort, which BDB should drive along, reporting to the economic staff. BDB should have two functions:

1   To make money available to small and medium-sized businesses which looked like succeeding at a cost not higher than would be paid by big business – equalize the cost of finance.

*Kreditanstalt für Wiederaufbau

2   To advise good small or medium business how to avoid
    going *out* of business. This could include changing the
    ownership, or management. The cost of such advice would
    be divided between the interested parties.

BDB's main skill would be in choosing which managements to
support, which to refuse and which to renew in case of failure.
This is a business skill, not a civil servant's or politician's skill.

To finance its operations BDB would need a capital of its own,
up to £500 million, drawn down as needed, to be supplied by
government as a grant which would not require repayment or
the payment of dividends. This capital should be increased by
BDB's retained profits. BDB should be exempt from tax and
credit restrictions. BDB would, of course, need far more money
than £500 million, and it should raise loans in world markets on
the best terms available at the time. Government ownership of
BDB's capital would be an implicit government guarantee. BDB
would lend (it would not subscribe ordinary capital) to small
and medium-sized business, for up to ten years. It would finance
this partly from its own capital and reserves, on which it would
pay no interest or dividend, and partly from the money it had
borrowed. BDB's lending rate to Britain's small and medium
business would have to cover:

• the cost of the money borrowed on the money market;
• the cost of running BDB (say 150 staff);
• a contribution to reserves required to cover bad debts and the
build-up of BDB:
• a commission to the commercial banks for carrying the risk
that the loan might not be repaid – BDB would not be on risk.

As a result, BDB would lend at approximately the minimum
lending rate, many percentage points below what British small
business now has to pay.
    The commercial banks would build BDB loans into the
financial packages which they put together for their customers.
No one can start or expand a business without a bank account,
and the first place the businessman goes for cash is to a bank.

Any bank would be ready to build a BDB loan into a customer's financial scheme because:

- BDB's money would come from outside the bank – another source of funds;
- BDB's money would be cheaper and longer-term, thus reducing the strain on the borrower;
- BDB would pay the bank an agreed annual commission for carrying the risk that the customer might fail;
- BDB's money could be applied for only through a bank, so instead of competing with the banks BDB would be a new source of medium-term cheap capital, which banks could choose to build into the financing of their small and medium-sized customers.

The Germans have made a great success of their credit organization for reconstruction. It is lending over £1 billion each year to some 20,000 borrowers. Britain's Finance for Industry (now called 3i), which is owned by the banks and has to pay dividends and tax, has lent £2 billion, but only over a period of forty years. In the steel closure areas of Britain we have used some of the proposed BDB techniques. So far we have supported 2,000 new or expanding businesses (we have lost 400) with the prospect of well over 36,000 new jobs. So I do know about this.

BDB's second function would be to save as many small or medium businesses as possible from failing. The evidence from receivers in bankruptcy is that, overwhelmingly, businesses fail because of management mistakes, many of which could have been corrected if taken in hand in time. Secondly, businesses fail for lack of capital; thirdly, from lack of markets for their products or services. It would be no good BDB financing new starts or expansion if it was not prepared to advise on the subsequent management of businesses in difficulty. Small businessmen often do not know why they fail, or what to do to get help, or how to pay for any help or advice they might want. Uncle Bill is needed just as much as Aunt Agatha.

The commercial banks are very much aware of this and they have set up 'intensive care' units to nurse sick companies back to health, but it tends to be the larger customers with problems who get this treatment. There are statistics to show that up to one third of new small businesses fail within three years. This is a high casualty rate and BDB should play a part in its reduction.

In the support of new and expanding companies in the steel closure areas our loss rate is less than one third over the last six years. These years have been the most difficult for small business since the thirties. We have done better than average by careful choice and continuing care and maintenance.

What BDB should do is to recruit a corps of local, reliable experienced business consultants, who would go in at short notice to a company in trouble and diagnose and prescribe what should be done. This should not usually be a laborious or expensive task. Most problems are obvious to an experienced businessman – Uncle Bill.

But now BDB has a problem! How to overcome the small businessman's determination not to disclose (perhaps not to acknowledge even to himself) that he is in trouble? This is deep in human nature. The last person to know may be the bank, because the small businessman will go to great lengths to conceal his trouble from his bank, fearing that it may 'pull the plug' on him. The banks have to change this image, because it damages their business.

BDB itself would be put on the alert if ever interest due or a repayment instalment of its loan was not paid on the due date. That is an infallible sign of trouble. BDB, with bank and customer consent, should then appoint a consultant to report urgently. Customer, bank and BDB would then decide on the remedial action to be taken. The priority for the bank would be to save its money; BDB's priority would be to save for the long term a potentially profitable business and the jobs in it. Between them they should be able greatly to reduce the casualty rate among small businesses in Britain. This procedure should be written into BDB's loan agreements, so that the drill did not have to be extemporized at the last moment and under duress. The essential is that whoever is employed to advise in these difficult situations should visit the business and investigate on site. Sending for a small businessman often ends in failure. You don't need to ask me why!

BDB should report to 'E' committee through the economic staff, and Parliamentary Questions about it would be for the chairman of 'E' committee – the Prime Minister. This would demonstrate government's real intention of a new start for Britain. It would recognize that there is need to repair a flaw in British society which began with the reluctant businessman, continued with the British preference for finance and trade and has recently permitted the closure of about a quarter of British manufacturing capacity.

America in the thirties, and other countries post-World War II, had immense structural flaws – political and economic – to mend. In every case an organization similar to BDB was successfully used. My fear is that Labour's hang-up about private enterprise and the Tories' hang-up about 'intervention' will between them perpetuate the inadequate, half-hearted treatment we have had so far. It is for precisely that reason that Britain has to start again. Tinkering with 'as is' won't mend anything. It is a radical new attitude of mind that is called for, to jerk us into a position to compete and succeed.

In the development state there would have to be a new Education Act, giving more powers to the Secretary of State; a new curriculum, giving more time to practical learning and 'technik'; and a new method of assessment, giving less emphasis to examinations and more to general performance while at school. Many schemes are being tried to find an interesting, thought-provoking school system. We should look for a curriculum suitable for British youth as it is and as it wants to be, not as idealists think it ought to be, which has proved too academic and theoretical and has led to widespread truancy.

In a technical age Britain is not producing enough educated young people whose minds have been opened to continuous learning. Even when a year's training has been provided for all who do not go on to further education, young Britons will be far less qualified for work in today's technical conditions than young Europeans, Americans or Japanese. This has created a huge gap in Britain's chances of recapturing success. The educational establishment appears to be impotent, except in Scotland. The economic staff would certainly need its own education unit. There are excellent men and women up and down the country who are desperate about the educational failure and full of ideas for its reform. Chapter 9, 'Ready for Work', covered many of these. The efforts of the real practical reformers need to be drawn together by a few powerful, radical people who know what should be done and who have the influence necessary to get the improvement made – the 'E' committee.

It is at the sharp end, the microeconomy where men and women work – or don't work – that the development state would have to be effective. It is easy to sit on the top of the heap, make plans, give instructions and get the sensation of managing an economy, a government department or a big business. Then, when you get out on the ground, you find that nothing is happening. That is what has made the clever macroeconomic people at the Treasury so pessimistic about getting the economy right. The truth is that *they* have to get their sums right and that there have *also* to be means of encouraging, facilitating, steering and accelerating the economy right down to the shop floor, the local bank and the schoolroom. We know this and we try to do it, but with more than a touch of that arrogant attitude, 'the man in Whitehall knows best'.

In the past, except in wartime, Britain has never done this well. Other countries have – with great advantage to themselves. We must not be simple about this. It is not a question of control, regulation or penalty. It is a matter of stated objectives for sectors of British life and business being followed up by intelligent, careful, determined, experienced managers working with government in companies and public services. If little is done, little will happen. If too much is done, there will be rejection. The trick is to find the correct amount of collaboration to get a positive response from most companies and public services.

The future of Britain is in the hands of the managers and entrepreneurs in companies big and small, and in the public services. Only they can cure the British disease and get a turnaround. They cannot maximize their efforts without help and encouragement from government. This is the reason for the move to the development state.

There is indeed, now, a fantastic opportunity for Britain to catch up lost ground. The new technology, the new sense of reality, the obvious danger of living off wasting North Sea oil – all are pointing Britain towards radical change. 'Too little and too late' has been Britain's besetting sin. Can we avoid it this time?

'For there is good news yet to hear and fine things to be seen
Before we go to Paradise by way of Kensal Green.'
(G.K. Chesterton, 'The Rolling English Road')

Finale: The Development Pack

I finish this writing in the summer of 1984. Economic recovery from slump is strong in America, Japan and Eastasia, hesitant in Britain and the rest of Europe, weak in Third World countries. Is this the start of a long, sustained growth movement, or do we face years of stagnation? Is it the calm before another storm? There are experts canvassing each of these futures.

Britain has to move whatever the future, either to catch a favourable tide or to resist further ebbing away of our markets. The reason is simple enough. Britain, like any other country, corporation, family or person throughout history, has in the end to cut its coat according to its cloth. Thatcher governments One and Two both tried desperately hard to cut the coat down to suit the shrunken cloth. It was right to try and to keep on trying, but this has had only marginal success. That option has not worked; the share of national wealth spent by government has not fallen. Britain gets to the end when the oil runs down, quite soon now, and the cloth shrinks again.

What British governments have not done was to set about increasing the amount of cloth available – increasing wealth – as the main plank of a new, long-term national attitude and strategy. The markets are there, as is proved by the huge volume of goods coming into Britain from Europe, America and Eastasia. But 80 per cent of British companies tell the CBI that lack of orders is the main constraint on production.* One can only conclude that Britain is not yet competitive and that to

* CBI Quarterly Survey, published April 1984

recapture these markets is the harder option for us and the end of the slack life to which we have all become accustomed. That means a turnaround – a new start!

Just look at the last page of charts! British labour costs are still running ahead of the competition, as they have done for many years now. On the competitiveness scoreboard Britain in 1983 (a recovery year?) fell back from thirteenth to fourteenth place. In 1983 our productivity rose less and our wages rose more than in the competition: that old devil is still at work, so our unemployment stays obstinately high. Manufacturing output is stuck at the 1980 level. The balance of trade in manufactures deteriorated further in the first three months of 1984: imports rose 12 per cent and exports (non-oil) by 7 per cent.

In March 1984 the Bank of England reported: 'The recovery continued to rely quite heavily on consumer spending, much of it financed by borrowing . . .' and, further on, 'The output measure again rose more slowly than those based on expenditure and on income, continuing the uncertainty about the precise scale of the recovery.' Private-sector borrowing rose in the six months to March 1984 from £5 billion to £8 billion.

If Britain carries on with the flawed capital/manager/work-force/ education system of the last forty years we shall become poorer, with more unemployment and less social security; we shall become less educated, more class-ridden and prone to social problems of rising severity. All this is as certain as many of the great tides in the past and we shall slide down to ever-worsening crises, like the Roman Empire of old.

That is why Britain has to move on to the development state – 'go-getter society' – call it what you will. It would retain parliamentary democracy, individual liberty and social security for the needy, but it would make high-speed growth and the advance of the real economy its top priority in action, in persuasion, in programming and in all the ways open to those who govern, administer, teach and manage. Government, civil service and management of all descriptions (what I have called the 'driving ten') would work together for the improvement of the whole economy and try to take with them their constituents, their workforce, their customers, their shareholders, their trainees and pupils. This combination would be much stronger than each paddling his or her own canoe; it could be joined at

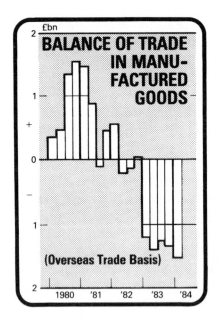

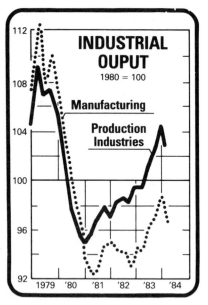

Source: Dept. of Trade

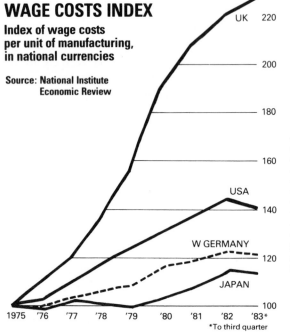

WAGE COSTS INDEX

**Index of wage costs
per unit of manufacturing,
in national currencies**

Source: National Institute
Economic Review

THE COMPETITIVENESS SCOREBOARD

1 Japan (1)
2 Switzerland (2)
3 U.S. (3)
4 W. Germany (4)
5 Sweden (9)
6 Finland (8)
7 Austria (10)
8 Norway (12)
9 Denmark (11)
10 Netherlands (5)
11 Canada (6)
12 Australia (7)
13 Belgium/Luxembourg (14)
14 UK (13)
15 France (15)
16 Ireland (16)
17 Italy (18)
18 New Zealand (20)
19 Spain (17)
20 Turkey (19)
21 Greece (21)
22 Portugal (22)

(Figures in brackets
are last year's rankings).

**European Management
Forum Jan '84**

FIGURE B2

UNEMPLOYMENT:

Unemployment as a percentage of total labour force, UK and rest of OECD

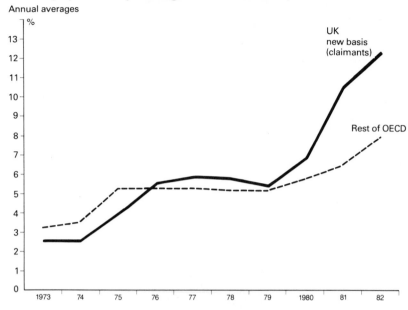

FIGURE E1

PRODUCTIVITY:

Industrial production per head in common currency

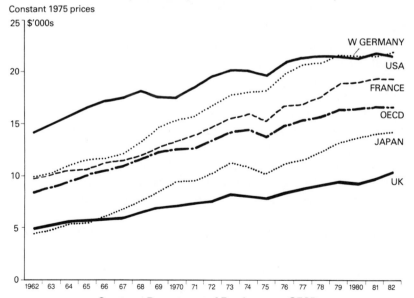

Sources: Department of Employment, OECD

national or local level by those trade-union leaders who believed in the objectives and purposes of the development state.

Britain needs to widen the action into what Dr Small-is-Beautiful Schumacher called 'a broad popular movement of reconstruction ... success cannot be obtained by some sort of magic produced by scientists, technicians or planners. It can only come through a process of growth involving the education, organization and discipline of the whole population. Anything less than this must end in failure.'*

Britain has not much time to lose. Thatcher One bulldozed and cleared the site. Serious construction should now begin. This cannot take the 'as is' inflation route; it has to take the development route, which has just started to open up, like the darling buds of May. To get June bustin' out all over will take positive, collaborative action to change the inherited and damaging anti-industrial culture in schools and pubs and clubs and where we work, or don't work, and to diminish the hostility between the managers and the managed.

This action should include:

• Establishing and making part of national life and expectation a continuous economic improvement strategy – not just an industrial policy – which would pursue 'more and better' in every activity into the development state, out of the declining welfare state.

• This purpose would be led by the 'E' Committee of the British Cabinet, which should be supported by a continuing economic staff, of which half should come from the private sector.

• Nudging important market rates and taxation to work, above all, to improve the real economy.

• Promoting intense competition between managements in the markets, but close collaboration everywhere else.

• Shifting exhausted or unprogressive old-style management, before it is too late.

• Encouraging investment and innovation in the new technologies on a greatly increased and wider scale, to catch up with Germany and others.

* Page 171 of the 1974 edition of *Small is Beautiful*

- Overcoming 'them and us' with 'all one family' reality.
- Fostering the decentralization of industrial unions into largely independent company and regional units, which collaborate in search of new markets, investments, revenues and jobs.
- Facilitating a big increase in the small-business population through a new Business Development Board.
- Introducing a new Education Act to improve management of schools and drop the non-achievement habit, to increase the practical *'technik'* curriculum and to provide school-leavers with a valid passport to the world of work.
- Starting to do all these things before the North Sea oil declines and Britain reaches the point of no return.

Taken singly, these actions cannot be effective. It is the package which would deliver the necessary new start and the turnaround. Many of these obstinate problems have, of course, been on the agenda of the Thatcher government and its predecessors, but they have never been drawn together as a coherent development policy, put over as the highest national purpose. The resources thrown at these problems have been too small. The ministers responsible for them have often not had enough 'clout'. They have been administered by non-entrepreneurial civil servants. They have been treated one by one and the results have got lost in the process. This is typically what happens if you try to 'do good by stealth'.

There has therefore not been the sense of urgency and unity needed to release a new spirit – a spirit which would not only improve Britain's material condition, but would spill over into behaviour and, indeed, into moral values, which thrive on hope and purpose and success, and on working closely with others.

If only Britain could confidently expect to get this improvement, all our problems would diminish. At home we could do more for the poor and disadvantaged, for education, research, the arts, to stop Britain falling to pieces, and above all for business, large and small. Abroad we would sit more comfortably in Europe, in NATO, in the Commonwealth and in the rest of the Third World. America prefers winners. It is all to play for.

The fat cats, those who are bogged down in 'as is', or who believe that all things are 'bright and beautiful' in Britain, will recoil from the development state in horror and alarm. Britain's establishment is in a state of uneasy balance, but it is extremely defensive: 'pooh-pooh', 'tried before', 'doesn't add up', 'won't work', 'look what happened to Bloggs', 'better not'!

But to those who are aware, who have high hopes and high spirits, to the non-conformists, to those who will not put up with 'it can't be done' and to the 'driving ten', this book says:

> You can get a turnaround in Britain,
>   if you want it enough.
> But, if you have not done so already,
>   you will have to start again.

Index